The Chi

and

The Bahá'í Faith

by

PHYLLIS GHIM LIAN CHEW

GEORGE RONALD

OXFORD

GEORGE RONALD, *Publisher*
46 High Street, Kidlington, Oxford OX5 2DN

A Cataloguing-in-Publication number for this book
is available from the British Library

ISBN 0–85398–358–5 Pbk

This book is dedicated to the Great *Tao*

Printed and bound in Great Britain by
Biddles Ltd, Guildford and King's Lynn

Contents

Preface

Why was 'Abdu'l-Bahá, the Perfect Exemplar of the Bahá'í Faith, brimming with optimism over the spiritual capacity of the Chinese people?

The Chinese people are most simple-hearted and truth-seeking ... In China one can teach many souls and train and educate such divine personages that each one of them may become the bright candle of the world of humanity. Truly, I say, the Chinese are free from any deceit and hypocrisies and are prompted with ideal motives. Had I been feeling well I would have taken a journey to China myself![1]

'Abdu'l-Bahá remarked of China that it 'ranks foremost among all nations in material, cultural and spiritual resources' and that its 'future is assuredly bright'.[2] Elsewhere Shoghi Effendi, Guardian of the Bahá'í Faith and grandson of 'Abdu'l-Bahá, acknowledges that 'Abdu'l-Bahá often spoke 'in most hopeful words' of 'its brilliant future and of the spiritual capacity of its people'.[3] Such overtly optimistic views on a people and country at the turn of the twentieth century and at a time when the Chinese people were generally held in low regard politically, economically and scientifically must naturally be surprising if not astonishing to many people. China was at this time virtually a colony of the imperialist powers of both East – Japan – and West. I found 'Abdu'l-Bahá's point of view most surprising.

To find the answer to 'Abdu'l-Bahá's optimism and faith in China and the Chinese people, one must look to the spiritual tradition of China. I decided that it was imperative for me to research the spiritual history of China to discover the particular elements of her spirit and culture which would enable me to glean

vii

a deeper understanding of these enigmatic remarks of 'Abdu'l-Bahá.

This book focuses on the Chinese civilization. It looks at the original spiritual teachings of Confucius and Lao-tzu as well as those of their most well-known disciples, chiefly Mencius and Chuang-tzu. In particular, it focuses on the mind and spirit of the Chinese people by examining their cultural foundations. In studying the culture, I have had to concentrate on religion as it is not possible to grasp the subtle meaning of Chinese culture without knowing anything about its primary beliefs, which may generally be summarized as Confucianist, Taoist, Buddhist and animist-polytheistic. In fact, in any study of the Chinese people one cannot help but notice that their culture and religions are so inextricably woven together that there are not even different words for them.

The reader may ask, 'Why "religion" rather than "religions".[4] Surely more than one religion has been important in China? What about Confucianism, Taoism, Buddhism?' The answer is that by using the word in the singular I can emphasize that the character of religious expression in China is above all a manifestation of the Chinese culture. 'Religions' is often used in such a way as to imply that the three systems are all religions and perhaps religions only. To the Chinese, the word *chiao* connotes three separate ideas: education, culture and religion.[5]

The term 'religions' also implies that Confucianism, Taoism and Buddhism are organized institutionalized churches. This may be true of Buddhism and Taoism, which have a hierarchy of priests; but this structure affects only the clergy who live apart from the people in monasteries and has no relationship to the masses. Although creed – what one believes – is of utmost importance in the West, in China there is no credo and religious life does not have anything to do with the acceptance of certain definite doctrinal propositions.

The word 'religions' also implies the erroneous view that a Chinese is either a Confucianist, a Buddhist or a Taoist. There are of course thousands of Buddhist monks, Taoist priests, millions of Muslims and Christians, all of whom follow only one religion. But the majority of China's millions, including the several thousand Jews who do not practise their original teachings, follow a religion which combines and overshadows Buddhism, Taoism and the ancient primitive cult. They do not follow three separate and conflicting religions but a syncretic religion embracing the ancient cult and Confucianism as its basis and Buddhist and Taoist elements as secondary structures.

Apart from my primary motivation to discover the reasons for 'Abdu'l-Bahá's enigmatic remark, there are other reasons for my writing this book.

First, despite the number of books written about China in recent years, it is remarkable how little authentic knowledge people, especially Westerners, have about the religion and culture of that country. If one asks the well-educated Westerner to list some of China's major philosophers or great spiritual leaders, unless they are China specialists, they will be unable to name more than Confucius and possibly Lao-tzu.

Second, although the humanistic system of values founded by Confucius is one of the greatest ideals ever devised as well as one of the richest and longest spiritual traditions in human history, it is also the least understood. There is, for example, a common misunderstanding about what Confucius stood for. It is often thought that Confucius was agnostic, atheistic or ritualistic. This leads to the further misconception that the Chinese are irreligious or indifferent to religion. There exists too an erroneous view that filial piety is the essence of Confucianism and that that is all there is to it.

Third, it is imperative for any citizen with a world consciousness to know about different cultures and different religions, especially the Chinese religion, which has a connection to almost one-quarter of mankind. Knowledge is the only way to promote cultural and religious tolerance, the only route to the understanding of the Chinese mentality. This is especially important in view of the fact that the Chinese, to Westerners, have always been 'inscrutable'.

Fourth, there is a need to redress a gross imbalance prevalent in Sinological literature. The majority of Chinese intellectuals, as well as China scholars in the West, have focused far too predominantly on what may be called the 'dark side' of Chinese culture — that is, the Confucian contribution to despotic, gerontocratic and male-oriented practices and tendencies in traditional and contemporary China. The upsurge of anti-Confucian campaigns in recent decades may be long overdue since Confucianism has lost its original spiritual vitality and become preoccupied with inflexible forms and rituals. However, it is one thing to evaluate Confucian ideas in a modern perspective and another to attack it from the vantage point of modern ideology, be it scientism, nationalism, socialism or communism. An attempt must be made to review the original writings of the Chinese sages, especially those of its foremost sage, Confucius, in the historical context in which they were written. Authentic possibilities for new interpretations may then present themselves again. There is a need to dig through the strata of partial and distorted writings on the matter.

Finally, there is a need to view the essence of Chinese religion from the fresh perspective of the latest prophetic revelation, the Bahá'í Faith. What did the central figures of that Faith have to say about the sages of China? Did China have a manifestation of God? What were and are the spiritual ideals of the Chinese people? What was and is their worldview? How do these compare with the central teachings of the Bahá'í Faith? Only in answering these questions can we say that we have arrived at some kind of understanding.

My central concern has been to learn as impartially as I could the distinctive characteristics of the Chinese philosophical and religious traditions. For the sake of focus, my priority has been to probe its 'inner dimension' (spiritual values) as a step towards a more comprehensive appreciation of the cultural, social and political manifestations of Chinese life. My preference has been to emphasize Confucian thought which has, in the judgements of its leading proponents, inspired many generations of sophisticated thinkers in traditional China.

Whenever the word 'Confucian' is used, I refer to the original thoughts of Confucius as well as those of Mencius, his most prominent disciple. Depending on the context, Taoism may also be included, especially the philosophy of Lao-tzu and that of his most famous disciple, Chuang-tzu. This is because Taoism complements Confucianism in various ways, besides being born in the same period of Chinese history.

The underlying cultural implication of the Chinese religion is not applicable to all the various Chinese societies in the same way. It goes without saying that the Chinese in mainland China are vastly different from their forebears who have not been strongly influenced by Maoism and Marxism. The Chinese in Hong Kong and Taiwan are also distinct from those in China, not to say from each other. Yet it should be recognized that the cultural implications of any traditional outlook or perspective are valuable points of reference in studying these societies which are still more or less under the sway of that outlook. The cultural implications are particularly relevant to tradition-bound societies and the vast agricultural populations which comprise the bulk of China.

I have retained certain important words in Chinese thought such as *Tao*, *li* and *jen*. Key terms in any great tradition are inevitably distorted or even falsified by translation and can be grasped in something like their true significance only by seeing their operation in many contexts. In studying Buddhism, for example, such words as *nirvana* and *sunyata* are rightly considered as technical terms and customarily left untranslated.

As to the transliteration of Chinese names, this is at present complicated by the fact that several systems are being used among scholars. The system each scholar chooses depends on his own special interests in the field of Chinese studies. I have decided to follow as a guide the modified Wades-Giles system of romanization, this being the system most familiar to readers in the West, since it is the one most commonly used by Western specialists working on Chinese culture. Occasionally, however, I may use the newer Pinyin system of romanization for the proper names of persons and places from contemporary mainland China.

There are essentially four major sections to this book. The first section (chapters 2 to 4) discusses the unique but rather confusing relationship of the terms of religion and philosophy in the context of Chinese culture. It clarifies how Confucianism could be viewed as both a religion and a philosophy. This is followed by a discussion of the Chinese conception of the nature of *Tao*, its attributes and how people may walk the way of *Tao*. The intriguing question of sagehood and prophethood in the context of a Chinese religion is then broached. An attempt is made to understand the enduring quality of Chinese philosophical and religious thought.

Section 2 (chapters 5 to 8) gives a summary of the Chinese worldview. It examines the Chinese concept of the harmonious working of nature as seen from the agrarian perspective and the famed cognates on Chinese thoughts – the *yin* and the *yang*. It describes the nature of man as taught by their sages. The Chinese affiliation for harmony is elaborated through their perception of the interrelationship of all religions as different paths to the same destination as well as in their dream of world unity.

Section 3 (chapters 9 to 14), relates the Chinese principles behind a successful and happy life. It examines the universal values of *jen* and *li* expounded by Confucius and their application in daily interaction with one's fellow men in domains such as education, the family and the state.

Section 4 (chapters 15 and 16) is a summary of the universal values of Confucianism as well as an analysis of possible reasons behind the fall of and disenchantment with a once dominant spiritual tradition.

Throughout the chapters, the little known but striking similarities of the spiritual insights of the Chinese sages with those of the Bahá'í Faith (and indeed with those of any of the revealed religions) emerge clearly.

We then begin to understand not only 'Abdu'l-Bahá's optimistic appraisal of the spiritual capacity of the Chinese people but also His exhortation that the West should turn to the East for spiritual ideas since 'the Spiritual Sun of Truth has always shone from the horizon of the East'.[6]

Finally, a word of appreciation to all my friends who encouraged and helped me in one way or another with this project. Many thanks to Counsellor Rose Ong for encouraging me to begin this study, to my husband for his patience and quiet support and to Mr Shum Yu-cheong for his many comments.

Phyllis Ghim Lian Chew
Singapore
January 1993

1

An Introduction to China

The spiritual tradition of China has resulted in a rich and unique civilization admired by many for the greater part of history and has contributed to the sense of national pride which the Chinese have for their heritage. To understand this tradition one must focus on the history of thought in China, for it is this which is the nucleus of the history of the nation. This great tradition can be traced to the 'axial period' in Chinese history.

An Axial Period

Each great civilization in human history has had what the existential philosopher Karl Jaspers called an axial period, during which the essential insights that spawn great cultures arise.[1] In China, this axial period was the 6th century BC and the two most important figures were Confucius and Lao-tzu.[2] Their teachings may be said to sum up the past and forecast the future. Although their teachings were not original since it is possible to find almost every important tenet of their philosophies before their time, nevertheless their great influence on subsequent Chinese culture places them in the period which succeeded them, rather than in that which came before.

Before Confucius and Lao-tzu were long centuries of nature- and ancestor-oriented responses to the sacred.[3] The ancient Chinese had polytheistic ideas of God and worshipped their many gods through shamans, a human being – usually male – thought to be capable of communicating with spirits from the other world while in a trance. These shamans were believed to be able to levitate, to make magical flights into the sky and magical descents into the underworld (presumably in a trance), to have mastery over fire and to cure sicknesses. Waley[4] described the shamans (the *wu* of China) as intermediaries in spirit-cults, experts in exorcism, prophecy, fortune-telling, rain-making and the interpretation of dreams, as well as magic healers.

There were many gods worshipped by the Chinese. There was the supreme God (*Ti*) represented as a remote and imperial creator, the nature deities such as earth itself and its products, such as grain, rivers and mountains. There were also the spirits of deceased kings and high ministers who had passed away as well as the many ancestral spirits of the governed. Pacifying these spirits kept the population busy and fearful. Archaeological discoveries of the Shang people (c.1500 BC) included bone fragments containing records of questions which the people of the time put to their ancestors and gods, for example, 'Shall we raise an army of 5,000 men?'[5] In the beginning, probably only the most momentous matters were asked but later, the oracle was used more and more in the manner in which some people today use the ouija board. Sacrifices of fowl and cooked food were frequent rituals practised by the majority of people as a means of protection from the spirits and for the asking of favours.[6] Shamans were consulted frequently for supernatural guidance in even the smallest matters.

These were long centuries of superstitious beliefs in spirits and ghosts. Spirits and ghosts were believed to constantly appear to men in dreams or simply as day-light apparitions and to communicate freely with men without the aid of a shaman. There were a lot of stories about ghosts and spirits. Shamans were credited with fakiristic performances such as tongue-slitting and belly-ripping.

Then in BC 551, Confucius came. His teaching readjusted the moral and spiritual fibre of the people, especially that of the intellectuals. He taught the people to keep spirits at a distance and to focus their energies instead on the cultivation of a good character as well as virtues such as human-heartedness and love for others. He gave the people a higher vision of themselves as human beings capable of perfection in character and morals. As a result, the shamanistic hold on the people receded gradually into the background. By the late Chou period (1122 BC – 256 BC), the teachings of Confucius had become a major influence, and by the time of the Han dynasty (206 BC – AD 220), it was adopted as the state orthodoxy. By then, the ruling class and the educated in society looked down on shamans as impostors who traded on the credulity of the masses. Five hundred years later, in 32–31 BC, when shamanistic performances at the Chinese court were abolished, the sayings of Confucius about keeping spirits at a distance were quoted by a minister who sponsored this reform.[7] Although shamanistic divination, sacrifices and seances did not entirely disappear from Chinese society, shamanism no longer had a stranglehold on the vast majority and especially the intellectuals and the educated. Its role had become marginal with the withdrawal of the support of the court and, with it, the intellectuals. In its place was an increased emphasis on rational thought. The mastery of Confucian literature became the basis for the civil service examination system and this survived until the waning years of the Ch'ing dynasty in the first decade of the 20th century.

In the place of gods, spirits and ghosts, Confucius revived the concept of one Supreme Being – that of 'Heaven' (*T'ien*) or 'Supreme Lord' (*Shang-ti*).[8] These were not new concepts, but they were concepts that had been forgotten with the political and social and spiritual deterioration of China after the last Golden Age, believed to be that of Kings Wen and Wu during the time of the early Chou (around 1100 BC). For the Chinese of that Golden Age, 'Heaven' referred to the supreme being and the personal god who has absolute power and who rules over the universe. At the same time, it also referred to an impersonal cosmic power or nature.

The axial period also comprised the foundation of the religious philosophy expounded by yet another remarkable Chinese sage, Lao-tzu, who lived during the same period as Confucius and who is the subject of chapter 3. Lao-tzu popularized the idea of *Tao* (Way) a concept which in time became just as important, if not more so, than 'Heaven' in Chinese thought. With the coming of Lao-tzu and his important work, the *Tao-te ching*, often called 'the Chinese Bible', the idea of a personal and supreme god was denied and, instead, an 'unknowable' *Tao* was introduced which was regarded as the Essence and the Ultimate Reality of the universe.

From the 6th century AD onwards, Confucian and Taoist ethics and metaphysics began to play a bigger and bigger part in the Chinese consciousness. They formed a system of social values, and fulfilled various spiritual and ethical functions very much like those of a religion. Thus, although they were historically speaking 'philosophies', they functioned like religions and became in all senses and purposes the Chinese religion. When referring to the Chinese religion in the axial period, one must speak of both Confucianism and Taoism. The former can be said to constitute the *yang* or positive aspect of life and culture and the latter the *yin* or passive aspect, the two balancing and complementing each other. It is useful to view these two religions as one whole. They are two halves, irretrievably linked in the cultural thought of the Chinese people, originating in the same century. While Confucianism manifests its influence predominantly in the ethical and political spheres, Taoism manifests its influence mainly in the literary, the artistic and the spiritual.

Taoism, however, was gradually overshadowed by Confucianism which was officially recognized by the Han emperor towards the end of the 2nd century BC and was declared the orthodox philosophy of the state, with a government university set up in the capital to teach its doctrines to prospective officials. This did not mean that Taoism was in any way suppressed. People were still free to read and study its literature, and it is certain that educated men of the Han continued to savour the literary genius of Chuang-tzu and Lao-tzu as they had in the past. It simply meant that Taoist writings were not accorded any official recognition as the basis for decisions of state and public affairs.

Thus it was Confucianism rather than Taoism which was the more dominant force in Chinese culture as it laid down the structural principles and supplied the key operational values for the basic Chinese institutions from the family to the state. The Confucianists – the scholars trained in the Confucian doctrine – staffed the offices of the government and constituted the elite of the society. Through them, the influence of Confucianism permeated every aspect of Chinese society for more than two thousand years.

A word must be added here on Buddhism, the subsequent 'third' party of the Chinese religion. Although the Buddha lived in approximately the same period as Confucius and Lao-tzu (563–483 BC), his teachings were brought into China by Buddhist devotees through the Silk Route only around the 1st century AD. Buddhism was propagated among the people in the southwestern region and gradually penetrated central China and flourished. It was very popular with the court in the time of the Divided dynasties (around 420–590 AD) and during the T'ang dynasty (618–907 AD).[9]

By then, however, Confucianism had entrenched itself as the state ideology and Buddhism was not able to take over its pre-eminent position. Nevertheless, some aspects of Buddhism were absorbed into the Chinese culture and, through the centuries, it was so interwoven with Confucianism and Taoism that it became quite indistinguishable from the two. At the height of its popularity in the T'ang dynasty, Buddhism was neither insepar-able from nor in conflict with native Chinese religious and cultural beliefs and practices. It became a part of the Chinese religion.[10] This phenomenon has been referred to as the Chinese conquest of Buddhism rather than the Buddhist conquest of China. Like Taoism, Buddhism played the role of a supporting structure essentially filling in certain metaphysical 'gaps' which Confucianism did not provide.

In view of these developments and in terms of the intention to understand the spirit, culture and psyche of the Chinese people, the focus of this book will necessarily be on the original teachings of Confucius since they are the undisputed core of the Chinese culture and religion.

The Significance of Confucius

Although it is difficult to measure the influence of religious or philosophical systems, it is possible to assert that Confucius was the greatest and most significant unifying force of the Chinese people and of civilization in Chinese history. In fact, Confucian-ism is synonymous with what is known as the 'Chinese Great Tradition'.[11] A disproportionately large amount of space must therefore be given to him as the originator of one of the greatest spiritual traditions in human history. Confucius set the pattern for later thinkers in China. As 'Abdu'l-Bahá expressed: 'These blessed souls whether Moses, Buddha, Confucius or Zoroaster were the cause of the illumination of the world of humanity. How can we deny such irrefutable proof? How can we be blind to such light?'[12]

Taoism, of course, has exercised tremendous influence on Chinese art, religion, government and philosophy of life, while Buddhism has contributed substantially to Chinese religion, philosophy and art, especially sculpture. There is no question, however, that Confucianism has been the controlling influence so far as government, education, literature, society, ethics and non-institutional religion in China are concerned whereas in all these both Buddhism and Taoism have played a secondary role. Confucianism was the official philosophy of China for about two thousand years until the birth of the Republic of China in 1911. It went through many phases and had various aspects, but its fundamental tenets have generally remained constant throughout the centuries. Furthermore, the metaphysics, epistemology and psychology of medieval Buddhism and Taoism were assimilated into Confucianism to constitute Neo-Confucianism in the 11th and 12th centuries.[13]

Confucianism has left an indelible mark on the social and political structure of the nation. Through the educational system, teachers succeeded in inculcating Confucian values into the minds of young people. Thus, the Chinese outlook on life has been immensely coloured by Confucian ideas which have been formulated since his day into a governing code of etiquette and morality for all the Chinese. Just as the sayings of Chairman Mao were reference points for policy decisions when he was alive, so in Imperial China, for over two thousand years, the sayings of Confucius were often the ultimate authority in all spheres of social and political life.

Dynasties have risen and fallen but Confucianism, although increasingly stereotyped and formalized through the centuries, abided, despite such changes. Because of Confucius, the large family system, with its special emphasis on filial and fraternal obedience, continues to be a dominant factor in society. In almost everything from their national to private life, in their culture, in their manners and behaviour, in their customs and traditions, in their mode of expression in speaking and writing, the Chinese are indebted to Confucius. Through centuries of enforcement and practice as a social doctrine, Confucianism won uncritical acceptance by the people and became an emotional attitude as well as a body of rational thinking.

In addition, Confucian teachings were brought to Korea, Japan and Vietnam in varying degrees and became a part of their national heritages. Each of these countries owe to it the best features of their social life and public institutions.

Who, then, is this man of which much has been written and of which so much has been misunderstood, whose teachings are indispensable to the understanding of the Chinese worldview, their character, their culture, their psyche?

Confucius, the Man

Confucius is the latinized rendering of the Chinese K'ung Fu-tze. K'ung is the surname. Fu-tze means 'the Master'. Confucius and his most well-known disciple, Mencius, are the only Chinese with latinized names. This can be explained by the fact that Chinese books were translated first into Latin (as the *Confucius Sinarum Philosophus* of the Jesuits published in Paris in 1687, copies of which still exist in specialized collections; one notes at this point that Jesuit missionaries of the 16th and 17th centuries saw in Confucianism a religion somewhat like the Greek philosophy of Plato and Aristotle and did much to publicize it as such). Having been made famous in Europe as Confucius, it was impossible thereafter to call him K'ung Fu-tze.

An attempt to understand Confucius is made difficult by the large mass of legend and tradition that has accumulated so thickly about him that over the centuries it has become very difficult to discern fact from fiction. These elaborations about Confucius stem from two different motives. On the one hand, his admirers wanted to exalt him and therefore built up an elaborate genealogy that traced his ancestry back to emperors. On the other hand, those whose interests were menaced by this revolutionary thinker sought to nullify his attacks on their entrenched privilege by distorting and misrepresenting what he had to say. The safest course therefore is to completely disregard the elaborate traditional story of his life and rely only on the documents that can be proved to be early and reliable.

Confucius was born in 551 BC in the state of Lu, in Shantung Province. We cannot be certain about his ancestry but there might have been aristocrats among his forebears. As a young man, however, he was without rank and lived in humble circumstances. He had to make his own living and was self taught. His father died when he was a child, and Confucius grew up under the care of his mother. Being fatherless and born into a society without the benefit of a well-organized social welfare system, Confucius learned poverty and hardship of life from an early age. This experience was probably one of the chief reasons for his strong desire and search for an ideal life and world. These experiences gave him a close view of the sufferings of the common people, about whom he became deeply concerned. He grew up convinced that the world was in a sorry state and that it was vital for drastic changes to be made.

Confucius lived during the time called the Period of the Warring States (8th–3rd century BC).[14] China was not yet unified but divided into many states which were ambitiously warring among themselves. The splendid Chou dynasty, established by the end of the 12th century BC, had reached its zenith in the 11th. By the 10th century, it had begun to decline. The feudal system had steadily disintegrated. As the consequence of the war, China experienced social, political, economic and moral chaos. The major question of the time was how people could live in peace.

Murders, intrigues, assassinations, rebellions and notorious immoralities were the order of the day. The poor and downtrodden were the greatest victims of the social disorder. Confucius witnessed glaring discrepancies between name and reality. The king was not like a king, the ministers not like ministers, fathers not like fathers, brothers not like brothers and friends not like friends. Men seemed to have lost their humanity, as evidenced in the unscrupulous behaviour and hypocrisies of the local princes and the ministers, the corruption of the royal house and the immoral behaviour of the nobility.

Of the aristocrats Confucius had a poor opinion. He saw that men who were born with every hereditary claim to rank and nobility often behaved like beasts while others without those advantages often conducted themselves in a manner far more worthy of respect. 'It is difficult to expect anything from men who stuff themselves with food the whole day, while never using their minds in any way at all. Even gamblers do *something* and to that degree are better than these idlers.'[15] The aristocrats used considerable ingenuity to devise ever more expensive adjuncts to their luxurious living, for which the people paid with taxes and forced labour. Above all, the aristocrats practised the art of war. As the nobility was of military origin, most felt that the arts of war were the only occupation worthy of the attention of gentlemen and made fun of those who concerned themselves with the need for good government and orderly administration.

Confucius spent about ten years of his life travelling from state to state in China seeking a ruler who would use his philosophy in government. Like the great spiritual leaders, he never found one in his lifetime.[16] In some places he was treated with scant courtesy; at least once an attempt was made on his life. In only one case did a noble who wielded the chief power in a state treat Confucius with great deference and frequently ask his advice; but this man was so corrupt that, when an invitation came to return to his own state, Confucius did so gladly.[17]

2

A Chinese Religion

In the morning hear the Way; in the evening die content.[1]
Confucius

In the *Analects*, Confucius exclaimed that if he could hear the
Way in the morning, he would be happy to die in the evening of
the same day. The Way, Heaven's Way, was one which Confucius
adhered to with religious fervour and which was his supreme gift
to his people.

Although there have been attempts to call the Confucian
ideology an atheistic or agnostic one,[2] it is not possible to do so on
the grounds that Confucius' concept of Heaven was not as
sharply and well-defined as the personal God in the Judaeo-
Christian theology. In fact, on closer examination of the
Confucian writings, one finds that Confucius recognized the
existence of Heaven (*T'ien*) as a sort of Supreme Being who rules
over man and the world. (The Chinese word *T'ien* was originally
the word for God.)[3] Heaven in this view is both transcendent and
immanent. Confucius stands in awe of this ultimate source of
creativity which works incessantly in the universe and the
human world. If religious belief is understood to mean faith in
something transcendent that has exerted profound influence on
our lives, then Confucius must be regarded as a deeply religious
man.

A Religious Faith

. . . verily, the philosophers have not denied the Ancient of Days.[4]
Bahá'u'lláh

Confucius had a lively faith in Heaven. This faith in Heaven was
the ultimate source of his greatness. He acknowledges, 'It is only
Heaven that is grand',[5] and 'He who sins against Heaven has no

one to whom he may pray'.[6] He himself admitted that at fifty he 'knew the Mandate of Heaven'.[7] Heaven was a term that often occurred in his teachings:

> The superior man stands in awe of three things. He stands in awe of the Mandate of Heaven; he stands in awe of great men; and he stands in awe of the words of the sages. The inferior man is ignorant of the Mandate of Heaven and does not stand in awe of it. He is disrespectful to great men and is contemptuous toward the word of the sages.[8]

His faith in Heaven convinced him that man's happiness depended upon the approval of Heaven rather than the praises of men, upon one's interior qualities rather than external things. Once he said:

> I do not murmur against Heaven nor grumble against men. My studies lie low, but my penetration rises high. T'ien alone knows me.[9]

This faith explains why Confucius could be so composed and serene when faced with the dangers of life. The idea of Heaven led Confucius to feel that somehow, somewhere there was a power that stood on the side of the lonely person struggling for what is right.

On one occasion, when a certain Huan T'ui, the Minister of War of the State of Sung, was apparently after his life, Confucius said, 'Heaven begat the power that is in me. What have I to fear from such a one as Huan T'ui?'

Faith in Heaven and a sense of heavenly mission could be seen in Confucius' declaration that since Heaven endowed him with virtue or power (te),[10] none could harm him, and that since Heaven would not destroy culture,[11] his enemy would not be able to harm him:

> When King Wen [the founder of the Chou dynasty 1122 BC – 256 BC and mentioned by Confucius as a model of virtue] perished, did that mean that culture ceased to exist? If Heaven has really

11

intended that such culture as his should disappear, a latter-day mortal would never have been able to link himself to it as I have done. And if Heaven does not intend to destroy such culture, what have I to fear from the people of Kuang?[12]

Like other great spiritual leaders, the security of his own life was of no consequence to Confucius. Once, in a touching episode which took place on the border of the two states of Chen and Ts'ai, he and his disciples were surrounded by an army sent by his political enemies. Their food supplies were running out, and many of the followers were sick and depressed. Confucius, however, was seemingly unconcerned – he continued to lecture and read, play music and sing.[13]

It is apparent that Confucius felt that he had been entrusted by Heaven with a mission to cure the ills of the Chinese people, and he hoped that Heaven would not permit him to fail. Believing he had this heavenly conferred virtue as well as a heavenly appointed destiny, he went about his mission as a great educator of his people resolutely and with great conviction. He regarded himself as Heaven's instrument on earth, a wooden bell to arouse the people from their lethargy. He was convinced that his teachings denoted a moral endowment, which, if fully cultivated, would make one worthy to rule the whole empire.

Confucius' view of Heaven was endorsed and further developed by Mencius, who acknowledged the existence of a Supreme Ultimate: 'Heaven gives birth to creatures.'[14] Mencius went even further to point out a concrete way to approach Heaven: 'He who exerts his mind to the utmost knows his nature. He who knows his nature knows Heaven. To preserve one's mind and to nourish one's nature is the way to serve Heaven.'[15]

In common with other great spiritual leaders Confucius was neither loved nor respected for his insights, especially by the intelligentsia.[16] In his lifetime, he was ridiculed and misunderstood. Up to the time of his death he was unable to make the Way prevail. At times of great distress, he was heard to remark: 'Alas! How is it that the Way does not prevail!'[17] On another occasion, he cried out in despair that there was no one who understood him, but added, 'But Heaven understands me!'[18]

These little cries should not be discounted although they occur relatively infrequently in the writings of Confucius. It is known that Confucius was usually a happy and serene man, at ease with all around him. He was not in the habit of 'murmuring against Heaven' or 'grumbling against men'.[19] If such cries were uttered at all by a man who was known to be normally serene and composed, then they must have been said at moments of extreme agony and, for this reason, should be taken all the more seriously.

Another thing which characterized the religious faith of Confucius was his belief in the power of divine beings. Confucius praised the strong power of spirits. When he offered sacrifices to his ancestors and other spiritual beings, he felt as if they were actually present.

The word 'sacrifice' is like the word 'present'; one should sacrifice to a spirit as though that spirit was present, the Master (Confucius) said, if I am not present at the sacrifice, it is as though there were no sacrifice.[20]

The ancient Chinese believed that the offering of sacrifices to beings in other worlds was a means of disciplining one's mind and nature. Confucius sacrificed to spirits as though they were actually present. It would not have been in keeping with his character for him to observe the ritual forms of sacrifice of prayers and foodstuffs, if he was not sincere in his belief in the existence of spirits. Confucius was not an insincere or hypocritical man: if he had felt that such acts were of no consequence, he would not have hesitated to speak out against them.[21]

As to sacrificial rites, we may note that Confucius announced his distaste for one item of ritual usage – the human effigy. These wooden burial figures were made with human limbs so as better to represent human beings capable of serving the dead. Confucius is reported to have condemned makers of such figures.[22]

Once, when Confucius was ill, his disciple Tze-lu prayed for him. Upon hearing this, the sage asked Tze-lu whether this was true. 'Yes,' answered Tze-lu. 'I have prayed for you to the gods above and below.' Confucius told Tze-lu: 'I have been praying, too, for a long time.'[23] What Confucius meant was that he had been praying all his life, not just during his current illness. There is also in the *Analects* a prayer by Confucius: 'Whatsoever I have done amiss, may Heaven avert it, may Heaven avert it.'[24]

There cannot be the slightest doubt that Confucius was deeply religious. He did not deny God or His evidences; rather he acknowledged, throughout his teachings, the glory and over-powering majesty of Heaven which overshadowed all created things.

A Humanistic Focus

The essence of Confucius' teachings lay in his conviction that serving man was equivalent to serving Heaven. Thus, the orientation of his philosophy was thoroughly 'this-worldly'. Confucius stayed close to the concrete. Not for him were the metaphysical speculations of Heaven or what comprised the afterlife. He avoided committing himself on theological questions and refused to be wafted on the wings of metaphysics into the realm of the Great Unknown where only pure ideas exist.

Like his historical contemporary, the Buddha, Confucius was basically a humanist and a pragmatist, avoiding speculation about the metaphysical ideas of God or the Supreme Ultimate.[25] He set the tone for later Chinese scholars who marginalized such controversial topics as the existence of God and the immortality of the soul, subjects extensively discussed by Western philosophers. Not for him were the debates on how many angels could dance on the head of a pin.

Not understanding the motive behind the 'this-worldly' orientation, many Western observers tended to view the followers of Confucius as areligious. A not uncommon comment from a Westerner is that the Chinese have a great moral tradition, but they lack religious faith in God.

What such Westerners do not realize is that Confucius' concern and focus on practical human problems was due to his belief that the best way to serve Heaven would be to serve man, rather than by making sacrifices to spirits, ghosts or to Heaven itself. Confucius' vision was centred on uplifting the moral fibre of society, the belief that human nature is capable of perfection once

14

certain rules of conduct are followed. His commitment was to the retrieval of the deep meaning of human civilization. Self effort was indispensable for a happy and better life for all. A truly religious man should be totally committed to the propagation of the ideal social and political behaviour.

Should one offer a Confucianist a comparable choice of rendering to Caesar what is Caesar's and to God what is God's, in which the kings minded political business and the Confucians were allowed to devote themselves wholly to spiritual matters, he would have to reject it. The separation of the sacred and the secular would be too arbitrary and superficial. What was sacred was not just meditation on God but also one's behaviour towards one's fellow men. What was sacred was not merely how one behaved in a temple or how one recited a holy text but how one's actions and attitudes manifested themselves in everyday occurrences of social relationships.

It may be noted here that in contrast to the major religions of the world which stress *belief* in God as the essential task of religion, Confucianism stressed *ideal human relationship* as the essence of its philosophy. For this reason, critics have asserted that Confucianism is not a religion, but a humanistic and ethical philosophy.[26]

One must note that although Confucius did not stress the necessity of belief in Heaven or a supernatural element, this did not mean that he disclaimed the necessity of belief. He did not stress the belief in a God for the simple reason that any man in his right mind in axial China would not disclaim the existence of God or Heaven. The key was therefore not to emphasize belief but to stress the importance of good character and good deeds.

It must be remembered that the age of Confucius was not an agnostic or atheistic age. In fact, it was an age of an infusion of all kinds of supernatural beliefs. There was an 'over-belief' in the presence of God and gods. The popular imagination invented various spirits, which were worshipped as gods, for various natural objects – the tree, the water, the river and even the garden wall. There was a belief in the malevolent ghosts of those whose sacrifices had been discontinued, or who had otherwise been wronged in their earthly term. The malevolent ghosts sought revenge on mortals and religion was concerned with protection against their attacks. Charms, exorcism, communication through mediums, the sounding of gongs, placing of spirit-walls to prevent entry of evil spirits through a doorway, offerings to placate them, the burning of incense, prayers, fasting – all are evidence of the fear of the uncertainties of the spiritual dimension.

What was necessary at that time was not a call for a belief in a God or in a supernatural being which would have proved to be redundant, but the responsible and rational behaviour that must come with such a belief. Confucius called to man to adhere to the moral code that such a belief in the supernatural world entails. Confucius reminded his fellow men that the right way of worshipping Heaven was found in good behaviour towards one's fellow men rather than in offering sacrifices as a means of placating gods, spirits and ghosts.

In the context of his time, Confucius believed that the people needed a 'this-worldly' emphasis more than an 'other-worldly' one. The people of feudal China needed to learn how to live the life rather than theories on metaphysics. A pragmatic approach was needed. Thus, by turning away from the vain search for the mysterious region of life after death, Confucius taught his followers to take a more realistic interest in present-day life.

Once, in response to a question as to what wisdom was, Confucius replied, 'To be devoted to one's duties regarding others, to honour the gods and spirits and to remain far from them, this may be called wisdom.'[27]

Thus, although Confucianism later became a state religion, it never developed or established a full-fledged priesthood which had the time to dwell on theories of metaphysics. Unlike the history of institutionalized religions such as Islam and Christianity, there was no protracted struggle between church and the state and there was no strong centrally organized religion in most periods of Chinese history. The separation of church and state was never made in Chinese culture.

Yet without the establishment or infrastructure of a 'church' in the Western sense of the word, one cannot help but notice the impressive historical record of the ability of the Confucians to moralize politics and to transform a legalist or military society into a moral community.

Religion or Philosophy?

The Confucian tradition stands on the boundary of philosophy and religion, a humanistic tradition and a religious tradition. It stands on the boundary of religious scripture and humanistic classics. For this reason, Confucianism should be defined as both a religion and a philosophy since there does not exist a word to cover these two concepts. It should not, as has been the case, be defined as only a religion or a philosophy.[28] This is because if we define it solely as a religion, we may not be able to understand its uniqueness, and if we define it solely as a philosophy, we may lose the dynamism and vitality that it has on the hearts and minds of the people.

The Confucian scholars themselves never considered whether their system of values was a philosophy or a religion.[29] This was simply not a question that had any relevance in their culture. Take, for instance, the question of dualistic terminologies, e.g. 'sacred' vs. 'secular', 'salvific' vs. 'pedagogic', 'spiritual' vs. 'practical', etc. which plays a large part in Western philosophical consciousness. These categories are quite alien to the Chinese since there is no concept of duality in the traditional Chinese mind. In the same way, philosophy and religion are neither separable nor clearly distinguishable in Chinese civilization.[30]

Nevertheless, the popular attitude is that Confucianism is not a religion but a philosophy. We have already seen how Confucius' emphasis on the concrete and the practical rather than the abstract and the metaphysical has led people to think that he did not believe in Heaven. There are, however, other reasons for this misunderstanding.

First, the writings of Western Sinologues such as Legge and Giles in the 19th and early 20th centuries helped mould such beliefs. Their well-known works emphasized the agnostic character of Confucianism. In addition, a later generation of Western scholars,[31] who grew up under the influence of Legge and Giles and who became acquainted with Chinese culture through Chinese classical studies and through association with the Chinese educated class, assigned a relatively unimportant place to religion in Chinese society, leaving unexplained the universal presence of religious influence.

Chinese scholars themselves who lived during the time of the Chinese Renaissance which came at the close of World War One were also happy to lend support to this view. They hoped to defend the dignity of the Chinese civilization by stressing the role of rationalism in the classics, given the Western contempt for superstition and magic as the signs of national backwardness.[32]

Two passages from the *Analects* were often quoted to support the supposedly non-religious stand of Confucius. One was a remark by Tzu-kung (a disciple of Confucius) that Confucius was reluctant to talk about the way of Heaven.

Our Master's view concerning culture and the outward insignia of goodness, we are permitted to hear; but about Man's nature, and the ways of Heaven he will not tell us anything at all.[33]

However, the fact that Confucius did not talk much about Heaven should not be misinterpreted to mean that Confucius did not have deep concern for Heaven. It is, after all, futile to talk about something that is beyond the comprehension of most people. Confucius himself admitted that only at fifty years of age did he know the Mandate of Heaven.[34] What would have been the point of discussing metaphysics with the average man, who most probably would not reach the age of fifty?

The other passage often quoted to prove Confucius' aversion to spiritual matters relates to the incident when his disciple asked whether one should serve ghosts and spirits and the dead. Confucius replied, ' "Till you have learnt to serve men, how can you serve ghosts?" Tzu-lu then ventured upon a question about the dead. The Master said, "Till you know about the living, how are you to know about the dead." '[35]

This passage was often quoted to illustrate the fact that Confucius did not have much influence on the religious lives of the Chinese people. Yet it should be made clear that although Confucius was against discoursing on spirits, he never disputed their existence. In fact, he exhorted his followers to worship the spirits with reverence and sincerity as though they stood before them. Thus, although he kept aloof from spirits and such, he did honour their presence. Such utterances of Confucius would also be best interpreted relatively rather than absolutely (as had been the case). He taught during a period when there was excessive spirit worship as well as the worship of the dead. Confucius wanted to turn the people away from such preoccupations to more practical concerns.[36]

A Definition of Religion

The question of a Chinese religion of which Confucianism forms the core can be clarified by defining what a religion is.

If one considers Paul Tillich's definition of religion as 'ultimate concern',[37] or A. N. Whitehead's concept of religion as 'the art of the internal life of man',[38] then there is no difficulty in naming the philosophy of Confucius (and Lao-tzu) a 'religion'. Tillich defines religion as the system of beliefs, ritualistic practices, and organizational relationship designed to deal with ultimate matters of human life such as the tragedy of death, unjustifiable sufferings, unaccountable frustrations, and uncontrollable hostilities that threaten to shatter human social ties. Such matters transcend the conditional finite world of empirical rational knowledge, and to cope with them as an integral part of life, man is motivated to seek strength from faith in the non-empirical realms as spiritual power inspired by his conception of the supernatural.[39]

Einstein's concept of wonder and the experience of the mysterious in daily routine corresponds to the Chinese concept of contemplating the intrinsic value of things. Julian Huxley's concept of religion as a way of life, an inner awareness and a sublimation, is also similar to the Chinese approach to religion.[40]

In addition, one notes that the thoughts of Pierre Teilhard de Chardin in *The Divine Milieu* are very Chinese.[41] His whole structure of the worldview coincides with the Chinese cosmological view of life. Likewise, his idea that God permeates all things and that we can encounter God in our own action resembles the Chinese concept of the Mandate of Heaven descending upon man and all things. The Chinese believe that the love of Heaven is in all creatures, and that in meeting them, man encounters God. The divine love energy is the unifying power of the universe. The universe has consciousness and is progressing towards the Great Unity that Teilhard de Chardin calls the 'Omega point'.

19

Similarly, both Confucianism and Christianity share a common basic ethic which may be said to be love for one's fellow human being. Five hundred years before the Sermon on the Mount, the *Analects* of Confucius had already stated the Golden Rule: 'What you do not wish others to do to you, do not to others.[42] Jesus was to emphasize this just as positively: 'Whatever you wish that men do to you, do so to them.'[43]

In light of these definitions, we should have no problem in referring to a 'Chinese religion'. It would be inadequate to term it a 'Chinese philosophy'. Yet, one must remember that the Chinese approach to the Holy and the Supreme God is a unique one. The Chinese concept of religion is that it is a religion that emphasizes the eternal now. It is a religion of life. It is a way of living, not just thinking about life. Humans must live and experience the beauty and goodness of the universe right here and now, not just hope for and aspire to the phantom of a future happiness. For Confucius and the Chinese sages, a religion is a set of moral codes for living a good life. The foremost duty of the sage was therefore to create a set of rules for rightful conduct.

In discussing the 'Chinese religion', one should note too that there is no Chinese word that corresponds exactly to the word 'religion'. To the Chinese, there is no difference between religion and education. The Chinese people use the word 'teaching' (*chiao*) to include all religions. The 'religion' of the Chinese people is implicit in the word 'teach'. Education, or religion, guides the people to live a good life, in harmony with the mystery of the Great *Tao*. Both 'teaching' and learning have the purpose of bringing enlightenment. A great teacher teaches one to understand the great principles of life and of the universe and how to reach the good and appreciate the beautiful. Although the Chinese notion of 'teaching' does not indicate an explicit belief in God, it is incorrect to say that the Chinese do not believe in God. Everywhere in the classical books of China, such as those of Lao-tzu, Confucius, Mencius and Chuang-tzu, there is reference to the presence of the Supreme Ultimate, of Heaven and of the Great *Tao*.

To conclude, Confucianism is both a religion and a philosophy. It is a religion because it shares with the major religions the acceptance of a God, the supreme being. It seeks strength from faith in the non-empirical realms. It also emphasizes mercy and love. It encourages prayer. On the other hand, Confucianism is a philosophy because there was no 'revealer', only an educator; he was not 'divine' and therefore did not have the authority to promise paradise or salvation or *nirvana* as a reward for belief. Bearing in mind terminological difficulties, I will refer to Confucianism as both a religion and a philosophy since there is no word that envelops both concepts.

3

The Great *Tao*

Something there is without form and complete,
Born before heaven and earth,
Solitary and vast,
Standing alone without change,
Everywhere pervading all things,
Mothering all beneath heaven.
I don't know its name;
I style it Tao,
And for want of a name call it great.[1] *Lao-tze*

While 'God' was the supreme concept in the West in terms of questions of the Highest Reality, *'Dhama'* (truth or law) took its place in the Indian tradition. But in the Chinese tradition, 'Heaven' and *'Tao'* occupied the place of the highest reality.

A prominent Chinese scholar summarized Confucianism in six words: 'follow Heaven's *Tao*: establish man's *Tao*'.[2] Although we know the existence of Heaven's Way, it cannot be described. We do know however that if it is not there, nothing can exist in the universe. Because of Heaven's *Tao* things exist and grow and die and are born again. The purpose of life is to establish one's *Tao*, which must be in harmony with that of Heaven.

An understanding of the Chinese religion must therefore include an understanding of the Great *Tao*. Since the Confucian emphasis was a predominantly 'this-worldly' one, it was left to the Taoist sages, particularly Lao-tzu and Chuang-tzu, to try to expound more fully the concept of *Tao*. Their exposition of *Tao* was absorbed into the Confucian ideology and together they form the Chinese worldview and religious orientation.[3]

Due to the success in the West of books such as *The Tao of Physics*, the word *'Tao'* has now gained currency and is listed in well-known English dictionaries.[4] However, such dictionaries describe *Tao* simply as a 'way' or 'path'. This is correct but not complete. One should note that as well as indicating the multifarious ways of communicating with this ultimate reality, *Tao* also denotes the ultimate reality in Chinese religious experience. *Tao* means *both* the way as principle and the way as the means to realize the principle.[5] We note, too, that *Tao* is the common term used by all Chinese religious thinkers to denote the essence of religion. It is used to exemplify their understanding of the most subtle nature of religious experience.

The most famous exposition of the *Tao* is found in the *Tao-te ching* which contains a consistent and coherent view of life and the universe. It is believed to be the most translated work next to the Bible. Not surprisingly, in the course of succeeding centuries, commentaries on this canon have been written in great profusion, attesting to the immense interest and importance attached to this work. About a thousand commentaries are known to exist: some 500 in Chinese, over 250 in Japanese and a small number in the Western languages.[6] There have also been numerous translations of the Taoist canon. The earliest was in Sanskrit and made by Tripitaka-Master Hsuan Tsang, a Buddhist luminary of the T'ang dynasty. The next earliest translation was in Latin and appeared about 1750. It was apparently made by a Jesuit missionary who had been to China. In 1828 the first Russian version appeared, and 40 years later the English version.[7] Today, there are upwards of 40 English translations in the field, competing with one another for superior merit.[8]

In relation to its small size (some 5000 characters), the influence directly or indirectly exerted by this extraordinary work on Chinese life and culture is profound and far-reaching. It has, for instance, contributed considerably towards the development of various classical schools of Chinese philosophy, notably Han Fei-tzu (d. 233 BC), a great leader of the Legalist school, and Chuang-tzu (369–286 BC), second only to Lao-tzu as a Taoist mystic and philosopher.

Like all the religions of humankind, Taoism has added to the pool not only of spiritual but also of physical knowledge. The development in China of such sciences as chemistry, mineralogy and geography can be traced to Taoism. In addition, Taoism has played a signal part in the development of medicine, acupuncture, and the practical arts and crafts, as well as alchemy, astrology, divination and martial art (kung fu).[9]

Lao-tzu, the Man

The author of the *Tao-te ching* is said to be Lao-tzu, who is
believed to be the first ancient sage of China who dedicated his
life to the study of *Tao*.[10] We cannot, however, be sure of his real
name. Lao-tzu is a description rather than an appellation. It can
mean 'old philosopher' or 'old sir', but it can also mean 'old child'
or 'old fellow'. Perhaps Lao-tzu followed his own dictate that one
should not be attached to names and thereby kept himself so well
hidden that today very little is known of him except his writings.

The story[11] goes that Lao-tzu was a custodian at the imperial
archives in the state of Chou and as such had access to the
ancient books of China. However, being disillusioned with the
depraved conduct of the nobility and their oppression of the
peasants and slaves, he left China to live outside its borders as a
sign of protest. The officer of the frontier, Yin Hsi, noted his
intention and urged him to write a book before he left his
homeland. Lao-tzu took up the suggestion and wrote a book
discussing *Tao* and virtue. At first the work was simply called
Lao-tzu. Later, during the Han dynasty (202 BC–AD 9), it was
dignified with the title *Tao-te ching* (Classic of the Way and Its
Virtue).[12]

Lao-tzu and Confucius

It is traditionally believed that a meeting took place between
Lao-tzu and Confucius. The earliest account[13] begins with
Confucius going to Chou to put questions to Lao-tzu concerning
the rites, although in the document itself nothing further is said
about them. All that is recorded is a lecture by Lao-tzu on the
kind of behaviour to be avoided. There are other versions of this
meeting, however. One version, which is of Confucianist origin
recounts that Confucius received instruction in the rites, while
another of Taoist origin concerns the censure of Confucius by
Lao-tzu. Lau[14] records four instances of Confucius recalling what
he learned about the rites from Lao-tzu, although there is no
account of the actual meeting. After the meeting with Lao-tzu,
Confucius is reported to have said:

I know a bird can fly, a fish can swim, and an animal can run. For that which runs a net can be made; for that which swims a line can be made; for that which flies a corded arrow can be made. But the dragon's ascent into heaven on the wind and the clouds is something which is beyond my knowledge. Today I have seen Lao-tzu who is perhaps like a dragon.[15]

Whatever the version, one notes that it is Confucius who sought advice from Lao-tzu and not the other way round. From this and other evidence I am inclined to believe that Confucius was at one time a student of and an apprentice to the older philosopher, Lao-tzu, whose influence in the conception of a non-anthropomorphic and all-pervasive *Tao*, in a laissez-faire (wu-wei) philosophy of government as well as in the advocacy of harmony, moderation and of deeds rather than words can be observed in the thinking of Confucius himself.

Tao as Absolute

The Chinese people, contrary to common belief, were very religious. From the oracle bones, a record of 13th–12th centuries BC, we find that the name of 'Supreme Dominator' occurred over 800 times in various writings. The words 'Heaven', 'Great Heaven', 'Immense Heaven', 'Supreme Heaven', 'Dominator', 'August Dominator' were often used to designate the Supreme Being.[16]

Regardless of the diversity of names given to the Supreme Being, the ancient Chinese always believed in God as the single source of life and of all existence. From this inexhaustible spring of life, one is able to draw life-energy to nourish one's own life. God is the ultimate source of life, imparting His life-energy to many agents, such as parents, earth, air and water. Abundant nutrition is distributed to all creatures and this can be seen in nature.

Thus, the Chinese concept of God is not mythological. Chinese history of the primitive period from 2000 BC is based largely on legends but there is no legend concerning God and no book that contains the acts of God as does the book of Genesis. No definition of God has ever been suggested. There was no myth, no legend, no miracle.

The ancient Chinese centred their daily lives around the idea of a Supreme Being who was benevolent, omnipotent, virtue-loving, just and therefore capable of punishing evil. In fact, their concept of God did not differ much from that found in the Old Testament, but unlike that description, the Chinese idea of the holy sage was not a mysterious person who walked among his people.[17] Instead, it was a God (*Tao*) who by definition was undefinable, indescribable and unknowable except as the single source of all creation.

The religious attitude of the ancient Chinese can thus be said to be monotheistic. It must be noted that the terms 'Heaven' and 'Earth' did not denote two gods, as has often been suggested. To the Chinese, Heaven was the male and Earth the female principle. They represented the harmonious operation of the centrifugal and centripetal forces (*yin* and *yang*), which, in turn, derive from the Ultimate.

Yin-yang is the pivotal theory in traditional Chinese thought so that no aspect of Chinese civilization, government, architecture, personal relationships or ethics can escape its influence. *Yin-yang* are two principles or archetypes whose interaction generates the five elements – metal, wood, water, fire and earth – which, in various combinations, constitute the foundation of the cosmos in all forms. They are also the manifestation of the *Tao*. It is a view of a wholesome nature made up intricately of halves. In other words, everything that is a half must be completed by another half: spirit and matter, subject and object, inside and outside, above and below, man and woman, light and darkness, etc. The two poles complement each other and there is a dynamic balance between them. Most Western philosophies have tended to be lop-sided by glorifying one pole at the expense of the other, e.g. the mind is considered to be better than the body, logic better than intuition.

The confluence of these two powers, like a symphony of love, produces infinite varieties of forms and colours of life. 'In the beginning was the *Tao*', goes a Chinese saying. 'The *Tao* became *yin* and *yang* and from these two principles emerged ten thousand things.' It is a concept of cosmic union involving the idea of the one and single God, immanent in everything. These work together and represent one single, all pervading vital impetus, not two gods.

However, during the 6th century BC, this monotheistic principle of the Supreme Ultimate was lost sight of, and spirits, ghosts, ancestors and other objects were worshipped. Thus it was the mission of Confucius and Lao-tzu to remind the people to look beyond the worship of spirits and other shamanistic practices to the Great *Tao*, the Supreme Dominator, as expounded in their ancient scriptures.

Tao as Unknowable

Since the Chinese did not have either a theology or an interest in speculation, their idea of God was neither philosophical nor theological. The Chinese were not concerned with the attributes of God. They believed in one Supreme Being which had no clear definition. As to who He was and what He looked like, that was better left to God Himself. The Chinese sages have expounded the belief that from a relative knowledge, absolute truth cannot be obtained;[18] in other words, it is impossible to fathom the Infinite with a finite measure.

The essence of Chinese religion can be said to comprise a belief in the presence of a Great *Tao* which is unknowable. Often represented by the Chinese word 'Heaven' (*T'ien*), the Great *Tao* was not so much the personal Creator, Ruler and Judge of the Jews and Christians but a remote, absolute and ultimate reality which cannot logically be well defined.

As the first chapter of the *Tao-te ching* recounts:

If *Tao* can be Taoed, it is not *Tao*.
If its name can be named, it is not its name.
Has no name: precedes heaven and earth;
Has a name: mother of ten thousand things
... Mystery of mysteries, the door to inwardness.

We may compare this with the opening lines of the *Gleanings from the Writings of Bahá'u'lláh*, a collection of passages from Bahá'u'lláh's Writings which His great grandson and Guardian of the Bahá'í Faith, Shoghi Effendi, put together in one volume.

Exalted, immeasurably exalted, art Thou above the strivings of mortal man to unravel Thy mystery, to describe Thy glory, or even to hint at the nature of Thine Essence.[19]

As the Origin of the Universe and 'mother' of all things, *Tao* is transcendent and defies all designation. The *Tao-te ching* explains that it is shapeless, soundless and bodiless.[20] The descriptions of *Tao*'s nature use terms such as cloudy, formless, obscure, elusive, silent and void. *Tao* is essentially indefinable in human language and inexplicable by human reasoning. It is beyond the distinction of personal or impersonal. *Tao* cannot be understood as 'God' in the sense of ruler, monarch, commander, architect, shaper or maker of the universe.

Immanent and Transcendental

The true Taoist knows that *Tao* is not only the Way but the Origin and End of all things, yet it cannot be identified with anything in particular. Immanent in the universe, it nonetheless transcends it. It is the mystery of mysteries which evokes in the minds of thinking people a perennial sense of wonder. Taoism never hides the mysterious nature of *Tao*; rather it glorifies it. The wiser the man, the more amazed he is by this mystery. Only ignorant fools think that they know.[21]

There is an interesting similarity between the metaphysics of *Tao* in Taoism and Brahman of Hinduism. Both *Tao* and Brahman are in essence and in themselves indescribable and nameless, while in manifestation and function both are identifiable with many and all things in the universe. In the *Bhagavad Gita*, Lord Krishna says '. . . the whole world does not know Me who am above them and inexhaustible' and at the same time announces paradoxically that 'I am in everyone's heart as a Supersoul' and 'I am the Self . . . seated in the heart of all creatures'.[22] The Taoist believes that 'the Great *Tao* is simple and near because He is present in everything'.[23] Confucius himself said that '*Tao* is not far from man'.[24] Confucius also elaborated that Nature (human nature) is ordained by Heaven; that taking command of nature is *Tao*, and that to cultivate or practise *Tao* is *chiao* (to teach/to educate). In other words, Confucius refers to the fact that *Tao* is to be found in a person's daily life.

Bahá'u'lláh Himself re-expresses this paradox:

How can I claim to have known Thee, when the entire creation is bewildered by Thy mystery, and how can I confess not to have known Thee, when, lo, the whole universe proclaimeth Thy Presence and testifieth to Thy Truth?[25]

Although the whole universe from the gigantic sun to the tiny ant may manifest the *presence* of Heaven yet its *essence* remains as hidden as ever. Moreover, before the universe came to be, Heaven eternally was, a concept reflected in another statement of Bahá'u'lláh's: 'Consider the hour at which the supreme Manifestation of God revealeth Himself unto men. Ere that hour cometh, the Ancient Being, Who is still unknown of men and hath not as yet given utterance to the Word of God, is Himself the All-Knower in a world devoid of any man that hath known Him. He is indeed the Creator without a creation.'[26]

Chuang-tzu and the Unknowable

Deeply influenced by the *Tao-te ching*, Chuang-tzu,[27] a literary genius with profound spiritual insights, composed many verses on the nature of *Tao*. Chuang-tzu was born in the city of Meng in the state of Sung (in the present Honan province) in the decade between 370 and 360 BC and died probably in his early eighties.[28] Chuang-tzu's notion of the *Tao* appears to be essentially the same as that of Lao-tzu; but whereas Lao-tzu was a sage, economic with words and pregnant in his utterances, Chuang-tzu articulated, by graphic descriptions and intriguing stories, what was implicit in the epigrams of his master.

With Chuang-tzu the philosophy of Taoism can be said to have reached its summit since later works have not contributed anything significantly new. Together, Chuang-tzu's and Lao-tzu's ideas became (like those of Confucius and Mencius) the leaven of Chinese thought.[29] These two thinkers can be called the 'pilgrims of the absolute' precisely because of their almost childlike faith and confidence in the *Tao*; both expressed their scepticism of the various schools which attempted to paint a more concrete picture of the Unknowable.

The following verse on the nature of the *Tao* is typical of Chuang-tzu:

It (*Tao*) may be obtained, but cannot be seen. Before heaven and earth, were, *Tao* was. It has existed without change from all time.

Spiritual beings drew their spirituality therefrom, while the universe became what we can see now. To *Tao*, the zenith is not high, nor the nadir low; no point in time is long ago, nor by lapses of age has it grown old.[30]

Since the *Tao* defies all human understanding and human language, what Chuang-tzu and Lao-tzu have attempted to do is to describe, obliquely and in a negative way, some of its effects in relation to the existent universe and human world. They reasoned that since the *Tao* alone is the absolute, it follows that everything else is relative, including all human opinions and traditions.

Sometimes Chuang-tzu enters into an 'I-thou' relationship with the *Tao* reminiscent of a Muslim or Bahá'í prayer:

O My Exemplar! Thou who destroyest all things, and dost not account it cruelty; thou who benefittest all time, and dost not account it charity; thou who art older than antiquity and dost not account it age; thou who supportest the universe, shaping the many forms therein, and dost not account it skill – this is the happiness of God![31]

The many titles of *Tao* referred to by Chuang-tzu include the Great Negative (Omnipotent), the Great One (Omnipresent), the Great Law (i.e. perfection), the Great Nomenclature (all inclusive), the Great Uniformity (all-assimilative), the Great Eye (that is, the Omniscient), as well as the Great Space, the Great Truth and the Great Unity. This is a forerunner of the many titles of Bahá to be revealed by Bahá'u'lláh such as the Most Great Spirit, the Pre-existent Root, the Supreme Heaven, the Most Great Name.[32]

A Benevolent *Tao*

Just as the sun rises on the evil and good and sends rain on the just and unjust, one characteristic of the Great *Tao* is that it does not differentiate but loves all nature and all men:[33]

The sage has no fixed heart.
He finds his heart

In the hundred families' heart,
He is good to the good;
He is also good to the not-good,
For virtue is good.
He is faithful to the faithful;
He is also faithful to the unfaithful,
For virtue is faithful.[34]

This bounty and generosity of *Tao* however does not mean that *Tao* does not take an active hand in redressing inequities because although 'the *Tao* of Heaven plays no favourites . . . it always succors the good'.[35]

Confucius has the same idea of Heaven and narrates what he terms the 'three impartialities'.

Heaven spreads over all without partiality; Earth sustains and contains all without partiality. Reverently displaying these three characteristics and thereby comforting all under Heaven in the tools which they imposed, is what is called 'the three impartialities'.[36]

Similarly, 'Abdu'l-Bahá taught that 'the good pleasure of God consists in the welfare of all the individual members of mankind'.[37] The Ultimate is not partial and is no respecter of persons. Provision is made for all and the harvest is for everyone.

The Promise of Immortality

The celestial Youth hath, in this Day, raised above the heads of men the glorious Chalice of Immortality . . .[38]

Bahá'u'lláh

We note that the assurance of immortality has always been and will always be important for man, for if there is no such assurance, then there is nothing left to work towards, no reason to strive, nothing to look forward to. Religion alone offers to the individual fulfilment of his quest for immortality and enables him to transcend his desire for the material and the mundane.

In pre-Confucian time, there had always been the belief in reward and punishment. The *Book of Changes* records that 'the family [people] that accumulates good is sure to have happiness, while the family that accumulates evil is sure to have superabundant misery'.[39] This has been passed down through popular sayings such as 'the virtuous will be rewarded, the wicked punished' and 'the reward of virtue and vice is like a shadow following man'. Such sayings generally assume an afterlife. This can be seen in popular Chinese mythological accounts which graphically describe the horrors found in the various chambers of Hell.

Because the people of his time were preoccupied with the worship of spirits, Confucius emphasized that a person should focus his attention on living a good life. The afterlife, with its rewards or punishments, is not within one's control and thus should not be the point of emphasis.[40] This is reminiscent of the Báb's teaching that 'that which is worthy of His Essence is to worship Him for His sake, without fear of fire, or hope of paradise'.[41]

When Confucius was asked whether men have consciousness after their death, he replied:

If I say that the dead have consciousness, I am afraid that the pious sons and obedient grandsons will harm their own lives for the dead; if I say that the dead have no consciousness, I am afraid that the unfilial and impious children will abandon the cadavers of their deceased parents and not even bury them. Why are you so eager to know if the dead have consciousness? It is not important now. We will know it naturally later (when we die).[42]

Nor did any of his disciples talk about the subject at length, their famous reply being; 'If we do not know about life, how do we know about death?'[43]

Thus, Confucius was non-committal on questions of immortality and was careful to rationalize why he was oriented in this way. He did not deny that the afterlife was a reality but he did not emphasize it. He accepted what the ancient Chinese had believed about God and afterlife, that is, that Heaven and afterlife are not clearly and dogmatically defined, but are vaguely recognized as real.

Yet it seems to be part of human nature to worry about death and the hereafter. Thus, it was left to the other Chinese sages to fill in the gaps about death and to satisfy man's greatest curiosity and psychological desire for assurance. Therefore, to understand the Chinese ideas about this subject we must turn to the writings of Lao-tzu, Chuang-tzu and Mencius.

In the *Tao-te ching*, Lao-tzu affirms the promise of immortality to those who adhere to *Tao*:

It is said that
He who preserves his life
Meets no tigers or wild buffaloes on the road
Remains untouched by weapons in the wars.
In him the wild buffalo
Finds no space for his horns,
the tiger no space for his claws,
the soldier no space for his blade.
How is this?
Because there is no place for death in him.[44]

As for Chuang-tzu, the promise of eternal life is so real that it makes life on earth seem like a dream, a metaphor that is not unfamiliar in Bahá'í scriptures.[45] He often spoke of life as a dream and death as 'the great awakening':

A man is dreaming, he does not realize that he is dreaming. Sometimes he even dreams that he is awake and goes on to interpret the dream he has just had. Only when he awakes does he realize that it was all a dream. So when the Great Awakening comes, one will realize, that this life is a Big Dream. Yet fools consider themselves as awake, knowing for sure that 'this is the prince and *that* is the shepherd'. Oh, what cocksureness! Confucius and yourself are both dreams; and I who say that you are dreams am likewise a dream.[46]

For Chuang-tzu, human beings were the passing shadows of their spirits or true selves, just as for 'Abdu'l-Bahá 'the human life is like unto a mirage and a reflection on the water'.[47]

Man's life in this world is like the flitting shadow of a white pony on its run as seen through a crack in the wall. A momentary flash and it disappears! Like jets of water from the bubbling fountain, men spring out and return to their source. By one transformation they are born, by another transformation they die. At the point of dying, all living beings become miserable and men feel sad. But it is only the removal of the bow from its sheath, or the shedding off of a shell. There may be some confusion amidst the yielding to this change, but the spiritual soul and animal soul are taking their leave, and the body will follow them. This is the Great Return![48]

There is, therefore, a belief in immortality, in the human spirit and in the soul. Death is just the beginning of a new stage of life.[49] However, death, being unknown, is commonly feared and Chuang-tzu, like the great spiritual leaders, reassured people that their fear of death might be unfounded:

The Lady Li Chi was the daughter of Ai Feng. When the Duke of Chin (a border chieftain) first got her, she wept until the bosom of her dress was drenched with tears. But when she came to the royal residence, and lived with the Duke and ate rich food, she repented of having wept. How then do I know but that the dead repent of having previously clung on to life?

Religions have often sought to comfort their believers by explaining that death is feared as a result of ignorance. In the Bahá'í Faith, the death that one shrinks from is imaginary and absolutely unreal, being only 'human imagination'.[50] It is explained that 'death proffereth unto every confident believer the cup that is life indeed. It bestoweth joy, and is the bearer of gladness. It conferreth the gift of everlasting life'.[51]

Mencius' confidence in achieving immortality was unmatched among the followers of Confucius.[52] His confidence is clearly shown in his description of the 'strong moving power' which may be said to be the equivalent of the Bahá'í 'soul' which, in its essence, is 'one of the signs of God, a mystery among his mysteries'[53]:

It is difficult to describe. As power it is exceedingly great and exceedingly strong. If nourished by uprightness and not injured, it will fill up all between heaven and earth. As power, it is accompanied by righteousness and the Way. Without them, it will be devoid of nourishment. It is produced by the accumulation of righteous deeds but is not obtained by incidental acts of righteousness.[54]

Mencius did not believe that a person's life ends with his physical death. This strong moving power is man's built-in link to immortality. Yet whether one preserves this power or not depends on the way it is nourished. It must be nourished by uprightness, righteous deeds, and most of all, the Way.

Later, for the popular mind, the afterlife came to be considered as a kind of reincarnation (introduced into China by Buddhism). This fitted in well with the popular imagination and saying that 'if during life, one is not sparing of the five grains, after death one will become one of the six domestic animals'. Later Taoist and Buddhist works catered to the popular taste and elaborated on pictures of Heaven and Hell with many features and grotesque descriptions.[55] An even later Taoist doctrine suggested that a good man could achieve long life and eventually become immortal. In popular belief, after great men died, because of their contributions in their lifetimes, they turned into deities. A conspicuous example of this belief is the popular deity Kuan Kung, a virtuous and just general of Chinese history, loved by many. It must be noted, however, that such ideas were absent from the original philosophy of Lao-tzu.

Heaven and Fate

Predetermination or fate (*ming*) occupied a prominent place in the traditional Chinese interpretation of life and life crises. By the time of Confucius, a variety of theories of fate had emerged.

One of the popular contemporary adages during the time of Confucius, and which is still quoted today, is 'Death and life have their determined appointment; riches and honour depend upon Heaven'.[56] Confucius himself spoke of fate thirteen times, one example of which is: 'If my principles are to advance, it is so ordered. If they are to fall to the ground, it is so ordered.'[57]

Mencius was even more explicit in regarding Heaven as a personified predeterminer. For example, 'To advance a man or to stop his advance is really beyond the power of other men. My not finding in the prince of Lu a ruler who would confide in me, and put my counsels into practice, is from Heaven.'[58]

The belief in fate is therefore a component of the Chinese psyche. Bahá'ís believe, however, that there are two kinds of fate: one decreed and the other conditional or impending. The decreed fate is that which cannot change or be changed while the conditional fate is that which may occur.[59] While one has control over conditional fate, one has no control over decreed fate.

Tao and Tao Alone

If *Tao* prevails on earth, prophets will fulfil their mission.[60]

The *Tao-te ching* advocates that the nature of great virtue is to follow *Tao* alone.[61] Once in harmony with *Tao*, everything is made whole, there being no metaphorical demons or spirits to upset the people's constitution:

When beneath-heaven is ruled with *Tao*,
Demons don't go spiriting.
Not only do the demons not spirit,
But the spirits don't harm people.[62]

The Chinese explanation of the nature of great virtue is not dissimilar from the Bahá'í belief that 'the beginning of all things is the knowledge of God' and the admonition by Bahá'u'lláh that one should 'barter not away this Youth, O people, for the vanities of this world or the delights of heaven'.[63] The *Tao-te ching* states that it is natural for men to turn to *Tao* and that it is separation from *Tao* which is unnatural. *Tao* is the one who gives life, nurses, raises, nurtures, shelters, comforts, feeds and protects.[64] Every creature who is conscious of its origin thus has a natural and intimate kinship with *Tao*. *Tao* is like the mother to the newborn.[65] Logically, then, turning towards *Tao* is life and turning away is death. Being on the path is as life-giving as reaching the end of it, while being off the path is more death-dealing than ignorance of where the path leads:

If I have a grain of wisdom,
I walk along the great *Tao*
And only fear to stray.[66]

For Chuang-tzu, the ultimate end of man was to be united with *Tao*. Once one attained a union with the *Tao*, humanity and justice would flow from one spontaneously 'like a stream from the fountain'.[67] These virtues would no longer be onerous duties imposed upon one by an external authority. In their performance, one would feel no sense of being virtuous, but only a deep joy incidental to any act gracefully done.

An Unbiased Mind

However, to be at one with the *Tao*, one should first empty oneself of all human learning so as to be objective in the partaking of divine knowledge. For Bahá'u'lláh, learning, after all, often 'cometh with arrogance and pride, and it bringeth on error and indifference to God'.[68] In His letter to the learned men of the Bayán in Persia, Bahá'u'lláh even begged them 'not to depend upon their intellect, their comprehension and learning'.[69]

To show the importance of an unbiased mind in the search for Truth, the *Tao-te ching* frequently uses metaphor in describing a human being's uncontaminated nature, variously likening it to 'uncarved wood', the innocence of a spewing infant, the seeming obscurity of muddy water and the openness of a valley.[70] Lao-tzu believed that man's original nature was constant although its pristine simplicity had been smothered by layers upon layers of the 'knowledge' and 'desire' generated in a contrived and unnatural society. For Lao-tzu, this encrustation of social norms, values and conventional erudition could be pared away through a cultivation of the Taoist way and a return to the beginning:

To get learning, add to it daily.
To get *Tao*, subtract daily.
Subtract and subtract
Until you achieve nothing-doing
Do nothing-doing
and everything will get done.[71]

The *Tao-te ching* stresses that one must unlearn conventional knowledge and reject all artificially-established values before one can return to a natural and uncontaminated state. The cultural accumulation around one's original nature – this unnatural carving of the 'uncarved wood' – represents a real deterioration of the human condition. Truth will only be distorted when seen through prejudiced eyes. Lao-tzu went on to elaborate on the fact that most people see the concrete aspect of the wheel, vessel or room not realizing that its utility or usefulness lies in its hollowness.[72]

Thirty spokes share one hub:
In emptiness lies the wheel's utility.
Kneading clay makes a pot;
In emptiness lies the pot's utility.
Cutting doors and windows makes a room,
In emptiness lies the room's utility.

Tao is to be known by 'nothing knowing', a clear and unobstructed state of mind, made possible only by first emptying oneself of all human learning. The mind should be opened to *Tao* by absorbing and becoming intimate with it and not by building mental constructions on top of it.[73] As Bahá'u'lláh puts it, one should 'be cleansed from the idle sayings of men' and 'cast away ... the things ye have composed with the pen of your idle fancies and vain imaginings'.[74]

Nothing-knowing can be achieved not only by the learned but the common people. As in the past revelations, men devoid of learning have comprehended the truth, 'a power whose reality men of learning fail to grasp'.[75] This is perhaps most clearly seen in the recognition of Christ by the illiterate and the rejection of Him by the intellectuals of His time.

Without going out of the door
You can know beneath-heaven
Without looking out of the window
You can see heaven's way
The further you go,
the less you know.[76]

Indeed, Lao-tzu warns that 'the wise are not learned; the learned are not wise',[77] as learning is more often a hindrance rather than an aid to spiritual insights.[78] In this context, *Tao* is attained not so much by knowledge but by an absence of knowledge accomplished through learning.

Conclusion

The Chinese concept of God as revealed in the *Tao-te ching* is that He is absolute, unknowable, immanent, transcendental and benevolent. There is a belief in immortality and in the operation of fate, and a realization that to follow *Tao* is to go by Heaven's Way, not man's way. To be at one with the Way, an unbiased mind is of critical importance. In addition, the *Tao-te ching*'s role as the greatest expounder of the *Tao* must be acknowledged. Like the Confucian *Analects*, the *Tao-te ching* dwells on the practical and the factual rather than the mystical. It is immensely social in terms of laying down the wisdom of happy living through the practice of humility, contentment, moderation and deeds. There is a model for a good ruler, lessons on what succeeds and what brings grief.

As a spiritual legacy, the *Tao-te ching* covers a vast variety of subjects ranging from personal culture to political ideals and expounds both the immanent and the transcendent aspect of *Tao*. It has played a major part in fostering a spirit of contentment, a deep love of nature, and a strong sense of humility, moderation, simplicity and innocence in the psyche of the Chinese people.

4

Sage or Prophet?

God leaves not His children comfortless, but, when the darkness of winter overshadows them, then again He sends His Messengers, the Prophets, with a renewal of the blessed spring. The Sun of Truth appears again on the horizon of the world shining into the eyes of those who sleep, awaking them to behold the glory of a new dawn. Then again will the tree of humanity blossom and bring forth the fruit of righteousness for the healing of the nations.[1] *'Abdu'l-Bahá*

One recalls that preceding every great civilization, there have always been divine teachers who taught that perfection on earth consisted in the continuous remembrance of the divine source of all things, a source called God or the *Tao*.

Since Confucius and Lao-tzu were both the founders of a system of beliefs which eventually became the 'state religion' of a great civilization, might they be considered prophets, divine messengers in the same sense that one considers Zoroaster, Krishna and the Buddha?

Before answering this intriguing question, it is pertinent to consider the many striking similarities between Chinese sages like Confucius and Lao-tzu and the prophets of other religions.

Continuity and Renewal

The compass and square produce perfect circles and squares. By the sages, the human relations are perfectly exhibited.[2] *Mencius*

Like the great religious teachers of other civilizations, both Confucius and Lao-tzu revived the great spiritual truths such as a monotheistic and unknowable *Tao* and the emphasis on good character and good deeds, that were buried deep in Chinese culture. They did not repudiate the past teachings, although they may have added to them or tried to change some of the more outmoded forms of worship. In this sense, they provided a transcendental anchorage for the Chinese people. Confucius himself made the humble admission that he had not contributed anything new to learning: 'A transmitter and not a maker, believing in and loving ancient studies, I venture to compare myself with our old P'eng.'[3]

Confucius did not renounce the worship of spirits by the Chinese people but portrayed empathy with the religious faith of his ancestors. He respected spiritual beings and insisted on preserving the elaborate sacrificial rites, especially the cult of ancestors. In the time of Confucius, the sacrifice to ancestral spirits and Heaven was an important observance; Confucius did not break with this custom. Instead, whenever he performed rituals of sacrifice, he would stand with great respect.[4]

It must be noted, however, that Confucius did not teach that one should attempt to reconstruct the ancient way of life in modern times. Instead, he advocated a coming together and blending of many diverse elements.[5] Confucius cautioned against the blind imitation of tradition: '. . . to be born into the modern era yet attempt to return to ancient ways – a person like this will suffer disaster in his own lifetime.'[6]

While repeatedly asserting that the ways of the ancients must be preserved, Confucius tempered this respect for antiquity with the practical consideration that this inherited knowledge must be made relevant to prevailing circumstances: 'He who in reviewing the old can come to know the new, has the makings of a teacher.'[7]

Thus, the teachings of Confucius as well as Lao-tzu were marked by continuity and creativity. The old was not rejected but it was made new to enable it to be applicable to changing times. One way of renewing the old truths was through the emphasis of the essence rather than the form. Both Confucius and Lao-tzu were confronted with the established order (the 'rites' or *li*) and criticized outer conformism and hypocrisy in this order in favour of an inner attitude. In the same manner, Jesus criticized some aspects of Jewish 'law' or Torah, such as the avoidance of work on the Sabbath; and the Báb criticized the unnecessary prolongation of prayer by stating that 'the most acceptable prayer is the one offered with the utmost spirituality and radiance'.[8]

Confucius broke sharply with the existing practice where motivation behind sacrifices to spiritual beings was concerned. Sacrifices to spiritual beings during his time had degenerated into a barter transaction, in which so many goods were sacrificed to the ancestors and their spirits in the expectation of receiving blessings. Condemning this attitude, he said that while sacrifices should be made, they should be made in the same spirit in which one is courteous to one's friends; not because of what one expects to get from them, but because it is the right thing to do. Whether the spirits conferred blessings as a result of these sacrifices was of no consequence.[9]

Rejection and Antipathy

The emergence of any new faith always attracts much scepticism from the masses and fierce opposition from the religious and political rulers – the latter with vested interests in preserving the status quo. Spiritual leaders with revolutionary 'new' insights are rarely loved during their lifetime, particularly by their own people. This was the case with Jesus, the Buddha, the Báb and Bahá'u'lláh, all of whom died without apparently having achieved their goals.

Both Confucius and Lao-tzu, in their hopes for a coming kingdom of peace, suffered disappointment. Throughout their lives, they opposed the ritualistic, the oppressive and the violent. Both were rejected by the leaders of their day. Confucius often remarked on 'the paradox of life': that the world finds it difficult to accept 'a true gentleman' or the Way, especially when it is 'extremely great'.[10] Both Confucius and Lao-tzu wandered around for many years of their lives trying to find an enlightened ruler who would listen to their ideas. They never did.

Lao-tzu left the country in disgust to live outside the Chinese border, with people whom the Chinese considered as 'barbarians'. This was a scandal as great to the Chinese as Jesus dying the death of a criminal was to the Romans, since the Chinese had traditionally believed themselves more intelligent, more cultured and more capable than other races. Just as the Jews denigrated temple prostitutes and the Romans as subversives, so the Chinese throughout their history denigrated 'barbarians' to the

north and west of their country. Indeed, the flight of Lao-tzu to
the people they despised persists as a symbol of the sage's
denunciation of the trappings of conventional success.[11]

His departure can be understood in the light of the rejection of
his ideas as heretical and incongruous with current social trends:

All beneath heaven say
My *Tao* seems like folly.
But it is great
because it seems like folly.
Were it not like folly,
Long indeed would it have been petty.[12]

So it is that people, particularly the intelligentsia, do not
usually recognize a sage when he is alive: 'The great *Tao* is easy
indeed but the people choose bypaths'.[13] Lao-tzu, reminiscent of
the founders of other religions, refers to this:[14]

My words are very easy to know,
Very easy to follow;
But beneath-heaven can't know them,
Can't follow them.[15]

He acknowledges that only the truly spiritual can see beyond
the personality of the sage to recognize the Original Source which
has always, throughout history, been the same:

My words have an ancestor;
My deeds have a lord.
People don't know Him,
So they don't know me.[16]

The Central Mission of the Sage

Despite the cool reception that a sage may receive, he continues
to work tirelessly to return the people to the light – the Great
Tao, the Universal Law or Truth, the Right Way. 'The sage', it is
said, 'returns the people to what they have lost' and 'helps all
things find their nature'.[17]

The central mission of the founders of religions can be said to be that of lifting the people 'from the darkness of ignorance, and guide them to the light of true understanding', as well as 'to ensure the peace and tranquillity of mankind, and provide all the means by which they can be established'.[18] With this in mind, the sage is thus the exemplar par excellence, the epitome of the ideal character – humble, selfless and spiritual, his life being an example of how one may walk along the path of *Tao*. Throughout the *Tao-te ching*, numerous verses expound the sage as one who desires but is desireless,[19] loving, brave, simple and generous,[20] as one who conquers without competing, answers without speaking, attracts without summoning[21] and one who completes his work but takes no credit.[22]

> The sage knows himself,
> But makes no show of himself.
> Loves himself,
> But does not exalt himself.
> He rejects the outward,
> Accepts the inward.[23]

A Loyal Group of Disciples

Without their own families playing a role, Confucius and Lao-tzu both attracted disciples or students, without regard to social background, who were to spread their message. In fact, their teachings inspired a remarkable number of men with the most complete devotion to their ideals.

This was true too of the Buddha, Muḥammad, the Báb and Bahá'u'lláh. Like these spiritual leaders of man, Confucius demanded the utmost zeal of his followers. He expected them, as a matter of course, to be prepared at all times to lay down their lives for their principles – and they did.

> A resolute scholar and a man of humanity will never seek to live at the expense of injuring humanity. He would rather sacrifice his life in order to realize humanity.[24]

'To realize humanity' as the ultimate value of human existence eventually became the spiritual self-definition of a Confucian. Tseng-tzu, a Confucian disciple who can very well be characterized as the knight of humanity, made the following pronouncement:

A knight must be great and strong. His burden is heavy and his course is long. He has taken humanity to be his own burden – is that not heavy? Only with death does his courage stop – is that not enough?[25]

Over the centuries, the Confucian legacy has produced a goodly company of martyrs who have given their lives in defence of the Way.[26] Some have died as revolutionaries who had taken up arms against tyranny; this was the fate of Confucius' own heir in the eighth generation. Others have died at the hand of the executioners, for daring to obey Confucius' injunction to criticize an erring ruler fearlessly, on behalf of the common good.[27] It is clear then that the function of the Way for the Confucianist has been much like that of other religions in terms of the existence of persecution and martyrdom.

A New Era

The founders of the great religions come in times of social crisis. As wandering teachers and masters (rabbi, guru, fu-tzu) they try to respond to the crisis with their message. Although their ideas are in all cases initially unpalatable to the great majority, their message takes root and triumphs, liberating greater forces for the collective progress of the human race. They become historically influential only after their deaths. Without a crown or a government, they have all, symbolically, become kings who rule the whole empire. It is in this sense that each new religion can be said to be the beginning of a new era in the history of humankind. Confucius was no exception to this rule.

In addition, prophecy has always surrounded the coming of the new era marked by the advent of a new messenger of God. In the case of Jesus, Bahá'u'lláh and the Báb, there were clear astrological signs. As for Confucius, there was a prophecy that a true king would arise every 500 years and, according to Mencius, Confucius was regarded as such a true king. This naturally strengthened Confucius' strong sense of social responsibility.[28] He himself acted as if he were the guiding star of this renaissance and it became a self-fulfilling prophecy. As for Lao-tzu, he was so near to prophethood that there is a popular legend that after he left his homeland, he travelled to India and was reincarnated as the Buddha!

The last 2500 years of Chinese history may rightly be called the 'Confucian Era', which officially came to an end with the establishment of the Chinese Republic in 1912. It was very different from the feudal era before it. With the spread of Confucian teachings, Chinese society became less stratified into classes and there was a sense of freedom. This freedom came largely from education. Confucius was the first man to give education to the common people, thus promoting social equality. It marked the beginning of what may be considered a period of enlightenment.

Lifestyle

Like the leaders of other major religions, both Confucius and Lao-tzu lived and preached and presented a highly individualized and personal ethic that expressed itself in clear moral demands. Neither was an ascetic, wishing to withdraw from the world. Instead, each worked in the midst of this life, ate, drank, and was criticized as such by the 'pious'.

Neither was a mystic practising psychological self-analysis, teaching the steps of meditation and in search of ecstasy or *Nirvana*. They were not metaphysicians speculating about God and ultimate questions in general; neither called himself God. Neither was sceptic or rationalist, bent on reducing all thought to the rational and all religion to morality without taking cognizance of a transcendent reality.

Both Lao-tzu and Confucius can be compared to religious teachers such as Jesus and the Buddha who travelled from village to village in order to teach and help people. Each gathered and trained a group of disciples and both laid the groundwork for a continuing spiritual reform that took the form of a new religion after their deaths. Their followers told such stories of their masters that they eventually came to be regarded as more or less godlike.

Both were concerned with the practical application of their messages, messages that were very similar, the heart of each being that their disciples should strive towards a pure mind, free from greed, anger, lust and anxiety.[29]

Religion without Revelation

However, although their teachings are very similar to those of the prophets of the great religions, Confucius and Lao-tzu were not themselves prophets. Confucius himself admits, 'I transmit but do not create.'[30] On another occasion, he elaborated: 'I am not one of those who have innate knowledge'[31] (that is, like the Buddha). 'I am simply one who loves the past and who is diligent in investigating it.'[32]

When asked specifically whether he was a prophet, Confucius said: 'As to being a divine sage or even a Good Man, far be it for me to make any such claim.'[33] He added: 'A Divine Sage I cannot hope ever to meet, the most I can hope for is to meet a true gentleman.'[34]

The Guardian of the Bahá'í Faith, Shoghi Effendi, expressed the Bahá'í view:

Confucius was not a Prophet. It is quite correct to say he is the founder of a moral system and a great reformer.[35]

Regarding Lao-Tse: the Bahá'ís do not consider him a prophet, or even a secondary prophet or messenger, unlike Buddha or Zoroaster, both of whom were Divinely appointed and fully independent Manifestations of God.[36]

However, 'Abdu'l-Bahá, the son of Bahá'u'lláh and the author-ized interpreter of the Bahá'í writings, acknowledged that 'Confucius became the cause of civilization, advancement and prosperity for the people of China',[37] and that Confucius was 'the cause of the illumination of the world of humanity'.[38]

Thus, Confucius was not God and neither was he a messenger of God. His spiritual insights, however relevant and endurable, were not 'revealed' to him as they were to other messengers. Moreover, Confucius made no claim to heavenly descent or divine revelation. He worked no miracles. In fact, he was opposed to such preoccupation with 'other-worldly' activities.

The Confucian texts as well as the *Tao-te ching* are therefore not based on the authority of any kind of transcendental power external to the human realm. They are not meant to be considered a form of 'revelation' or even a manifestation of the will of God. They are not intended to be used as a means of 'salvation' but rather as a guide to the transformation of lives and the way of the *Tao*.

Neither Confucius nor Lao-tzu claimed to have specific missions given them by the one true God, the process by which the prophet becomes the direct representative of God, making known the word and will of God – 'Thus says the Lord', 'This is the word of the Lord' – as has been the case with the founders of the world's great religions.[39]

An intriguing and necessary question remains: if neither Confucius nor Lao-tzu were prophets, how then do we explain their enduring spiritual insights? How do we explain their bright gems of wisdom, both profound and provocative and which, like those of the great scriptures of the world, produce an irresistible tug on the heart of the reader? How do we explain the durability of a system of beliefs which is more than half way through its third millennium?

Waves from India

The essence and the fundamentals of philosophy have emanated from the Prophets.[40] *Bahá'u'lláh*

One hypothesis is that both Confucius and Lao-tzu were immensely spiritual men sensitive and attuned to the spiritual waves emanating from the coming of the Buddha in India in the 6th century BC. They were able to tap the spiritual currents of the time and formulate them in a way that was especially relevant for their time and people.

Thus it may be said that, although the 6th century BC has been acknowledged as the commencement of the Confucian era, it was only so from the perspective of Chinese history; from the perspective of world history, it was the start of the Buddhist era, a religion which was to have great impact on the world, founding civilizations both within and without its native land as well as influencing widespread changes in values and thinking.

A Prophet of Antiquity

Another hypothesis, and perhaps a more plausible one, is that both Confucius and Lao-tzu, being lovers of learning, were able to research the ancient books of China, many of which were considered scriptures by the literati of their time.

Both Lao-tzu and Confucius drew heavily from the *I Ching* and the *Shu* of *The Book of History*, traditionally considered to be the oldest books in China, although they did not quote explicitly from these or from other books.[41] Nevertheless, whatever ideas both may have derived from the ancient Chinese cultural heritage, it must have been spiritually digested by them before expression in their unique styles. In a sense, the contribution of Lao-tzu may be considered greater because he gathered together all the spiritual wisdom scattered throughout ancient documents and put them into a small volume.

Is it possible that in the prehistory of China, there was a Manifestation of God so ancient that His name is now unknown, who appeared on the Chinese horizon long ago but who was so influential that the civilization of the ancient Chinese people has always been considered great and much more advanced than that of other nations? Is it possible that the remnants of His teachings were preserved in some ancient documents and that it was Confucius and Lao-tzu, students of the divine, who rediscovered them, reflected on them and reshaped them into a moral philosophy, the spiritual insights of which were so powerful that in the course of time, they became once again the basis of a vital religion of the Chinese people?

One remembers here Shoghi Effendi's comments on the scarcity of references to the Asiatic prophets:

The only reason there is not more mention of the Asiatic prophets is because their names seem to be lost in the mists of ancient history. Buddha is mentioned and Zoroaster in our scriptures – both non-Jewish prophets or non-semitic prophets. We are taught there always have been Manifestations of God, but we do not have any record of their names.[42]

In the *Analects*, for example, it is apparent that some historical periods were accredited with having attained the Way while the age in which Confucius himself lived is viewed as falling far short of this ideal: '. . . never has anyone fallen into error who followed the laws of the ancient king'.[43] The *Analects* convey the general impression of an upward trend in the development of human society from ancient times until the early Chou peak, when society entered a period of steady decline.

Mencius also mentioned the existence of 'sages' in the distant history of China:

From Yao and Chun down to T'ang were 500 years and more. As to Yu and Kao Yao, they saw those earliest sages and so knew their doctrines, while T'ang heard their doctrine as transmitted, and so knew them. From T'ang and King Wen were 500 years and more, Yi Yun and Lai Chu, they saw T'ang and knew his doctrines, while King Wen heard them as transmitted and so knew them. From King Wen to Confucius were 500 years and more. As to Tai-kung Wang and San Yi-sheng, they saw King Wen, and so knew his doctrines, while Confucius heard them as transmitted, and so knew them.[44]

Throughout the *Mencius*, ancient sage kings are extolled.

We know, too, from archeological evidence, that there were Stone Age men who lived in China but since we have nothing of what they wrote, we can only guess what they may have thought or believed. The earliest Chinese writings were found during the era of the Shang kings around 1400 BC. It was an age of large buildings, beautiful bronze vessels, elaborately woven silks, etc. Although there were books, they have not been preserved and we are only left with short inscriptions on bone and stone.[45] (Whatever books that remained were mostly destroyed in 213 BC as part of Emperor Ch'in Shih Huang Ti's attempt to wipe out opposition.) These remnants give us a tantalizing peep at the elaborate religious ceremonials and considerable political organizations of the time, but are insufficient to tell us much beyond their visual form. Is it possible that in China's ancient history a Manifestation of God appeared who inspired a golden period of Chinese civilization – a period to which Confucius in his writings always referred and looked back on with longing and inspiration?[46]

To conclude, one may speak of the Chinese 'religion' while referring to the teachings of both Confucius and Lao-tzu because the 'religion' gave an entire civilization a unified conscience, a single standard of morality and a faith in Heaven. It could also be called a religion in the sense that Confucius restored and revived a decadent religion; he observed its tenets and advocated their observance. He recognized an invisible power and advocated sacrifice and obedience to that power. The Chinese people derived religious comfort from the teachings of Confucius. The 'religion' emphasized a balance of the spiritual and the material. History shows no record of any civilization unless sustained by the power of some moral code deriving from the teachings of some great religion. It is only religion which deals with spirit and faith. History is the story of religion; and in the 6th century BC that historical force was contributed by Confucius and Lao-tzu, inevitably influenced by the spiritual vibrations emanating from the lost scriptures of their ancient past and/or from the Buddha in India.

Thus in China we have the unique case of a 'religion' without a prophet or divine messenger, a religion not divine in origin but to all intents and purposes a religion in terms of function and its depth of spiritual insights. It is a religion without revelation.

5

Unity of Nature

The operation of Heaven and Earth proceed with the most admirable order, yet they never speak. The four seasons observe clear laws, but they do not discuss them. All of nature is regulated by exact principles, but it never explains them. The sage penetrates the mystery of the order of Heaven and Earth, and comprehends the principles of nature. Thus the perfect man does nothing, and the great sage originates nothing; that is to say, they merely contemplate the universe.[1] *Chuang-tzu*

From time immemorial the Chinese have viewed nature as being sufficiently orderly to suggest an overseer and a path. By observing the workings of nature, one is able to penetrate the mysteries of Heaven and acquire a deep understanding of the meaning of existence. Thus, 'the perfect man' and 'the great sage' need do nothing but look to nature for an understanding of the secrets of the universe and the manifestations of the Supreme Ultimate. No theology is needed to uncover the secrets of nature, only common sense. Thus no tradition of theological thought like those of the West has developed in China.

The Agrarian Perception

... the peasant class and the agricultural class exceed other classes in the importance of their service.[2] *'Abdu'l-Bahá*

Since China is a continental country, the Chinese people have to make their living predominantly by agriculture. From the very beginning of Chinese civilization to the present day, the majority of the population have been farmers. Farmers are, generally, simple earth-bound people and their understanding of the Ultimate Reality is through their simple conception of life. As peasants, they are not speculators or analysts and much of their wisdom derives from the observation of nature and from common sense.

The greatest experience for a farmer can be said to be the mystery, the joy and the beauty of life. When the trees bud and the flowers bloom, the miracle of life reveals itself. It is apparent that the earth, the soil, the rain and the sun are all involved with the creation of life. Life gushes forth rhythmically with every season and appears to be good and beautiful as well as a wonder and mystery. The farmer is surrounded by his family, trees, vegetables, poultry and all kinds of animals. The land is a beautiful place in which the beauty of life unfolds in various forms and colours.

Long ago the Chinese peasants realized the 'oneness' of all beneath Heaven – nature as seen in the forests, the stars, the ocean and humankind. Because of their closeness to the land, farmers are impressed by the regular and orderly transformation of natural phenomena, such as the alternation of day and night and the rotation of the four seasons which determine their sowing and harvesting. These have a strong impact upon their livelihood. Thus developed the belief that natural phenomena are inseparable from human affairs. This belief was later conceptualized by the Chinese sages as the principle of the 'oneness between Heaven and man'.

It is easy for the farmer to understand that life comes from harmony and love. Compared with the notion of love in other cultures, the Chinese idea of love means the 'power that gives life'. Love is the originating power of Heaven or God. The *Book of Changes* calls the universal generating power 'love' (*jen*). This universal generating power *jen* was greatly enhanced by Confucius in his teachings.[3] He used the idea of *jen* as the central theme of his teachings. In the *Analects*, which is divided into 20 short chapters, 16 of the chapters contain the word 'love', all within 58 short sentences. Altogether, 'love' is used 107 times.[4] The Chinese believe that this universal life-giving love of God is the universal principle (*Tao*) that creates, sustains and perfects.

The principle of love as the cause of existence of all phenomena is not unfamiliar to the Bahá'í religion. 'Abdu'l-Bahá declares that the absence of love is the cause of disintegration or non-existence:

Love is the conscious bestowal of God, the bond of affiliation in all phenomena ... It is therefore evident that in the world of humanity the greatest king and sovereign is love. If love were extinguished, the power of attraction dispelled, the affinity of human hearts destroyed, the phenomena of human life would disappear.[5]

When Heaven and Earth are in harmony and love, there is life, growth and vegetation. Correspondingly, the Chinese peasant understands that when a man and woman are in harmony and love, a new life comes to the world. The farmer loves his family and gives life to his children. He loves the life of his ancestors in himself and in his family. In this sense, ancestor worship can be said to be the demonstration of man's love of life beyond time and space. It is apparent to him that there is life everywhere and thus there must be harmony and love in the universe.

The Chinese concept of 'trinity' is that of Heaven, Earth and Man, with Heaven as the source of creativity, Earth as the source of sustenance and Man as the source of cultured achievements. The three work together in harmony. However, they are not equal because Heaven in this context should still be understood as the ultimate creative source of all things. As such it is not to be put on the same level with Earth and Man.

In fact, man occupies a rather insignificant place. In the traditional classification of painting, paintings of landscapes and flowers-and-birds are more important and valuable than paintings of people-and-things. In landscape paintings, the crowning art of China in which the greatest artistic talents have been immortalized, men are depicted as being subordinated to nature: human figures are usually very small, often incidental, and sometimes totally absent. There is no Chinese equivalent of the study of the human form by Michaelangelo or Raphael.

Yin and Yang

Yin and yang are the famed cognates of Chinese thought[6] about nature and it is interesting to note that the contrast of yin and yang is also reflected in the dominant trends of Chinese thought. Confucianism can be generalized as being masculine, active and dominating. Taoism on the other hand can be generalized as being feminine, intuitive, mystical and yielding.

The belief of the Chinese sages was that all changes in nature are manifestations of the dynamic interplay between the polar opposites *yin* and *yang*. Any pair of opposites constitutes a polar relationship where each of the two poles is dynamically linked to the other. Negative and positive are opposites but not enemies. They are not contradictory to each other but tend to compensate for each other. *Yin* and *yang* should, therefore, not be viewed as 'either-or' but 'both-and'. They are opposing and complementary at the same time. They are balancing powers in the universe for regulating cosmic order.

Generally, *yin* stands for a constellation of such qualities as shade ('on the north side of the hill'), darkness, cold, negativeness, weakness, femaleness, etc., while *yang* ('on the south side of the hill') denotes light, heat, strength, positiveness, maleness, etc.[7]

For the Western mind, this idea of the implicit unity of all opposites may be difficult to accept and understand. It is difficult to believe that values which one has always believed to be contrary should be, after all, aspects of the same thing. By comparison, the Chinese mind is not used to dualism and there is no struggle. The concept of *yin-yang* is not a dualism, but a dualistic monism whereby each completes the other in total harmony.

Apparent disunity and disharmony, e.g. life and death, joy and unhappiness, are natural phenomena of the perpetually changing process of the universe. Night is always followed by day; winter cold always leads into spring and then summer, and a long and blistering drought inevitably ends in needed rainfall. One cannot exist without the other. An understanding of the unity of opposites is considered essential for the achievement of enlightenment.

Thus it may be observed that while the Westerners are fond of putting each thing in its place, the Chinese are fond of mixing things together. The Chinese like a harmonious perspective. We have already seen how, for the Chinese, religion, philosophy and education are inseparable while to the Westerner, at least from the age of science in the 19th century, they are obviously distinct.

There are other examples. The Chinese Heaven and the Chinese man are inevitably one, but the Western God and the Western man are two. Spirit and matter are also inseparable for the Chinese – there cannot be matter without spirit, nor spirit without matter.[8] To a Westerner, these are different things.

This concept of harmony, oneness and interrelatedness is applicable to the relationships between the individual and the group, between freedom and discipline, between the component parts of any set of 'opposites' which are opposites by Western criterion but which, to the Chinese mind, do not oppose each other at all – rather, they are not opposites to the Chinese who is not yet converted to Marxism, pragmatism or logical positivism, and who still agrees with the author of the *Hsi-ch'ih-chuan* in the *Commentary on the Book of Changes* that there is a thing called *t'ai-chi* which contains both the *yin* and the *yang* without being *yin* or *yang* itself.[9]

Further, one notes that the *yin-yang* theory is very useful in explaining certain phenomenon such as cultural imbalance. Western culture has tended to favour *yang*, or masculine values and attitudes, and has neglected their complementary *yin*, or feminine, counterparts. Westerners have tended to favour self-assertion over integration, analysis over synthesis, rational knowledge over intuitive wisdom, science over religion, competition over cooperation, expansion over conservation, etc. Today, it is obvious that this one-sided development has reached an alarming stage: a crisis of social, ecological, moral and spiritual dimensions.[10]

Another relationship onto which the *yin-yang* theory throws light is that between good and evil. To the Chinese philosophical mind, good and bad are, first and foremost, opposites which are interrelated in the same way as *yin* and *yang*. The Chinese sages have never conceived of a Satan or an active evil source, the deliverance from whom might be secured by prayer.[11] Indeed, there can only be one Infinite. If there were any other power outside or opposed to the One, then the One would not be Infinite. Good and evil are movements along the same spectrum. This is a very advanced realization for its day, bearing in mind that 'Abdu'l-Bahá had to emphasize with great thoroughness in the 20th century that just as darkness is but the absence or lesser degree of light, so evil is but the absence or lesser degree of good – the undeveloped state. A bad man is one who has not developed the better side of his nature, just as a good man is one who has.

Going and Returning

To be great is to go on
To go on is to be far.
To be far is to return.[12] *Lao-tzu*

Among the laws that govern the changes of things, the most fundamental is that which states, 'When a thing reaches one extreme, it reverts from it.' These are not the actual words of Lao-tzu, but a common Chinese saying, the idea of which no doubt derived from him: 'returning is the motion of *Tao*', and 'to be far is to return'.[13] The idea is that if anything develops certain extreme qualities, those qualities invariably change into their opposites.

For the Chinese, this is a fundamental law of nature. Therefore 'Good fortune rests on bad fortune; Bad fortune aids in good fortune'[14], or as Bahá'u'lláh puts it: 'Be not troubled in poverty nor confident in riches, for poverty is followed by riches, and riches are followed by poverty.'[15] Lao-tzu continues: 'Squalls do not last the morning, nor downpours the day';[16] 'The softest things beneath Heaven overcome the hardest';[17] 'You may gain by losing, and you may lose by gaining'.[18] All these paradoxical theories are no longer paradoxical if one understands the fundamental law of nature; but to people who have no idea of this law, they seem paradoxical indeed. Therefore, Lao-tzu says, 'When an inferior man hears about *Tao*, he laughs loudly at it.'[19]

In fact, Lao-tzu says that to achieve anything, one should always start with the opposite. This is deduced from the notion that the movements of the *Tao* are a continuous interplay between opposites:[20]

What is going to shrink has first been stretched.
What is going to weaken has first been made strong.
What is going to be ruined has first been raised up.
What is going to be taken away has first been given.

Call this the subtle truth:
The soft and weak conquer the hard and strong.

One may ask what the Chinese notion of 'limit' is. A limit is relative to the objective circumstances. When one overeats, what is ordinarily good for the body becomes something harmful. One should eat the right amount of food. But this right amount depends on one's age, one's health and the quality of food one eats. These are laws that govern the changes of things.

Unity in Diversity

Consider the flowers of a garden: though differing in kind, colour, form and shape, yet, inasmuch as they are refreshed by the waters of one spring, revived by the breath of one wind, invigorated by the rays of one sun, this diversity increaseth their charm, and addeth unto their beauty.[21] *'Abdu'l-Bahá*

The basic oneness of the universe is not only known by the Eastern mystics but is also one of the most important revelations of modern physics. It becomes apparent at the atomic level and manifests itself more and more as one penetrates deeper into matter, down into the realm of subatomic particles.[22] It is also coming to light in other areas of inquiry as the emergent paradigms in neurology, psychology and ecology demonstrate.

In the natural world, for instance, there is a symbiosis of patterns which cannot exist without each other. There is a mutually beneficial partnership between organisms of different kinds, for example, in the association where one organism lives within another. Of course, when one looks at the natural world section by section or piece by piece, there is apparent conflict. It appears at first glance that the natural world is a mutual eating society in which every species is the prey of another. But if there were a species not preyed upon by another, that species would increase and multiply to such an extent that it would lead to its own self-strangulation. In the same way, by eliminating certain species of animal life, human beings run the risk of upsetting the whole ecological order and thereby of ultimately destroying themselves.[23] For this reason, anyone who sets out to 'conquer' the world by putting himself first and disregarding all other forms of existence, who ceases to see the earth as a community to which humanity belongs and views it instead as a commodity for our use and possession, puts everything, and especially himself, in danger since all are mutually interdependent.

The Taoist would explain that people see things relatively, that they observe differences and tend to discriminate things from one another. But from the standpoint of the universal *Tao*, such differences will be reconciled and discrimination cease. Although diverse, all things contribute to one another. In fact, the essence of Chinese philosophy and religion is the awareness of the unity and mutual interrelation of all things and events, the experience of all phenomena in the world as the manifestation of a basic oneness.

Hinduism and Buddhism also refer to this ultimate indivisible reality which manifests itself in all things and of which all things are parts. It is called *Brahman* in Hinduism, *Dharmakaya* in Buddhism and *Tao* in Taoism. Because it transcends all concepts and categories, Buddhists also call it *Tathata* or *Suchness*:

What is meant by the soul as suchness, is the oneness of the totality of all things, the great including whole.[24]

This awareness of the interelatedness of all things was known by the prehistoric Chinese who even then understood that trees, rivers, animals and humans altogether compose something whole. As a result, natural phenomena could be portents, while human actions, whether good or evil, influenced both Heaven and Earth. Just as the American Indians identified closely with their forest, so the oldest Chinese were citizens of nature, not a species standing outside and apart from it. Consequently, they did not consider the human being as 'emperor' or 'conqueror' of the other creatures of the cosmos. It was understood that all have to live in harmony so that each and every thing would benefit the others.

A famous Chinese poem expresses this concept beautifully:

Heaven is my father and Earth is my mother, and even such a small creature as I find an intimate place in their midst. Therefore that which fills the universe I regard as my body and that which directs the universe I consider as my nature.[25]

Confucius did not depart from this ancient awareness but instead reinforced and emphasized it in his teachings. As a result, a Confucian sage will always have a feeling of compassion and harmony with the entire universe and a realization that whatever he does carries cosmic significance.

Harmony in the universe, however, does not imply equality.[26] Every person under heaven has a different part to play. Each has his or her proper place, e.g. a servant can be different from and even the opposite of his master, yet unified with him, and as long as both play their roles 'properly', a kind of harmony results. In the same way, generals in the army play one role and privates another. In corporations some are chief executive officers, others clerks and janitors. It is like the different parts of the body, which, although having many different functions, assist one another and are one and equal. A sensitivity to the mutual interdependence of all members of a society, as well as all created things, provides a sound basis for harmony.

The Bahá'í Notion

. . . all beings are connected together like a chain, and reciprocal help, assistance, and influence belonging to the properties of things are the cause of the existence, development, and growth of created beings. It is confirmed through evidences and proofs that every being universally acts upon other beings, either absolutely or through association.[27]

The Bahá'í view is in intrinsic harmony with the Chinese worldview that all the members and parts of the universe are very strongly linked together in a limitless space, and that this connection produces an inevitable reciprocity in material effects. All things are created in a complete and perfect relationship. Not only are the members and elements connected with one another but they also influence one another spiritually and materially, although these connections have yet to be discovered by science.

This brings to mind Bahá'u'lláh's exhortation: 'Be ye as the fingers of one hand, the members of one body.'[28] It is obvious that there is a great diversity of form and function in a body as reflected in its various parts – hands, legs, ears, the backbone, and so on. Although one treasures one's sensory organs such as eyes and ears much more than one's legs and hands, yet all receive the full support of the body. If one of our toes is bruised accidentally while walking, the whole body feels the pain and may be immobilized for a while because all the organs and sensory perceptions rush to the aid of the toe. Similarly, if one applied this attitude to the people in the world, we would no longer live in a world where people ignore the sufferings of others but rather rush to one another's aid whenever one part of humankind was ailing.

Similar to the Chinese conception, the units can never be equal but every unit has its service to render to the whole body. Egalitarianism is the false interpretation of justice. Only in unity can people find fulfilment. Harmony and unity amidst diversity is the operating principle of the universe. 'Abdu'l-Bahá states:

The wonderful law of Attraction, Harmony and Unity, holds together this marvellous Creation.[29]

and:

Association, harmony and union are the source of life . . . Shouldst thou reflect on all created things, thou wilt observe that the existence of every being dependeth upon the association and combination of divers elements the disintegration of which will terminate the existence of that being.[30]

Living with Nature

Does anyone want to take the world
And act on it?
I don't see how he can succeed.
The world is a sacred vessel
Not to be acted on.
Whoever acts on it spoils it:
Whoever grasps at it loses it.[31] *Lao-tzu*

'The world', said Lao-tzu, 'is a sacred vessel.' Nature is the sacred essential context of human existence. This is not to say that nature was worshipped as a god or that the Chinese religion was pantheistic. It is clear that the painting and the painter are two different entities: the painting is not the painter. The effect is not the cause. Thus, nature is a creation of the Creator and in that aspect it is 'sacred' and to be respected. How one behaves towards it is symbolic of one's relationship with the creator of that nature. Any tension and extremism with nature destroys harmony and unity.

One notes that the traditional Chinese view of man in intrinsic partnership with Heaven and Earth is rather different from the Judaeo-Christian tradition which makes man in the image of God and grants him dominion 'over the fish of the sea, and over the fowl of the air and over every living thing that moveth upon the earth'.[32] While 'dominion' does not equal destruction since it has an implication of nurturing and caring (for example, the gardener tending a garden) nevertheless, the Chinese has never been given to understand that he is to have dominion over everything on earth. Such a position is considered to be power-hungry and greedy, characteristics frowned upon by Confucius.

Man must not try to dominate nature but rather to live in harmony with it, just as he should live in harmony with his fellow men. Living harmoniously with nature is indispensable for the growth and existence of humankind. This concept is vital today when the planet is threatened with extinction. If nature is destroyed, man's own spirit is destroyed since people and nature share the same spirit. The Chinese sages have always known that the struggle for gain and power brings chaos to society and nations.[33] Bahá'u'lláh, for His part, has always exhorted His followers to set their hearts on 'whatever will ensure harmony'.[34]

The Chinese emphasis on living harmoniously also discourages the use of superlatives to describe everything. The 'world's biggest, tallest buildings', 'longest bridge', 'most beautiful women', 'most expensive painting', are phrases often heard in the West today. There is a tendency to slot things into categories of 'best', 'worst' or 'in-between'. It appears that the West lives in extreme tension and bifurcation. Competition is everything – business, scholarship, health, sports, beauty, leisure. There are competitions as to who can eat the fastest and the most. The popular *Guinness Book of Records* describes all kind of incredible feats and physical characteristics. Everything is categorized in physical terms as the best or the worst, the tallest or the shortest. This kind of thinking does not generally pertain among the Chinese.

The Physical and Spiritual Worlds

The Chinese believe that there is an interconnectedness not just between beings in the material realm of existence but also between souls in this world and the next. Examples of this idea are provided by episodes in the life of Confucius. While he preferred to serve man rather than spirits yet 'when the villagers were going through their ceremonies to drive away pestilential influences, he put on his court robes and stood on the eastern steps with all due respect, as if he were a true believer'.[35] On another occasion, he freely praised the spiritual beings: 'How abundantly do spiritual beings display the powers that belong to them ... They cause all the people in the kingdom to fast and purify themselves, and array themselves in their richest dresses, in order to attend their sacrifices.'[36]

Mencius taught that all spirits and ghosts reflect the presence of God and that regardless of how great and powerful a particular spirit or ghost is, they are all under the control of Heaven.[37] Their position is not permanent, due to the possibility of promotion or degradation. That is, since the spirits are deceased human beings, the conduct of their descendants can influence their present status.[38]

This belief in the interconnection between the physical and spiritual worlds of God is not unlike the Bahá'í view which postulates that unity is relevant not only on this physical plane but also between the physical and spiritual planes:

The worlds of God are in perfect harmony and correspondence one with another. Each world in this limitless universe is, as it were, a mirror reflecting the history and nature of all the rest. The physical universe is, likewise, in perfect correspondence with the spiritual or divine realm. The world of matter is an outer expression or facsimile of the inner kingdom of the spirit.[39]

Thus the unity of humankind as taught by Bahá'u'lláh refers not only to living things but also to the departed. The living and the dead are parts of one and the same organism and these two parts are intimately dependent, one on the other. Spiritual communion between these two parties, far from being impossible or unnatural, is constant and inevitable.[40]

Conclusion

We may conclude that the Chinese temperament is one which strives for wholeness in general. It seeks the union of Heaven, Earth and Man. These three are not equal in status or function but work together to achieve a wonderful unity for the benefit of all three. A harmonious and peaceful life with the sense of wholeness is the ideal to be achieved in the Chinese tradition. Such a way of life is called *Tao* and it is the essence and goal of the Chinese mind, at least in the traditional sense. There is a belief in the universal generating power of love in the universe which gives birth to and sustains all things. Everything is in balance and harmony through the operation of *yin* and *yang* and the law of 'going and returning'. Thus, the Chinese religion can be said to be a religion of optimism and one which has served the Chinese people well, in addition to having given them hope in times of crisis and natural disaster.

6

Unity of Religion

The names are different but the source the same.
Call the sameness mystery:
Mystery of mystery, the door to inwardness.[1] *Lao-tzu*

This is the changeless Faith of God, eternal in the past, eternal in
the future.[2] *Bahá'u'lláh*

Being significantly and spiritually advanced for his time, Lao-tzu
in the 6th century BC preshadowed the 19th century notion found
in the Bahá'í teachings that all the great spiritual truths come
from the same source and that there is in essence no fundamental
differences between their words and their messages. Thus, very
early in Chinese history, the Chinese people realized that each
religion has something good and valuable to offer. The acknowledgement of mutual goodness in all religions eventually led to the
affirmation that all religions are harmonious in having the same
origin and goal. It can be said that the unity of all religions has
thus become one of the unwritten decrees of the Chinese
believers.

This tacit feeling in the Chinese mind has been evident since
the beginning of the Han dynasty (206 BC – 220 AD) where with
the establishment of Confucian bureaucracy, the Confucian
officials and intellectuals began to develop a new metaphysics
which they called 'the way to Heaven' and which could
encompass all philosophical and religious ideas.

Berling describes the way to Heaven as follows:

This belief in the Unity of the Way of Heaven established a
foundation of syncretic thought; unless religious ideas could be
shown to be outright fantasies they had some claim on truth even
if a distorted or partial truth. Distortion or partiality could be
rectified; the believers were seldom called upon to choose one God

or one truth over all others. The Way of Heaven included all Truths of men.[3]

As the Taoist Ku Huan (c. 392–453?) puts it, 'Taoism and Buddhism are equal in illuminating and transforming people. Different religions develop under a variety of conditions to meet basic needs of the times, but they are all "convenient means" to the same end.'[4] Sun Ch'o of the Ch'in dynasty (265–420), also states: 'Confucius sought order and peace in society, and the Buddha sought enlightenment in the fundamental nature of existence, but their goals are the same.'[5]

These exclamations bring to mind the Báb's teaching that:

The process of His creation hath had no beginning and can have no end, otherwise it would necessitate the cessation of His celestial grace. God had raised up Prophets and revealed Books as numerous as the creatures of the world, and will continue to do so to everlasting.[6]

The sending of messengers by the Supreme Ultimate at different periods of history to different peoples can be likened to the Chinese saying that distributaries branching out from the same river may start off at different points and times and bear different names; but the water which each receives from its source does not vary. It is the water which serves a purpose to people, not the names of the distributaries. To the Chinese, each religion has always been understood as a branch of the educational system, and all founders and sages are but 'teachers' of a particular school. The Chinese people, after all, called their religion 'Chiao' or 'Teaching' or 'Education', and the founders of religions as 'Chiao Tsu' or 'Teaching Master'.

This Chinese analogy is not unlike the Bahá'í concept which teaches that the messengers of God are not rivals in the world, competing for their share of the human race, but are like teachers in the same school. As a wise teacher adapts his teachings to the capacity of his students, these teachers have given teachings in accordance with the capacity of the people among whom they appeared. Many of their teachings are identical, these reflecting the eternal spiritual laws which are repeated from age to age; for example, to be loving and generous, humble and truthful and to return good for evil. Social laws and teachings, however, have not been alike in each religion. For example, the laws of marriage, divorce, diet and cleanliness differ from religion to religion.

Certainly, the Bahá'í concept of 'progressive revelation' is unlikely to be too unfamiliar to the Chinese. From very ancient times, the traditional attitude was one of tolerance rather than dogmatic discrimination and ideological opposition. The sense of wholeness has always led the Chinese mind towards the sense of relativity of particulars within the universal totality.[7]

The Way of Mutual Penetration

All these religions have their source in Heaven which they obey.[8]
K'an Tse

Traced to the source, the three sages are no different.[9]
Emperor Wu

The idea of the unity of religion is not alien to the Chinese mind. In Chinese terminology, it has been labelled as 'the way of mutual penetration'. Historically, there was an attempt by Imperial China to implement this concept, but here I am referring to how Hua-yen Buddhism during the T'ang dynasty (618–907) developed the Way.

The T'ang dynasty was a cosmopolitan age in Chinese history. It was a time when there was a great influx of travellers from Central Asia, the Middle East, Korea and Japan who came to China to trade and to learn Chinese culture. China became the melting pot of the East.

Interestingly enough, it was during the reign of Empress Wu Tze-t'ien (684–704), the first and only female emperor in China, that Hua-yen Buddhism, as it came to be called, developed a universalistic view called the *Dharmadhātu*, which was adopted to promote the spirit of cosmopolitanism, not only in politics but also in religion.

67

The story goes that in order to demonstrate the subtle truth of the *Dharmadhātu*, the Buddhist abbot Fa-tsang (643–712) asked the Empress Wu to order the construction of a hall with all the walls, ceiling and floor covered with reflecting mirrors. Then, as he placed a statue of Buddha in the centre of the hall and lighted a torch, he invited the empress to enter the hall to see the instantaneous and simultaneous interpenetration of the Buddha images in all the mirrors. Different sides of the Buddha image and the viewers were reflected mutually without destroying one another. The Empress Wu realized instantly the truth of 'all in one' and 'one in all'.[10] During her reign, she actively promoted this concept.

Syncretism

In the world there are many different roads but the destination is the same. There are a hundred deliberations but the result is one.[11] *Book of Changes*

Another classical saying is that 'there are hundreds of roads to the capital but any one of them can take you there'. This desire for religious unity has led to the development of the famous Chinese syncretic attitude – sometimes called 'mere eclectism' – although it is much more than that. This doctrine applies to the Chinese spirit of harmony in the realm of the intellect and in the realm of religion, as well as in the practical and ethical life of man.

Syncretism is an interesting religious phenomenon. It may sound corrupting, random and superficial but it is not a mere slogan of unity of all faiths and an utopian dream of the peaceful coexistence of the world's religions. It is a concrete effort and serious enterprise to prevent religious persecutions as well as to work out a harmonious view of religion to meet the spiritual needs and desires of the time. It may be defined as 'the borrowing of affirmation, or integration of concepts, symbols, or practices of one religious tradition into another by process of selection and reconciliation'.[12]

This has led to the phenomenon of one religion adapting some religious elements from other religions. Confucianism, Taoism and Buddhism have all in one way or another borrowed or adapted certain religious concepts, practices and structures from one another as well as from other religions. In fact, religious doctrines, symbols, ceremonies and even deities have been so intermingled and interlocked that it is difficult to tell whether they are of Confucian, Taoist or Buddhist origin.

In Chinese religious history, the Chinese rationalize the existence of their three major religions: 'Confucianism has been chiefly concerned with the social order, Taoism with the individual, particularly his peace of mind and tranquillity of spirit, and Buddhism with previous and past lives.'[13] This rationalization stems from their belief that all religions although distinct from one another, having come from different social periods and regions, complement one another in the sense of helping man to recognize universal truths.

Religious syncretism has been manifested in various ways. In some Chinese temples, Taoist gods, Buddhist gods and even Confucius deified as a god are worshipped under the same roof. Moreover, it is not unusual for a Chinese to proclaim belief in more than one religion. This is unimaginable for those in a culture which takes an absolute stand on the truth of a certain religion.

It is also common for members of the same Chinese family to adopt different religions and to live peacefully with one another. Furthermore, if a Chinese has any objection to intermarriage, cultural or racial difference will be the issue, rarely the religious difference. When Chang Jung (444–97), hailed in history as 'an exemplary Chinese', died, he held in his left hand copies of the Confucian *Classic of Filial Piety* and the Taoist classic, the *Tao-te Ching*, and in his right hand the *Buddhist Lotus Scripture*.

Open-mindedness in religious affairs is also reflected in the funeral rites and solemnities accorded to the dead, especially during the days immediately after their passing. Before the spirit tablet (a slab of wood bearing the name of the ancestor) will be set offerings of food and wine in the Confucian tradition and Taoist and Buddhist monks invited to perform rites turn by turn. Outside China, occasionally a Christian pastor is asked to pray for the dead man's soul – just in case. The last may involve deception, as even a Chinese pastor cannot be depended upon to do his part if he knows his rival Taoist and Buddhist monks have had a hand in the affair.

Although there were occasional squabbles and conflicts among the Confucianists, Taoists and Buddhists, these were not as bloody or as prolonged as disputes in other parts of the world. Neither did the disputing sections condemn each other as untrue and wicked. They conceded a degree of truth in each of them and granted that others were as good a way of life, if not quite as good, as their own.[14]

Modern Attempts

Attempts at religious unification and tolerance proceeded right up to the 20th century. The beginning of the 20th century in China saw the rise of new religious societies, which extended their syncretism not only to Confucianism, Taoism and Buddhism but also to Christianity, Islam and Judaism.

They were founded by men of Confucian persuasion who were influenced by the concept of Confucian sagehood. Confucius had taught that the sage is on the same 'wavelength' as Heaven and that all men should attempt to be sages by imitating the manner and characteristics of the sage.[15] According to this idea, a sage can be born at any time and any place in the world and no sage of any particular place or particular time has the privilege of being the only sage. As all sages have the same fundamental virtue, *jen* or universal love, so all the sages walk the same way of *Tao*, share the same spirit of mind, and live with the same principles. This idea has taught the Chinese people to believe that there can be sages in different religions of different peoples.[16]

The imported doctrine of Buddhism also introduced to the Chinese the concept that there were going to be infinite numbers of future Buddhas. All these Buddhas, with an infinite number of suitable means, would save all living beings and enable them to dwell in the Pure Wisdom of the Buddha.[17] It also taught that the *Tathāgatas* (the ones who realized the truth) will propagate the teachings of salvation by all suitable means.

This background helps to explain the proliferation of societies promoting the unity of religion. In the early 20th century there were formed, among others, the Society of World Religions founded in 1915; the International Society of Holy Religions and the Hsi-hsin (Purification of the Heart) Society founded in 1917; the Tao Yuan (The Academy of *Tao*) in 1921; the T'ung Shan (Fellowship of Goodness) Society in 1918; and the Wu-shan (Society for Understanding of the Good) in 1915. These still function although not as actively as in their beginning years. These societies equally venerate the founders of the world's major religions – Confucius, Lao-tzu, the Buddha, Abraham, Jesus and Muhammad – and they have read the major scriptures of the world religions and selected from them the important texts they believe to represent the essence of each religion, thus composing their own bible.[18]

They echo the ancient truth that religions have evolved from the same source and that all religious communities are moving towards becoming one family. They abhor religious wars and seek a world peace supported by world religious communities.

In their temples are altars or halls to venerate the major sages of world religions but above them they worship a godhead whom they call T'ai-shang Lao-chun (The Supreme Primordial and Eternal Lord) whom they believe to be the transcendental ultimate reality of the universe. Some also believe this entity to be Lao-tzu. They are open and tolerant of all religions, having a desire to share their beliefs and to promote world fellowship.[19]

The beliefs of these societies are very close to the Bahá'í concept of the unity of religions, that is, that all the great religions emanate from the same source although originating at different periods of history. However, the societies are not familiar with the concept of 'progressive revelation', that is, that it is the latest religion of God that brings the purest spiritual insights and has the key to the solution to the world's current social problems. The older religions, although indispensable for their times, have become encrusted with doctrines and dogmas not their own to the extent that they can no longer be relied upon to provide the medication needed for the current ills of society.

These societies are focused on extracting bits and pieces of what they consider 'the essence' of the past religions and putting them all together in one compilation. Although having similar goals, they are essentially disunited since they disagree on what comprises the 'best elements' of each religion.

Conclusion

By studying the whole panorama of religious tradition, the Chinese have generally realized that truth – essentially the Golden Rule – in one form or another underlies the gospel of all the religions. It can be said in essence that there is but one religion and that all the divine messengers have taught it. In China, there has always been an emphasis on the similarities of religion rather than their differences. This was made possible by the emphasis on religion as a way of life rather than structure, authority, clergy or other institutional elements.

The syncretic tendency in the Chinese religion should not be viewed as apathy or indifference of the Chinese to religious matters, as has been interpreted by some observers, but rather as pragmatism as well as a logical correlate derived from a belief in the harmony of the universe.

Although the unity of all religions is a high ideal, it is difficult to realize in this present situation of divisiveness. Each religion and each school of that religion claims superiority and absoluteness. Dogmatism and sectarianism have been the disease of religion and this has been manifested in religious hatred and religious wars. Thus, it is a refreshing change to find that religion has been less of an issue in Chinese culture than in any other major culture. Such tolerance is a fresh breeze away from the sectarianism in the world which has so often been the cause of malice, slander, pain and bloodshed. It is also a refreshing change from one religion branding the others as false.[20]

7

The Great Unity

The most important principle of divine philosophy is the oneness of the world of humanity, the unity of mankind.[1] *'Abdu'l-Bahá*

Heaven is my father and Earth is my mother . . . all people are my brothers and sisters, and all things are my companions. Respect the aged . . . show deep love toward the orphaned and the weak . . . The sage identified his character with that of Heaven and Earth . . . Even those who are tired, infirm, crippled, or sick; those who have no brothers or children, wives or husbands, are all my brothers and sisters . . . In life I follow and serve Heaven and Earth, and in death I will be at peace.[2] *Chang Tsai*

Juxtaposed with the statement of 'Abdu'l-Bahá are the famous words of Chang Tsai (1020–77), a pioneer of Neo-Confucianism, who wrote this inscription on the Western wall of his lecture hall to inspire himself, as well as his students, to cosmic aspiration. His words best illustrate the fervent desire of the Chinese people in the yearning for a cosmopolitan understanding of the world community and a universalistic approach to solve the problem of cultural divisiveness and religious pluralism.

Arnold Toynbee, the great philosopher of history, included Chinese civilization among the five survivors of a number of ancient and medieval civilizations that once existed (the other four are the Indian civilization of Asia, the Islamic civilization, the Greek Orthodox in Greece, Russia, etc., and Western Christianity in Western Europe and America). He found that the Chinese civilization was the only one which aimed to eliminate war by establishing a world government of Great Unity (or Great Harmony) guided by the humanistic precepts of Confucius.[3]

From the very earliest times, the Chinese people have entertained the lofty thought of the 'pacification of the world'. Throughout the history of Chinese religion, such calls have come from its charismatic leaders and visionary prophets.

This may be understood in the Chinese word *p'ing* which means equality, justice and peace. The Chinese believe that all contention can be traced to the absence of *p'ing*. Contention arises when equality and justice are absent. Contention leads to strife. Strife may be put down by the stronger party but this does not bring true and lasting peace. This is because the vanquished are not submissive to the victor at heart. They may bow to him but only because they were defeated, not out of love or respect. This will not last; the vanquished only wait for a moment to strike back. Therefore, in the pursuit of *p'ing*, the basic thrust must come from love and respect, not force.

In light of this concept of *p'ing*, 'Abdu'l-Bahá goes even further to express that one should treat one's enemies as friends since it is love, consideration and respect and not force which conquer hearts. He taught that if people were obedient to this principle, the greatest unity and understanding would be established in the hearts of humankind.[4]

The Great Society of Confucius

All within the four seas are brothers.[5] *Confucius*

The first messengers of God taught family unity, Moses tribal unity, Krishna and Zoroaster racial unity, and the Buddha, Muḥammad and Christ national unity. By the 19th century, it was logical for Bahá'u'lláh to talk about world unity.

However, it is interesting to note that long before the advent of Bahá'u'lláh, Confucius dreamt of a united world which he termed the Great Unity (*ta t'ung*). He urged his disciples to strive to produce a paradise covering the whole world. This idea has been a motivating force to many Chinese statesmen, scholars and authors, especially to reformists and revolutionaries such as Dr Sun Yat-sen, the founder of the Chinese Republic in 1912.[6]

It was Confucius' belief that his teachings, if followed, would lay the foundation for a utopian world where everyone would abide by the Great *Tao*, the Great Way. This would, in turn, lay the foundation of a world community:

I have never seen the realization of the Great Tao and the eminent sage rulers of the Three dynasties, but I have always envisioned them.

When the Great *Tao* is realized, the spirit of openness and fairness will prevail all under the sky. The men of talents, virtue, and ability shall be chosen equally, and sincerity and harmony shall be cultivated. Therefore, men did not only love their parents and not treat their children as only children. A sufficient provision shall be secured for the aged till their death and competent employment for the able bodied and adequate means of upbringing for the young. Kindness and compassion shall be shown to widows, orphans, childless people, and those who are disabled by disease, so that they will have the wherewithal for support. Men will have their proper works and women will have their homes. They shall hate to see the wealth of natural resources underdeveloped, but also dislike to see the hoarding of wealth for their own pleasures. They shall regret of not exerting themselves (of their given talents) but also hate to exert themselves only for their own benefit. Thus, the selfish schemes shall be repressed and found no development. Robbers, filchers, and rebellious traitors shall not appear, and hence the outer doors shall be left open. This shall be the period of what I called the Great Unity (*ta t'ung*).[7]

According to this passage, when the Great *Tao* is realized, there will be universal love. Morality will be the prevailing influence between the ruler and the ruled. On the one hand, the ruler will be morally good; the masses on their part will work hard in their respective occupations and will be content with the security of their lives. The world will be well-governed and the people well-behaved. During the time of the Great Harmony security will be rendered practically unnecessary since the people will be unselfish, warmly clad and well-fed. The people's conscience and self-respect will be the most important safeguard of security. People will be affectionate towards one another.

There will be an emphasis on production, with the purpose of providing a job and a living for every member of the community, thus freeing them from unemployment, want, suffering and fear. There will also be an emphasis on mutual aid, so that nobody will want to hide away his treasures but will gladly offer them to the public. Nobody will want to remain idle but will like to do his utmost for the public. There will also be ample provision made for the poor, the sick, the aged, the disabled and the orphaned. In short, it will be a world where humanity will suffer the least.

In addition, with mutual confidence and good neighbourliness established among nations, there will be external peace and internal order. Trustworthiness will be emphasized in international relationships, so that each country will inspire trust from all the other countries and live peacefully with them, thus eliminating war once and for all. Most important of all, the world community will share in government expenses related to security and education, thus laying the foundation for the practice of the Great Way.

Being based on a humanitarian concept, the principle of *ta t'ung* promotes the well-being of humankind by teaching people to share, to live together, to have mutual sympathy and mutual love. *Ta t'ung* is a public-spirited principle which makes no distinction between race, religion, party or class. It embraces the whole human family.

It is clear, then, that Confucius sought to find integrated and holistic solutions to sociopolitical problems. His approach is comprehensive in character and is oriented towards a peaceful but fundamental transformation of the world.[8] His vision was to have a complete solution, and he aimed for a radical, not a gradual, transformation of existing society. The true Confucian believes that, deep in human nature, there is a secret yearning in man to get along well with his fellow human being: 'All men within the four seas are brothers.' If this longing is not properly satisfied, he will inevitably feel a sense of deficiency in life, even though other desires may be fulfilled.

It may be observed that although it is within the Confucian character to harmonize with rather than master existing conditions, a true Confucian often stands in tension with the status quo. A central concern in the Confucian tradition is how to be an integral part of a social collectivity without losing one's sense of being an individual moral person.

The Great Love of Mo-tzu

Other Chinese philosophers were also fascinated with the utopian ideal of the Great Unity. One of these was Mo-tzu.

Whatever we know of Mo-tzu is derived from the book that bears his name. He was a student of one of the disciples of Confucius and, during his life, organized a cultic community to defend the oppressed and the slaves. He is especially known for his elaboration of Confucian teaching, especially on the concept of universal love. He felt that the Confucian emphasis on loving one's family was not adequate and would, he predicted, eventually lead to nepotism. He believed that the ideal would be to love everyone in the world without distinction.

This is not to say that he was entirely different in his attitude from Confucius. For both of them, the final goal was that of the Great Unity or Great Harmony 'in which people cherish not only their parents and children but also the parents and children of others'. However, while the Confucians believed in radiating their love by degrees, starting with their own family and eventually extending their love to those whom they did not love at first, Mo-tzu wanted immediately to extend love to all, without distinction of blood ties.

Mo-tzu developed a concept called 'all-embracing love' (*Chien ai*), which emphasized a love of all humankind rather than just the love of one's family:

> Suppose that everyone in the world practised universal love, so that everyone loved every other person as much as he loves himself. Would anyone then be lacking in filial devotion? If everyone regarded his father, his elder brother, and his ruler just as he does himself, towards whom could he be lacking in devotion? Would there then be anyone who was not affectionate ... Would there be any thieves and robbers? If everyone looked upon other men's houses as if they were his own, who would steal? ... Would noble clans contend among themselves? Would states attack each other... then the whole world would enjoy peace and good order.[9]

For Mo-tzu, the goal of humanity was to promote the greatest benefits for the greatest number of people in the world and to remove dangers such as wars, quarrels between families and mutual injuries among individuals, and to promote altruism and loyalty between the rulers and ministers, parental affection and filial piety between parents and children and peace between brothers and sisters. The absence of such positive objectives arose, he argued, from a lack of 'an all-embracing love'. This lack of love, if not reversed, would lead to oppression, hatred and exploitation as well as calamities, usurpations, hostilities and animosity.[10]

Mo-tzu explained that such love was difficult to realize simply because the people of the world failed to recognize its benefits and understand its reason. Thus, it is important that people be made to understand that it is useful and in their own interest to cultivate empathy and love for one another. This reminds us of the Bahá'í teaching that if once humankind experienced the fruits of universal peace, it would give up war immediately. Unfortunately, the world of humanity has never enjoyed the blessings of universal peace and thus, not having tasted it, appears to prefer the present condition of war and strife. Out of ignorance, humanity seems to prefer the known to the unknown.

Mo-tzu's explanation of the benefits of universal love can be looked upon as the Chinese doctrine of 'enlightened self interest'. He provided a good many arguments to support this concept. One of his arguments was that a ruler who practises universal love will be liked and trusted by his people while one who is selfish and partial will not.

Mo-tzu was, of course, much too advanced for his time and the people could not conceive how such an abstract principle as universal love could be depended upon to make a person act unselfishly in a crisis. Predictably, the Mohist cause was short-lived and Mo-tzu's teachings were ignored for many centuries. Thus, it was not Mo-tzu's doctrine which assisted in the formulation of the Chinese national character but rather the *jen* of Confucius and its corollary, filial devotion. Today, however, many Christian missionaries and Communist leaders have rediscovered the great value of Mohism and re-advocated the Mohist cause.

It should be noted too that Mo-tzu's ideas were inspired by a religious belief in Heaven. While Heaven was for Confucius a vague divine presence, a distant supreme Being who controlled the destiny of man and the world and whose decree was that man should be moral, Mo-tzu's conception of Heaven was the closest to a personal God that is to be found in ancient Chinese thought. Here, Mo-tzu was probably influened by the ancient Chinese notion of *T'ien* (Heaven) or *Ti* (Supreme God), as represented in the songs and hymns of *The Book of Poetry*. In these ancient scriptures, *T'ien* (or *Ti*) was depicted as a knowing, feeling, loving and hating supreme ruler of men and the universe. Mo-tzu taught that it was the will of Heaven that men should love one another without discrimination, and that those who failed to do so would be punished.

The Cosmology of Tsou Yen

Another famous Chinese advocate of the Great Unity was Tsou Yen (305–240 BC?), who was one of the great scholars of China. He exhorted the Chinese people to be less ethnocentric and more humble, and emphasized that the political powers of the dynasties were not absolute but would have their rise and decline. He reminded the people that what scholars claimed to be the Middle Kingdom (China) only constituted one ninth of the whole world.

The Middle Kingdom is only one of the nine districts in the Divine Continent of the Red Regions ... Besides the Middle Kingdom there are continents similar to the Divine Continent of the Red Region totaling nine, which are called the Nine Continents. Around each of these is a small encircling sea. People and beasts cannot pass from one to another, thus making each a separate continent ... But ultimately all human relations shall culminate in the virtues of humanity, righteousness, restraint, frugality, and the practice of the proper relations between the ruler and minister, superior and inferior, and among the six family relations.[11]

Thus, throughout Chinese history, there have been attempts by enlightened men to rid the Chinese of their ethnocentrism and undue pride in their great ancient culture. They have not succeeded in doing so entirely, but it is to the credit of the Chinese people that their sages had this insight early in their history.

The Universality of K'ang Yu-wei

We now come to the most elaborate universalism that has ever been developed in China. This was expounded by the Confucian scholar K'ang Yu-wei (1858–1927). K'ang was a prominent, if ambiguous, figure in political and intellectual circles associated with the late 19th century reform movements, particularly that of 1898, and with the futile attempts in the early years of the republic to restore the Manchu dynasty. In the intellectual history of the period, he is best known for his controversial books on revision of the Confucian classic tradition and his vigorous lobbying for the adoption of his own version of Confucianism as the state religion in both the moribund empire and the young republic.

The following are some of his major statements concerning the Age of Great Peace.

In the world of great Unity, the whole world becomes a great unity. There is no division into national states and no difference between races. There will be no war . . .

In the Age of Great Peace, there are no emperors, kings, rulers, elders, official titles or ranks. All people are equal, and do not consider position or rank as an honour either. Only wisdom and humanity are promoted and encouraged. Wisdom is to initiate things, accomplish undertakings, promote utility and benefits, and advance people, while humanity is to confer benefits extensively on all the people and to bring salvation to them, to love people and to benefit things. There is no honour outside of wisdom and humanity . . .

In the Age of Great Peace, since man's nature is already good and his ability and intelligence is superior, they only rejoice in matters of wisdom and humanity. New institutions appear every day. Public benefits increase every day. The human mind gets stronger every day. And knowledge becomes clearer every day. People in the whole world together reach the realm of humanity, longevity, perfect happiness, and infinite goodness and wisdom . . .

In the Age of Great Peace, all people are equal. There are no servants or slaves, rulers or commanders, heads of religion or popes.[12]

This view was propounded by K'ang towards the end of the 19th century and into the 20th century. Although he had his supporters, he was received on the whole with great scepticism and branded a traditionalist and an idealist whose views were not in keeping with the urgency of a China facing the technological and imperial might of the West.

Certainly, it is ironic that someone with what we would deem a utopian vision should be branded a traditionalist and a conservative rather than a futurist and a progressive. But this is precisely what makes the Chinese philosophical tradition unique!

Universalism and Mao

Although Mao Tse-tung was influenced by Marx and Lenin early in life, his philosophy is interestingly often in tune with the principles and attitudes of traditional Chinese philosophy. Like the philosophers of the past, Mao's ambition was also to establish the Great Harmony – the age-old Chinese utopia. In his 28th anniversary address, Mao outlined the aims of Communist practice in China:

When classes disappear, all instruments of class struggle – parties and state machinery – will lose their function, cease to be necessary, therefore will gradually wither away and end their historical mission; and humanity will move to a higher stage. [The last phase reveals his concern for the human condition – the hope of the Confucianists] ... The party function is that of working hard to create the conditions in which classes, state power and political parties will die out very naturally and mankind will enter the realm of the Great Harmony.[13]

It is clear that the Chinese people, whether Confucianist or Communist, have always dreamt of a Great Society where there would be equality in diversity and where everybody would play their respective roles peacefully and happily, a time when the whole world would be at peace. In such a world there would be justice, and people would refrain from doing evil, not so much from fear of punishment or want of reward but more from their own conscience and sense of self-respect. One may label this as a strong streak of idealism in the Chinese psyche but it is an idealism generated by long years of strife and contention due to selfishness and individualism.

The Most Great Peace

The earth is but one country, and mankind its citizens.[14]

Bahá'u'lláh

The Chinese dream of an age of great peace parallels the prediction in all ages of the great spiritual leaders such as Zoroaster, the Buddha and Christ that there would be the coming of an era of peace on earth and goodwill among men. Today, the Bahá'í Faith confirms these prophecies and declares that their fulfilment is at hand:

. . . in this marvellous cycle, the earth will be transformed, and the world of humanity arrayed in tranquillity and beauty. Disputes, quarrels, and murders will be replaced by peace, truth and concord; among the nations, peoples, races and countries, love and amity will appear. Cooperation and union will be established, and finally war will be entirely suppressed . . . Universal peace will raise its tent in the centre of the earth, and the Blessed Tree of Life will grow and spread to such an extent that it will over-shadow the East and the West. Strong and weak, rich and poor, antagonistic sects and hostile nations – which are like the wolf and the lamb, the leopard and kid, the lion and the calf – will act toward each other with the most complete love, friendship, justice and equity. The world will be filled with science, with the knowl-edge of the reality of the mysteries of beings, and with the knowledge of God.[15]

However, it must be noted that absolute equality as far as the distribution of wealth (such as is advocated in the theories of K'ang and Mao) is concerned, is impractical because people's abilities and aptitudes are different. The order of the world would be upset if we were all forced to live alike, and justice and the motivation for work would be handicapped if the hardworking and the lazy were given the same material rewards. However, Bahá'u'lláh teaches that society must not permit extremes of either wealth or poverty and to this end He has established certain economic principles such as graduated taxation and profit-sharing in public and private enterprise.

Conclusion

Reviewing the history of universalistic thought in China, one concludes that the slogans 'one world' and 'a world shared by all' are not unknown to the Chinese psyche. There has always been a dream of a popularly-elected government and an efficient one in the meantime. There has always been the image of a full-fledged welfare state more advanced than the ones we have today. It is a kind of socialism more ethical than socialism itself. People in socialist countries often have to be coerced into doing something for the public when there is no reward for themselves. However, in the Chinese dream of the Great Unity (and in the Bahá'í era of the Most Great Peace), people are described as willing to do things for others on their own initiative.

Little are the Chinese aware that a non-Chinese School or Way echoes their age-long dream of the Great Society, the Great Harmony, the Great Unity. The dream is coming true for the time is now ripe. In the past, there was the dream but not the conditions to fulfil it. Until now, the world had not yet reached a stage where it had become imperative to unite; but we are beginning to realize that the alternative is self-destruction.

There is a pressing goal to achieve in our much-troubled and much-divided world. The mission is to convince people of all countries, all sects, all parties, all races, all classes to pay attention to their similarities; to realize that every man and woman is basically good, as good as one's self; and to see clearly that it benefits all if there is harmony among all. We are all linked in an inevitable chain.

The medicine to unite has been given and prescribed. It is a spiritual solution to the problem of social estrangement, political corruption and economic imbalance. Yet it has often been said that the effectiveness of any remedy depends upon the patient's willingness to take the cure.

8

The Nature of Man

We have many times demonstrated and established that man is
the noblest of beings, the sum of all perfections. . .[1] *'Abdu'l-Bahá*

Man is not an Animal

Confucius affirmed that man is the noblest being in the universe,
the only being with a consciousness of himself, hence with the
capacity for self-improvement and perfection. 'All man', he said
'is born righteous.'[2] The main concern of Confucius is how to be
human. Confucian thought takes a humanistic orientation and
advocates a humanistic way of life. For Confucius, man is *jen* and
jen is the basis for all human relationships. *Jen* is written with
two components, the symbol for 'man' on the left and a word for
'two' on the right. The reason is that *jen* refers to the closeness of
two persons – the friendship and love between two individuals.
Put together, the two components mean 'the essence of man'. 'To
be *jen* is to be man.'[3]

Therefore, man is not an animal. He is not descended from the
apes and monkeys. Neither is he created in the image of a deity or
reincarnated from some form of previous life. Man is a moral
being, distinct from all other forms of creation:

Water and fire possess power but no life, grass and trees have life
but cannot know, birds and animals know but are without the
sense of righteousness. Man has power, life, knowledge and the
sense of righteousness. Therefore, he is the most precious of all
species. His strength is not equal to that of an ox. He cannot run
as fast as a horse. Yet horse and oxen are used by man. Why?
Because man has the ability and intelligence for organization and
community.[4]

The human is a species in his own right. He may share many
similarities with the animals but there is an essential difference

84

between him and the wild beasts of the field. In other words, there is a difference in kind between man and the animals, not just of degree. In the same way, there is a difference in kind, not just degree, between man and God. Some people may be 'godlike' but they are not God. 'Divine men', according to Confucius, 'are divine to man, but ordinary to God.' Chuang-tzu develops this idea by saying that 'the meanest being in heaven would be the best on earth; and the best on earth, the meanest in heaven'.[5]

This saying is the Chinese acknowledgement of the differing levels of existence: although man may be the noblest of all created things, yet he cannot transcend his station to reach the station of God or other divine beings. From the perspective of God, even the most perfect man is still a man. In the same way, a dog can only be a perfect dog, never a man.[6]

The Chinese view of man as the noblest being in the universe parallels the Bahá'í view. Man is different from the animal for he is able to intellectualize and to understand abstractions. He is the only creature which can resist nature. For example, man can defy gravity through the invention of the aeroplane. He is, in the words of 'Abdu'l-Bahá, 'the end of imperfection and the beginning of perfection'.[7] That is to say, man has the animal side as well as the angelic side, and the mission of the great educators is to train him so that his angelic tendencies come into ascendancy.

The True Nature of Man

It was left to Mencius to elaborate the Confucian theory of the nature of man. Mencius, which is the latinization of Meng-tzu, was born in the state of Tsou in the province of Shantung in 317 BC, about 108 years after the death of Confucius. He died around 289 BC. He lived during the time of Plato, Aristotle, Zeno, Epicurus, Demosthenes and the other great philosophers of the West. He is acknowledged to be the greatest successor of Confucius.

Like Confucius, Mencius lived in a period of political, social, moral and ideological chaos and, like him, he travelled for many years to offer advice to rulers about moral leadership. Like his mentor, he was more often scorned than admired during his lifetime. Mencius' relationship to Confucius can be said to be generally similar to that of Chuang-tzu to Lao-tzu.

Mencius systematized Confucian philosophy and elaborated key Confucian concepts. He took up and developed much that was merely suggested or implicit in the sayings of Confucius. Mencius carried Confucius' theory to, and sometimes even beyond, its logical conclusion.

Mencius' unique contribution was his exposition that the original nature of man is good.[8] He speculated at great length on this theory. He postulated that men possess an innate knowledge of good and a natural ability to do good.[9] Mencius did not deny that there was an animal side to man. In fact, he admitted that there were 'many similarities and only a minute difference'. He said, for instance, that sex and nourishment are the two great desires of man but that these characteristics also belong to animals and therefore do not constitute the essence of a human being. It is man's moral and intellectual nature that is his essence. Without such a nature he might as well be an animal in the wild or a beast of burden.[10]

In a human being, some elements are noble, while other elements are small. The great must not be injured for the sake of the small, nor the noble for the sake of the element of inferior value. He who nourishes the small elements in him is a small man; he who nourishes the great elements is a great man.[11]

Mencius further illustrated this by saying that the man who is devoted to excessive eating and drinking is not fit to be a man because he has nourished the little at the expense of the great.[12] One eats to live and not lives to eat. To be a human being is to live like a human being rather than like the beasts in the field. If one behaves like an animal, then one does not deserve to be a human being.

This corresponds to the Bahá'í conception of the nature of man. 'Man', 'Abdu'l-Bahá said, 'is a child of God, most noble, lofty and beloved. . .'[13] He added that were man without virtue, he would be little better than a mere animal, and exclaimed that 'Verily, it is better a thousand times for a man to die than to continue living without virtue.'[14] Man is also referred to as being 'in the highest degree of materiality, and at the beginning of spirituality.'[15]

Man is Born Good

As for man's ethical nature, the Confucian tradition considered the question of whether human beings were born with a potential for moral growth. Mencius emphatically believed this to be the case. He argued that since human nature comes originally from Heaven, it cannot be otherwise.

He believed in man's 'natural equality', that is, the equal potential that every individual has for moral growth: 'Everyone may become a Yao or Shun.'[16] (Yao and Shun were legendary sage kings renowned for their moral uprightness.) One may not be capable of being an Einstein but one can be a Lao-tzu or a Confucius.

Concerning humanity Mencius said that all men have minds that cannot bear to see the sufferings of others.[17] He illustrated the good-heartedness of man by saying that when a man suddenly observes a child about to tumble into a well, he experiences a sense of alarm and sympathy. He instinctively stretches out his hands to protect the child from falling. He does this not to make friends with the child's parents, nor to seek reputation from his friends or neighbours nor to avoid the cries of the child.[18]

Mencius believed that should a man lose his original goodness, he could still regain it through his own effort and cultivation. This idea is contrary to the Christian idea of a universally fallen nature or depravity of man and man's inability to restore his original nature by his own strength or actions. It is also rather different from the view that mankind, as descendants of Adam and Eve, has sinned. The Chinese are free from this sense of guilt. A Chinese is taught that his nature is intrinsically good and that he is born directly from his parents rather than from his historical ancestors.

Equality and the Environment

In the estimation of God all men are equal.[19] *'Abdu'l-Bahá*

Confucius believed that man's differences were due essentially to disparities in their education rather than in their genetic make up: 'By nature near together; by practice far apart.'[20] Indeed, as recently as 1950 Confucius' simple observation was used by a group of international experts to support their plea for equal opportunity regardless of race or racial differences in the UNESCO 'Statement on Race'.[21]

Although the equality of man may not be stated explicitly and directly in the Confucian *Analects*, it is implied in almost every other utterance. In the *Analects*, for example, is a story about a man who had four brothers. However, all were in political difficulties and he feared for the life of one. He lamented to Confucius that having brothers was in his case like having no brothers at all. The reply from Confucius was 'All within the four seas are his brothers. How can any true gentleman grieve that he is without brothers?'[22] This latter part means that if a gentleman is himself always respectful and without fault and if he deals with others in accordance with proper manners in all things, then everyone will want to be close to him and therefore is his brother.

Mencius developed this idea of equality among men by showing that most differences were due to environmental influences:

In good years the young people often acquire a habit of dependence. In bad years the young people often take to violence. This is not due to the differences in their natural endowments as conferred by Heaven. It is owing to the different things by which they allow their minds to be ensnared and engulfed.

Take, for instance, the barley. Let the seed be sown and covered up. The ground being the same, and the time of planting again the same, it will grow luxuriantly and ripen in the fullness of time. If there be inequalities of produce, it must be due to the thickness and thinness of the soil, to the sufficiency and insufficiency of rain and dew, and to the different ways of farming.

In fact, all things which belong to the same kind or species are similar to each other. Why should we doubt in regard to man, as if he were a solitary exception to the rule? The sages and we are the same in kind.[23]

Mencius stressed that man's nature is like seeds which require time to sprout, grow and ripen. 'Of all seeds', he continued, 'the best are the five kinds of grain, but if they do not come to ripeness, they are not as good even as the tares. So it is with the virtue of humanity: all depend upon its maturation.'[24] The whole duty of man is thus to actualize his essential nature, and this is to be accomplished by cultivating and nourishing the moral virtues until their influence pervades his whole being.

Mencius explained that if man's nature was left uncultivated, it would become like that of the animal and this, for Mencius, explains the existence of evil:

The trees on the Ox Mountain were once beautiful. Being situated, however, in the suburbs of a large city, they were hewn down with axes and hatchets; how could they retain their beauty? Still through the growth from their vegetative life day and night, and the nourishing influence of the rain and dew, they were not without buds and sprouts sprung out. But then came the cattle and goats, and browsed upon them. This is why it appears so bare and stripped. When people see its bare appearance, they tend to think that there was no wood from the beginning. But is it due to the original nature of the mountain? Similarly, it cannot be said that there is no love and justice in the inherent nature of man. But the way in which a man loses the proper goodness of his mind is just like the way in which those trees were denuded by axes and hatchets. Hacked at, day after day, how can it retain its excellence? Still, there is some growth between day and night, and in the peaceful air of the morning, the mind feels in a degree those inclinations and aversions which are proper to humanity; but the feeling is very feeble. And then it is fettered and destroyed by what the man does during the day. The fettering takes place again and again; the restorative influence of the night is not sufficient to preserve the original goodness of his nature; and when the still small voice of the conscience is smothered, his nature is scarcely distinguishable from that of the irrational animals. When people see that man is like an irrational animal, they tend to think that from the beginning he had no capabilities for good; but is this due to his nature?[25]

Therefore, Mencius taught that the supreme task of being human is to be human. Human beings owe their nature to Heaven and they are accountable to Heaven for what they have done with it. The essential nature with which Heaven has endowed them is the same. One can see these tendencies in the small hours of the morning when the conscience is more active than at other times when one is distracted by many things.

The Vital Spirit

An interesting phase in the realization of a man's essential nature is the gradual permeation and assimilation by it of what Mencius calls the 'vital spirit'.[26] This can be said to correspond quite closely to the concept of the human spirit or the rational soul described in the Bahá'í writings. This spirit cannot be perceived by the material senses of the physical body but can only be expressed in outward signs and works. The spirit is also placeless since placement is characteristic of bodies and not of spirits.

This may be compared to Plato's 'passionate or spirited prinicple'.[27] According to Plato, the soul of man has three parts: the rational principle, the passionate or spirited principle and desire.[28] In the conflict between reason and desire, the passionate principle should be arrayed on the side of the rational principle.

With Mencius, this passionate principle or vital spirit is a necessary ally of the rational principle if the unruly desires of man are to be kept in order. Without the help of the vital spirit, the essential nature of man would be like a powerless monarch.

The important thing is to inform the vital spirit with the spirit of justice, thus keeping it in the service of the will. Mencius shows us clearly that when the vital spirit is nourished by the spirit of justice, it is lifted up to a higher plane and, instead of weakening, will grow immensely:

I know how to nourish my vast vital spirit . . . it is not easy to describe it in words. For it is a spirit extremely great and extremely strong. When nourished by rectitude and kept integral, it fills up all between heaven and earth. It is a spirit that must be mated to justice and natural law. Without these it would be starved. In fact, it is born of an accumulation of justice, not something which justice invades from outside and takes to itself.

Its very life depends upon justice. For whenever your conduct does not satisfy your conscience, the vital spirit suffers starvation.[29]

The Mission of Man

All men have been created to carry forward an ever-advancing civilization.[30] *Bahá'u'lláh*

According to Mencius, man's mission is to nourish the vital spirit. It may take a lifetime but this act is in accordance with the *Tao*: 'Strive always to accord with the law of Heaven. This is the proper way of seeking much happiness.'[31]

To be true to our nature means to pursue the good, and these are the virtues of humanity, justice, propriety and prudence. Avoiding evil means to avoid that which is contrary to these virtues. For Mencius, any person who practises the principles of humanity and righteousness with sincerity, radiates the spiritual influence of the universe. It is the only way to attain happiness:

> For a man to give full realization to his heart is for him to understand his own nature, and a man who knows his own nature will know Heaven. By retaining his heart and nurturing his nature, he is serving Heaven.[32]

However, Mencius realized that the mission of man, which is to acquire a high moral standing, must inextricably be tied to some measure of suffering. One recalls in this context that most of the great sages of China were faced with the pain of rejection during their lifetimes.[33] The mission of man is to rise above suffering such as this, knowing that suffering is a necessary step towards self-improvement:

> When Heaven is about to bestow a great mission or charge upon someone, it invariably begins by exercising his mind with suffering, toughening his sinews and bones with toil, exposing his body to hunger, subjecting him to extreme poverty, and frustrating all his plans. All these methods are meant to stimulate his mind, strengthen his nature, and increase his abilities.[34]

A parallel idea exists in the Bahá'í scriptures:

91

The mind and spirit of man advance when he is tried by suffering ... Just as the plough furrows the earth deeply, purifying it of weeds and thistles, so suffering and tribulation free man from petty affairs of this worldly life until he arrives at a state of complete detachment ... Man is, so to speak, unripe: the heat of the fire will mature him.[35]

The mission of man is not to be a Homeric hero, a Ulysses to outwit nature as Scylla and Charybdis were outwitted or to conquer enemies like Cyclops. He is not to conquer the highest peaks or the deepest seas. He is to conquer himself. As Confucius once said to his favourite disciple, one's mission is 'to subdue oneself and to return to propriety'.[36] The great man is one who 'prefers stillness of the heart to quiet the restlessness of mind'.[37]

In addition, when Confucius was asked what the meaning of being 'human' was, he said, 'It is to love others.'[38] Elaborating, he added:

Courtesy, generosity, good faith, diligence and kindness. If you behave with courtesy, then you will not be insulted; if you are generous, then you will win the multitude; if you are of good faith, then other men will put their trust in you; if you are diligent, then you will have success; and if you are kind, then you will be able to command others.[39]

It is clear from what has already been discussed that man's glory and greatness do not, in the Chinese psyche, consist in his being avid for might and blood. Man's glory rests in conquering the animal side of his nature, in conquering himself. It rests, as 'Abdu'l-Bahá puts it, on 'his reputation for justice, kindness to the entire population whether high or low, his building up of countries and cities, villages and districts, his making life easy, peaceful and happy for his fellow beings, his laying down fundamental principles for progress, his raising the standards and increasing the wealth of the entire population'.[40]

The famous Confucian dictum is recalled: 'Man is born for uprightness.'[41] Moreover, Mencius cautions that the difference between man and animal is minute and that the task of man is to widen this difference by uplifting himself. As is stated in the *Book of Great Learning*:

> From the son of Heaven down to the mass of the people, all must consider the cultivation of their person as the root of everything besides.[42]

The Sense of Shame

Since man is essentially noble, it is not the rule of law which must be employed in the cause of enabling man to control his actions. What should be emphasized is his sense of shame, something which must come from the inner self, the conscience. This sense of shame is probably emphasized more in China than in any other cultural tradition of the world. To label a man 'without shame' is to degrade him to the level of animals and seriously to insult all his ancestors.

Confucius himself said that a sense of shame is more powerful than fear of punishment: 'Guide through orders of government and enforce uniform obedience through (the threat of) punishment, people will avoid the punishment but will not know shame. Guide through virtues (as demonstrated by those in the government), promote uniform observance of etiquette/ethical code, people will know shame and correct themselves (of past wrong doings).'[43] Mencius elaborated by saying that the difference between human beings and animals is that the former know shame and the latter do not. Shame was therefore believed to be the driving force for the progress of humankind. It was believed that only where there was knowledge of shame could there be a vigorous effort on the part of man to be moral. Man would become degenerate, numb, listless, licentious and mean if he did not have this sense of shame. In short, he would become no different from the animals. The duty of the sage was therefore to teach the people the concept of shame.[44]

This concept of shame is prevalent throughout Chinese culture. Thus, it is uncommon for a Chinese to confess his sins publicly because it would be shameful for him to do so. One searches in vain in Chinese literature for 'a confession'. Apologies are not common. This is quite different from the Judaeo-Christian tradition where confession is encouraged.

The concept of shame found in the Chinese religion and philosophy is rather different from the concept of guilt found in the Judaeo-Christian tradition. Western society, under the influence of Judaeo-Christianity, views the nature of man as basically sinful and, through the centuries, has devised the rule of law as the primary means of restraining his sinful nature. The Chinese sages have, on the other hand, stressed the role of education as the main way to shape behaviour.

The Bahá'í Faith states that the presence of shame prevents man from doing what is unworthy and unseemly but recognizes that this sense of shame is confined to only a few people.[45] Therefore, by itself it is not sufficient to prevent the occurrence of immoral deeds. The prevention of immoral acts will not come about just from moral education per se but only through a moral education which begins with the recognition of the existence of God and His manifestations. For the Bahá'ís, this is the only lasting solution, for if a crime is prevented by violent or retaliatory measures, the effect will only be short term. Moral education which does not include an acknowledgement of the spiritual does not have any hold on the hearts of the people. The most effective method is to train, spiritualize and enlighten people through what we may call divine education, so that without any fear of punishment or vengeance, they will, through their own will, shun all criminal acts.[46] 'Abdu'l-Bahá elaborates on this concept of divine education as one which marks the difference between the material and divine civilizations:

As to the difference between that material civilization now prevailing, and the divine civilization which will be one of the benefits to derive from the House of Justice, it is this: material civilization, through the power of punitive and retaliatory laws, restraineth the people from criminal acts; and notwithstanding this, while laws to retaliate against and punish a man are continually proliferating, as ye can see, no laws exist to reward him. In all the cities of Europe and America, vast buildings have been erected to serve as jails for the criminals.

Divine civilization, however, so traineth every member of society that no one, with the exception of a negligible few, will undertake to commit a crime. There is thus a great difference between the prevention of crime through measures that are violent and retaliatory, and so training the people, and enlightening them, and spiritualizing them, that without any fear of punishment or vengeance to come, they will shun all criminal acts. They will, indeed, look upon the very commission of a crime as a great disgrace and in itself the harshest of punishments. They will become enamoured of human perfections, and will consecrate their lives to whatever will bring light to the world and will further those qualities which are acceptable only at the Holy Threshold of God.

See then how wide is the difference between material civilization and divine. With force and punishments, material civilization seeketh to restrain the people from mischief, from inflicting harm on society and committing crimes. But in a divine civilization, the individual is so conditioned that with no fear of punishment, he shunneth the perpetration of crimes, seeth the crime itself as the severest of torments, and with alacrity and joy, setteth himself to acquiring the virtues of humankind, to furthering human progress, and to spreading light across the world.[47]

Conclusion

The Confucian view of the human being sees him as what he ought to be – the noblest being in creation. In this sense it is not unlike the view of the Bahá'í Faith, which tries to uplift a person's spirit, to challenge him to be a human being and humane. For example, in the Confucian classics, it is hard to find a word which would give offence even on the most sensitive and most delicate issue.

A search for impropriety in Chinese poetry, for sly innuendo and for other marks of the unclean will be unsuccessful. Such a view instils in the educated person a desire to cultivate the nobler part of his nature. Certainly, if one takes seriously the process of learning to be human, the Confucian persuasion, far from being a static adherence to a predetermined pattern, signifies an unceasing spiritual self-transformation.

Critics of this aspect of Confucianism say that history is a strong witness that man is incapable of purifying his nature. They argue that Confucian ethics are too confident about the ability of man to achieve the ideal society and do not acknowledge the depravity of human nature. Nevertheless, for certain periods in Chinese history, the Confucian ethic worked especially well, not only in unifying the country but in ensuring peace and spiritual and material progress.

9

Leading the Life: *Jen*

Man must bring forth fruit. One who yieldeth no fruit is, in the words of the Spirit [Christ] like unto a fruitless tree, and a fruitless tree is fit but for the fire.[1] *Bahá'u'lláh*

In the *Analects*, Confucius echoed the long-time dream for a society in which people would grasp at good and shrink from evil instinctively: 'When they see what is good, they grasp at it as though they feared it would elude them. When they see what is not good, they test it cautiously, as though putting a finger into hot water.'[2]

The essence of Confucian teachings is expressed in the idea that by developing one's inner humanity a person can become great in private as well as in public life. When all individuals try to develop this, goodness will abound and happiness will be achieved.

It must be emphasized that Confucius put nothing, including personal survival, above doing what was right; and he argued that one must do what was right solely for its own sake. This meant that his morality not only eschewed utilitarian consideration, that is, concerns about the actual or forseeable results of the act, but also the promise of future religious reward. In this sense, it may be said to differ significantly from the major religions which remind people that their good deeds will prepare them for other worlds of God into which they will pass at death.

The central concept here is *jen* which has been variously translated into English as love, filial piety, righteousness, propriety, shame, trust, compassion, benevolence, human-heartedness, perfect virtue or humanity. It can be found in oracle records, in inscriptions on bronze ritual vessels, in documents preserved by the *Book of History*, etc., which existed before the time of Confucius. The meaning of the word, in most of these instances, was kindness.[3]

It was Confucius, however, who created an entirely new concept from this word by assigning to it many new meanings. He broadened it to become a comprehensive virtue covering all individual Confucian virtues and elevated it to the centre of his philosophy. Although he treated *jen* occasionally as a particular virtue, in most cases it represented for him behaviour such as honesty, love for fellow man, sincerity and justice.

If we combine the views of various interpreters, we might be able to enumerate six characteristics of *jen*: universality (love for all persons without discrimination), permanence (*jen* is the *Tao* of Heaven and Earth, therefore existing all the time), creativity (*jen* is life in the sense it is the seeds which produce life), susceptibility (it is the opposite of numbness, that is, the capacity to respond to stimuli), flexibility (*jen* is soft in appearance but very firm when in action) and protectiveness (*jen* is love for all persons, disapproval of war and extravagance). It is therefore quite an inexhaustible subject.[4]

To practise *jen* is to practise man's *Tao*. This *Tao* for man, established as *jen* by Confucius, was to become the nucleus of all Chinese thought. It permeated the heart of every Chinese. There is generally no other insult in the Chinese language as infuriating as 'You are not a *jen*' (person, man or woman). As mentioned, to practise *jen* was to practise *Tao* and to practise *Tao* is to walk in Heaven's way. Since Heaven loves all men, a *jen* man also loves all.

Although the principle of *jen* may sound rather mundane and commonplace today, it was a brilliant and daring principle of reform in the context of axial China, bearing in mind the degenerate and unruly condition of the society at that time. It was the principle essential for an ideal society.

As 'Abdu'l-Bahá said, 'When we speak of man, we mean the perfect one, the foremost individual in the world, who is the sum of spiritual and apparent perfections, and who is like the sun among the beings.'[5]

The Golden Rule

O Son of Being! Ascribe not to any soul that which thou wouldst not have ascribed to thee, and say not that which thou doest not.

This is My Command unto thee, do thou observe it.[6] *Bahá'u'lláh*

The basic manifestation of *jen* is seen in the operation of the Golden Rule. Once a disciple asked, 'Is there a single word that one can live by all one's life?' Confucius replied, 'Is not *shu* such a word? Do not do to others what you do not want done to yourself.' Confucius further stated that 'The truly virtuous man, desiring to be established himself, strives to help others succeed. The principle for his conduct towards others is the method of true virtue.'[7]

Confucius himself said that there was one thread that ran through all his teachings: *chung* and *shu*. The Chinese word for *chung* is made up of the components of 'middle' and 'heart'. With one's heart in the very centre, one will be able to achieve *chung*, which is faithfulness to oneself, to one's own nature and to the humanity that is in one. Only then can one be faithful to one's fellow men, as shown in the virtue of *shu*. *Shu* has the meaning of 'as one's heart', that is 'to do to others as your heart prompts or urges you'. *Shu* connotes altruism, a feeling of fellowship, a desire to cherish the other's heart as if it were one's own. One should treat other people as one would want one to be treated. The art of being human, according to Confucius, is to be able, from oneself, to draw a parallel for the treatment of others.

In his writings, Confucius elaborated on this Golden Rule. The most effective way of determining what not to do to others is to ask oneself whether one would approve of this action or quality in another person. For example, if a person does not wish others to show arrogance or jealousy towards him, he should refrain from showing such arrogance or jealousy.

What a man dislikes in his superiors, let him not display in the treatment of his inferiors; what he dislikes in his inferiors, let him not display in the service of his superiors; what he hates in those who are before him, let him not therewith precede those who are behind him; what he hates in those who are behind him, let him not wherewithal follow those who are before him: what he hates to receive on the right, let him not bestow on the left; what he hates to receive on the left, let him not bestow on the right – this is what is called 'the principle', with which, as with a measuring-square, to regulate one's conduct.[8]

This principle abounds in the sacred literature of the world. In the words of Jesus, it is said, 'Therefore all things whatsoever ye would that men should do to you, do ye even so to them, for this is the law of the prophets.'[9] In the *Mahabharata* of the Hindus, we read: 'Do not to others what ye do not wish done to yourself; and wish for others too what ye desire and long for, for yourself. This is the whole of Dharma, heed it well.'[10]

The Bahá'í Faith may be said to go a step further by teaching that one should cultivate in oneself an acceptance that others are higher and dearer than we are ourselves; indeed, they are as esteemed as high as Bahá'u'lláh Himself: 'O Son of Man! Deny not my servant should he ask anything from thee, for his face is My face; be then abashed before Me.'[11]

Moderation

In all matters moderation is desirable. If a thing is carried to excess, it will prove a source of evil.[12] *Bahá'u'lláh*

There is a saying of Confucius: 'To go beyond the mark is as bad as to fall short of it.'[13] In his life, there was a remarkable sense of balance that kept all his qualities from degenerating into their opposites. Although holding to the Mean was a treasured teaching in pre-axial China, Confucius was the first person to clarify this concept and to call it 'the Doctrine of the Mean'. He realized that both excess and inadequacy were extremes and that only by understanding the Mean and holding on to it could harmony be achieved.[14]

The Chinese sages taught that when the Mean is applied to others, it involves the practice of faithfulness and reciprocity, in which a person is concerned not only with himself but with others. In this process a person establishes and enlarges others while seeking to establish and enlarge himself. He does not do unto others what he would not have them do unto himself. When the Mean is applied to social affairs, it prevents the possibility of paying attention to one side only while neglecting the other and thus lays the foundation of justice and equality. Finally, when the Mean is applied to reasoning there is no excess or inadequacy, and contention between the part and the whole is avoided.

Confucius also taught that in maintaining the Golden Mean, man must always return to the root of the universal principle. A tree grown too tall for its root will not receive enough nutrition to grow further. A man who does not frequently return to his heart, where he can find the root of his being (a term which probably refers to his spirit and his soul), will lose his true nature and his vitality of life. To return to one's origin is the first manifestation of the eternal principle.

In the *Tao-te ching*, Lao-tzu espouses moderation as the key to successful living. This idea is supplemented by the theory that there is 'cyclical reversion' in *Tao*'s movement.[15] Cyclic reversion refers to the idea that *Tao*, after reaching the climax in its movement, will revert from one pole to the opposite pole. The lesson we should learn from this principle is moderation or contentment. In other words, one should not push any activity to the extreme limit, thereby avoiding the reaction or setback which will inevitably occur when the limit is reached. Thus, the true sage eschews excesses, extremes and extravagances. His life is one of moderation and fairness, for he realizes that anything that passes the limits of moderation ceases to exercise a beneficial influence:

Therefore the sage is
Severe, but he doesn't cut;
Exact but he doesn't hurt;
Straight, but he doesn't strain;
Bright, but he doesn't dazzle.[16]

Moderation in thought and behaviour should be the aspiration of all those who flow with *Tao*. 'Abdu'l-Bahá was known to tread the spiritual path with practical feet. In the *Kalimát-i-Firdawsíyyih*, Bahá'u'lláh gives great importance to moderation: 'If a thing is carried to excess, it will prove a source of evil.'[17] He told the rulers that moderation is a necessity since freedom in excess would 'exercise a pernicious influence upon men'.[18] In all matters, moderation is desirable.

Confucius gave similar advice and warned that even the highest values – for example, hierarchy, love and justice – degenerate when practised to excess. Justice descends into fanatical revenge and persecution, and unbridled love leads to indulgence. The fact that even the norms of ethics have inherent limitations was known to Confucius: 'Courtesy uncontrolled by the laws of good taste becomes laboured effort, caution uncontrolled becomes timidity, boldness uncontrolled becomes recklessness, and frankness uncontrolled becomes effrontery.'[19]

Needless to add, the principle of moderation is very important today in view of the ecological threat from indiscriminate industrialization. It is not that technology and industry are evil in themselves, but an excess of them threatens to devour us.

Non-Violence

Fighting, and the employment of force, even for the right cause, will not bring about good results. The oppressed who have right on their side must not take that right by force; the evil would continue. Hearts must be changed.[20] *'Abdu'l-Bahá*

All the founders of the great religions have been opposed to violence, oppression and cruelty. The theme of all major religions can be said to be love, peace and non-violence. According to Lao-tzu, the signs of the anti-*Tao* are such acts as civil disturbance and war. 'The countryside will be out of joint and man will hear the cry of loyalty and allegiance.'[21] 'Rulers will be taxing their people heavily.'[22] It will be a time when the court will be resplendent, while the fields are weedy and the granaries empty:

The court is very resplendent;
Very weedy are the fields,
and the granaries very empty.
They wear gaudy clothes,
Carry sharp swords,
Exceed in eating and drinking,
Have riches more than they can use.
Call them robber-braggarts;
They are anti-*Tao* indeed![23]

This description by Lao-tzu condemns people of any epoch, not only the early Chinese epoch, who are autocratic, competitive, class-conscious, deceitful, violent and oppressive.

While Bahá'ís today cherish the hope that 'the weapons of war throughout the world may be converted into instruments of reconstruction and that strife and conflict may be removed from the midst of men',[24] Lao-tzu in 600 BC foreshadowed this ambition:

Killing multitudes brings weeping and sorrow;
treat victory like a funeral.

And:

Fish should not leave the depths;
Neither should weapons of state ever be aired.[25]

Weapons may be necessary but they should be used sparingly. In fact, Taoism believes that it is wise to ignore provocation and never to have aggressive attitudes toward Nature and men. According to Lao-tzu, man cannot achieve his aims by aggressive action. In fact, to yield is to be preserved whole since the sage 'does not compete with anyone, hence no one beneath Heaven can compete with him'.[26]

Confucius, on the other hand, believed that there are times, regrettably, when force must be used by moral men in order to protect themselves from enslavement by those for whom force is the only argument and the only sanction.[27] But he considered force the last resort and one that must always be subordinate, not only ideally but as a matter of hard fact, to the power of justice. This, of course, is completely in harmony with the teachings of other great spiritual leaders.

Self-Conquest

True humanity, according to Confucius, comprises the conquest of oneself and a return to right and proper deeds. This call for self-conquest is very similar to the call of the divine messengers of God who exhorted the believers to submit themselves to divine law, to control their carnal desires and to direct their lives by the highest values so as to adopt divine virtues and perfection. At the end of this self-knowledge and self-conquest, this morally educative process, we find the moral person, the new man, what the different scriptures variously describe as 'the righteous', 'the children of God' or, as in the *Analects*, 'the superior man'.[28]

The superior man ought to be 'watchful over himself even when he is alone'.[29] This is important in the Confucian tradition because a man's conscience is his guide. This concept appears three times, twice in the *Book of Great Learning* and once in *The Doctrine of the Mean*. It is in the same vein of thought that Tseng-tzu, a disciple of Confucius, said:

> I examine myself on three points: whether in transacting business for others, I may have been not faithful; whether in intercourse with friends, I may have been not sincere; whether I may have not mastered and practised the instructions of my teacher.[30]

Since to 'err is human', it is impossible to be free from fault. Thus, self-examination and self-inquiry is imperative for self-improvement. One should censure oneself strictly without blaming others so as to guard against future mistakes. Whitewashing of faults is discouraged by Confucius as it not only deceives others but also deceives oneself. This is expressed in the familiar proverbs, 'There should be heavy censure of oneself and light censure of others', and, 'He who censures himself strongly and others lightly will keep himself far away from resentment'.[31] This is not unlike the Bahá'í admonition: 'Breathe not the sins of others so long as thou art thyself a sinner.'[32]

Honesty

> Beautify your tongues, O people, with truthfulness, and adorn your souls with the ornament of honesty.[33] *Bahá'u'lláh*

Everyone would like others to be honest with them. In the same way, Confucius exhorted his followers to be honest in their personal and business dealings, especially when profit was to be made: 'At the sight of gain, he thinks of what is right'[34] and, 'Any thought of accepting wealth and rank by means that I know to be wrong is as remote from me as the clouds that float above me.'[35]

The Confucian attitude to profit-making is that as long as wealth is accumulated without contravening moral principles, there is nothing wrong with it:

> Wealth and rank are what every man desires; but if they can only be retained to the detriment of the Way he professes, he must relinquish them. Poverty and obscurity are what every man detests; but if they can only be avoided to the detriment of the Way he professes, he must accept them.[36]

Profit can be made provided it is made honestly. Should profit be made for selfish, individual interests against the greater good of the community, then that profit is wrong.[37] For government, this means that the mandarinate should not engage in profit-seeking at the expense of the people.[38] When profit is made, a part of it should be shared and spread out to the family and community at large. This would impose some restraint on capital formation but not put a total ban on it.

For the true Confucian, then, there is a clear line of demarcation between moral values and money-making. 'A gentleman takes as much trouble to discover what is right as lesser men take to discover what will pay.'[39] If necessary, one should even lay down his life in order to uphold moral principles.

> If a gentleman abandons his humanity how can he fulfil his name? A gentleman never quits humanity even for the space of a single meal. In moments of stress he cleaves to it; in seasons of peril he cleaves to it.[40]

In fact, in the Confucian worldview, whether one is rich or poor is determined entirely by one's destiny; consequently, material comfort should not be one's main concern in life.[41]

Contentment

> Put away all covetousness and seek contentment; for the covetous hath ever been deprived, and the contented hath ever been loved and praised.[42] *Bahá'u'lláh*

Most therapists would agree that a reasonable dose of contentment would be excellent medicine for the ambitious modern city-dweller of today who is raring to get ahead of his competitors and keen to amass more and more wealth for himself. The divine educators have preached the virtue of contentment and practised it to a remarkable degree. The Chinese sages were no different.

Thus, although the Chinese are not innocent of greed and lust and overteeming ambition, it can be said that most of them have shown an unusual talent for happiness, even in the midst of poverty and suffering. This is especially true of the Chinese peasants. They have been able to find joy in things that many people overlook, such as the interesting and humorous things that happen to people around one, the dramatic unfolding of the life of one's family, a bird, a flower or even the singing of a cricket.

By comparison, the life of the city-dweller is characterized by aggressiveness and competitiveness. Undoubtedly these are qualities that are good only in moderation. The problem today is how to be contented within an urban setting. Somehow the stress of city life promotes an extreme materialism leading to much aggression and quarrelsomeness.

The aggressive and competitive tendency shows itself in one of the attributes of which humankind seems to be most proud – expansionism. Individuals and businesses must make more money this year than last. Governments must always show a table of economic growth. Nations must export or 'die', find new markets, and constantly widen their territories or at least their spheres of influence. This is unhealthy, for sooner or later, expanding empires must meet. The result is conflict and acrimony.

The scriptures of the major religions warn their believers of the variable fortunes of the world and exhort them not to be attached to material wealth. For example, Bahá'u'lláh warns: 'Be content, O people, with that which God hath desired for you and predestined unto you,'[43] and Christ said the same thing: 'For what is a man profited if he should gain the whole world and lose his soul?'[44] The *Tao-te ching* contributes the following:

No calamity is greater
Than not knowing what is enough

No fault worse than wanting too much
Whoever knows what is enough
Has enough.

And:

Attachment comes at wasteful cost;
Hoarding leads to a certain loss;
Knowing what is enough avoids disgrace;
Knowing when to stop secures from peril.
Only thus can you long last.[45]

The Root and the Branch

... thou thinkest thyself rich in its [gold's] possession, and I
recognize thy wealth in thy sanctity therefrom.[46] *Bahá'u'lláh*

It is strange that the things people seem to want the most –
wealth and power – are the very things the great religious
teachers have always cautioned against. Confucius taught that
one may strive for wealth and power but he certainly considered
this less important than striving for virtue.

Confucius regarded virtue as the root and wealth as merely a
branch. Hence, 'Possessing virtue will give him [the ruler] the
people. Possessing the people will give him the territory,
possessing the territory will give him its wealth. Possessing the
wealth, he will have resources for expenditure. Virtue is the root,
wealth is the result.'[47] In other words, the spiritual condition of
human existence (virtue) should precede its material condition
(wealth). The position of the root and branch should not be
reversed nor their order of sequence confused.

For the Chinese, although wealth is indispensable, it cannot be
regarded as the root; although strength cannot be ignored, it
cannot be relied upon as the long term factor; while technical
knowledge is essential to human life, true wisdom consists of
knowing what virtue is and possessing the courage to practise it.
The position of the root and the branch has always been
paramount in Chinese thought.

Our world today is, however, strongly materialistic: both
capitalist and communist systems hold material advancement to

be the highest good. Development is seen entirely in material terms. The Bahá'í view, on the other hand, is that development must be seen in a much broader perspective. Material progress is useful but by itself cannot uplift man. On the contrary, the more man becomes immersed in material things, the more his spirituality becomes obscured. This is not a denunciation of wealth or a commendation of poverty; it depends on how that wealth is used and the distribution of wealth in a country:

> Wealth is praiseworthy in the highest degree, if it is acquired by an individual's own efforts and the grace of God, in commerce, agriculture, art and industry, and if it be expended for philanthropic purposes . . . Wealth is most commendable, provided the entire population is wealthy. If, however, a few have inordinate riches while the rest are impoverished, and no fruit or benefit accrues from that wealth, then it is only a liability to its possessor. If, on the other hand, it is expended for the promotion of knowledge, the founding of elementary and other schools, the encouragement of art and industry, the training of orphans and the poor – in brief, if it is dedicated to the welfare of society – its possessor will stand out before God and man as the most excellent of all who live on earth and will be accounted as one of the people of paradise.[48]

Unfortunately, the emphasis on wealth and strength over virtue has now pervaded every aspect of life, be it in China or other parts of the world. Modern educators emphasize technique and art at the expense of morality. Teaching morality, they feel, is the task of religion. As progress has been made in the natural sciences, religious faith has steadily dwindled in importance. Since moral education is not stressed in schools, few pay any attention to it. As a result, society progressively comes to worship money and power, while the family system and morality in general rapidly disintegrate.

Humility

> Humility exalteth man to the heaven of glory and power, whilst pride abaseth him to the depths of wretchedness and degradation.[49] *Bahá'u'lláh*

From a survey of religious history one may conclude that the truly great men have been those who thought least of their own glory or interests but were focused only on giving peace and rest to the people. This observation is born out by Lao-tzu's comment: 'Therefore the sage puts himself last, finds himself first; abandons his self, preserves his self. Is it not because he has no self, that he is able to realize his self?'[50] Again, 'The Way of Heaven is to benefit but not to harm', and 'the way of the sage is to work but not compete'.[51] Many of the verses in the *Tao-te ching* extolling the life of the sage remind us of the life led by 'the Servant of Bahá', 'Abdu'l-Bahá:

> The sage does not hoard,
> The more he does for others,
> The more he has himself.
> The more he gives,
> The more he gets.[52]

In the *Tao-te ching* lowliness or humility is the foundation of greatness: 'Pride in wealth and fame breeds its own collapse.'[53] Therefore the sage 'holds to the One and becomes beneath-heaven's model. He does not show himself, hence he shines. Does not assert himself, hence he is seen. Does not boast his merits, hence he gets credit. Does not vaunt himself, hence he survives. Does not compete with anyone, hence no one beneath heaven can compete with him.'[54]

The Chinese have been taught that it is only from low places that it is possible to look upon heaven and earth: 'Rivers and seas become kings of the valleys because they lie lower.'[55] From high places, the temptation is to look down on earth and think oneself superior to it. Chinese landscape painters, for instance, always lifted up their eyes into the hills, never looked down from them.

In his writings, Lao-tzu equates water with the highest form of goodness. Water knows how to benefit all things without striving with them. It stays in crevices and unattractive low-lying areas not often frequented and usually loathed by men. 'Therefore it comes near to the *Tao*.'[56] The paradox with water is that nothing is as soft and as weak as itself, yet nothing is better to attack the hard and strong through attritive action, and nothing can take its place.[57]

According to Taoism, softness overcomes toughness. The Taoist notion here foreshadows the words of Jesus five hundred years later: 'Blessed are the meek, for they shall inherit the earth.'[58]

The weak overcome the strong;
The soft overcome the hard.
There is no one beneath heaven
Who doesn't know this,
And no one who practises it.
Therefore the sage says:
To bear the dirt of the country
Is to be master of the grain-shrines,
To bear the sins of the country
Is to be lord of beneath-heaven.[59]

Lao-tzu gives other examples. Apparent weakness may be real strength. A man who is confident is also humble. When one is young, one is not afraid to be called old. A world-renowned scholar does not advertise his knowledge. Those who are arrogant are also ignorant. Ambitious people are often filled with emptiness. Agitators are insecure. Those who find no inner peace are noisy. Those who find no joy of life are frenzied. Those who jostle and bustle are lonely. Those who whistle in a cemetery are afraid. The weak pretend to be strong. Sages appear to be simple.[60]

As for Confucius, his humility was legendary. Although he taught his disciples how to become sages or virtuous men, yet he often said that he himself could not be compared with either. It may simply be said of him, he insisted, that he was 'one who strived to become such without satiety and to teach others without weariness'.[61] (Of course, these were the very qualities which his disciples could not imitate.)

Confucius' greatness was built upon the solid foundation of deep humility, which of course is nothing else than self-knowledge:

There are four things in the moral life of man, not one of which I have been able to carry out in my life. To serve my father as I would expect my son to serve me: that I have not been able to do. To serve my superior as I would expect my subordinate to serve me: that I have not been able to do. To act towards my elders as I would expect my juniors to do to me: that I have not been able to do. To be the first to behave towards my friends as I would expect them to behave towards me; that I have not been able to do.[62]

It has been commented that not a single Confucian scholar in the long history of China has made such a good confession of his failings as his master did.[63]

Stories about Confucius' humility and modesty also take on a humorous flavour. The *Analects* contain an interesting self-portrait of Confucius. A certain duke asked Tze-lu, a disciple of Confucius, what he thought about his Master, but Tze-lu did not reply because he did not know what to say. Upon being told, Confucius said, in good humour: 'Why did you not say to him, "He is simply a man, who in his eager pursuit [of knowledge] forgets his food, who in the joy of its attainment forgets his sorrows, and who does not perceive that old age is coming on."'[64]

This emphasis on humility as exemplified in the life of Confucius and carried down to the general populace in terms of stories and fables has made its mark on the Chinese character. As a result, it is a widely acknowledged generalization that the East Asian is modest in his speech, expectations and demeanour.

Work is Worship

Can a man who is loved be exempted from labour?[65] *Confucius*

Waste not your time in idleness and sloth. Occupy yourselves with that which profiteth yourself and others . . . The most despised of men in the sight of God are those who sit idly and beg.[66]
Bahá'u'lláh

The Chinese religion and the Bahá'í Faith both stress the importance of work. The Chinese believe that human beings should regard labour as sacred because only through labour can there be life. Any person who does not labour is looked upon as a poisonous element within a group of people. Mencius often told a story of a man of Ch'i who supported his wife and concubine by begging and he ended the story by admonishing such 'shameful behaviour'.[67] In the Chinese psyche, idleness is frowned upon and work is extolled. A person without work is believed to be miserable. Idleness promotes gloominess and the best solution for this is to find relief in activity.

> The scholar who cherishes the love of comfort is not fit to be deemed a scholar. With all his knowledge, if such a man allowed himself to become accustomed to comfort and idleness for his enjoyment and even avoided work, he would be of no use to society, no matter how rich his knowledge. It has been said that such a man is 'not fit to be deemed a scholar'.[68]

The superior man, according to Confucius, is one who not only performs his own labour but also urges others to do the same. Should he, out of a kind of blind love for a loved one or friend, permit him to remain idle, he is only destroying his friend's future. Thus, all over the world, the Chinese are generally renowned for their industrious nature. In fact, the work ethic of Confucianism is given credit for the rapid economic development of the Pacific Rim.

The Bahá'í Faith teaches that work is good but it is even better when that work profits oneself and others. For the Bahá'ís, work performed in the spirit of service to humankind is elevated to the rank of worship of God. Spiritual attainment in both the Chinese religion and the Bahá'í Faith must be expressed in acts of service to others rather than in, for example, a life of monasticism and asceticism.

Backbiting

On no point is the Bahá'í Faith more unequivocal than in asking the believer to refrain from fault-finding and backbiting:

> O Son of Man! Breathe not the sins of others so long as thou art thyself a sinner. Shouldst thou transgress this command, accursed wouldst thou be, and to this I bear witness.[69]

> O Son of Being! How couldst thou forget thine own faults and busy thyself with the faults of others? Whoso doeth this is accursed of Me.[70]

It is thus fascinating to compare these with the many sayings of Confucius on this subject. The following is a sample:

He [the superior man] hates those who proclaim the evil of others. He hates the man who, being in a low position, slanders his superior.[71]

Mencius said, 'What future trouble have they and ought they to endure, who talk of what is not good in others.'[72]

Tzu-kung was in the habit of criticizing others. The Master said, 'Is Tzu really worthy? As to me, I have not leisure for this.'[73]

He who reproaches himself strongly and others lightly will keep himself far away from resentment.[74]

The self-righteous according to Confucius are the 'spoilers of morals'.[75]

In short, Confucius described slander as slow-soaking poison and calumny as having sharp stings. The person whose mind is proof against these, he called clear-sighted and far-seeing. Similarly, Bahá'ís believe that gossip, backbiting and slander or ill thoughts against others are the most grievous sins.

Forgiveness

God hath forgiven what is past. Henceforth everyone should utter that which is meet and seemly, and should refrain from slander, abuse and whatever causeth sadness in men.[76] *Bahá'u'lláh*

Confucius was able to imbibe this spirit of charity and forgiveness from his learning and reflection and he taught this spiritual truth to his disciples: 'If someone purifies himself to come forward to me, I approve of his purification without looking into his past conduct. I approve of his coming forward, and not his going backward. Why should I be so severe?'[77]

In addition, Confucius said, 'Po-i and Shu-ch'i did not keep the former wickedness of men in mind, and so the resentments directed toward them were few.'[78] These two were legendary brothers. The old ills were the misdeeds of the last Yin ruler.

When he was attacked by the Chou tribe, the brothers refused to take up arms against their sovereign, despite his great wickedness. Their lack of rancour was a classical theme.

In the *Tao-te ching*, Lao-tzu balances the concept of forgiveness with justice. He calls for requiting hatred with virtue:[79]

> Why did the ancients prize *Tao*?
> Because if it is sought, it is found;
> Because the guilty are forgiven.
> That is why it is beneath-heaven's treasure.[80]

In the Chinese view, forgiveness, however, must be balanced with justice. Thus, while Heaven forgives, Heaven also dispenses justice to the wicked:

> When people don't fear force,
> Greater force is on the way.
> Vast is heaven's net and wide-meshed
> Yet nothing slips through.[81]

Similarly, Bahá'í prayers ask for God's forgiveness and mercy and Bahá'ís are assured that although 'justice and equity are twin Guardians that watch over men'[82] and that 'all your doings hath My Pen graven with open characters upon tablets of chrysolite',[83] God is at the same time 'forgiving and compassionate toward the concourse of the faithful'.[84]

Deeds Not Words

Let deeds, not words, be your adorning.[85] *Bahá'u'lláh*

Both the Bahá'í and Chinese scriptures stress the preeminence of deeds over words. The famous Chinese saying that 'he who speaks does not know, and he who knows does not speak' resounds throughout the *Tao-te ching*.[86] Bahá'u'lláh Himself warns that 'the tongue is a smouldering fire, and excess of speech a deadly poison',[87] and that the most negligent of men is one that

114

'disputeth idly and seeketh to advance himself over his brother'.[88]
In inimitable paradoxes, Lao-tzu continues his words of wisdom:

> True words are not nice;
> Nice words are not true,
> A good man does not argue;
> An arguer is not good.[89]

The *Tao-te ching* argues that the sage manages without doing and teaches without talking.[90]

> Many words exhaust Truth
> Keep to the empty centre![91]

And:

> When prudence and wit appear
> Great hypocrites are here.[92]

Confucius was always markedly contemptuous of eloquence and of ornate language: 'A man who is strong, resolute, simple and slow to speak is near to *jen*.'[93] His own writings, like those of Lao-tzu, are generally brief and pithy. He believes that speech must be truthful and practical: 'A man with clever words and an ingratiating appearance is seldom a man of *jen*.'[94] Speech should not be excessive; indeed it is sufficient if it conveys the meaning. A spade must be called a spade. This will prevent hypocrisy as well as dishonesty: 'In language it is simply required that it convey the meaning.'[95]

Neither empty words nor fine words, it is stressed, constitute benevolence. It is only by deeds, or vigorous conduct, that benevolence can be manifested. As to what constituted the superior man, Confucius said 'he acts before he speaks, and afterwards speaks according to his actions'.[96] In addition, he is slow in his speech and quick in his conduct.[97] Finally, the superior man, being modest in his speech, naturally excels in his actions.

Caution must be exercised where words are concerned for the logical reason that one should not readily give utterance to words because one's action might not live up to them.[98] Besides, 'He who speaks without modesty will find it difficult to make his words good.'[99] After all, a man is judged not by what he says but by what he has done. Confucius was known to judge a man by his actions rather than his words.[100]

A disciple said: 'My master speaks when it is time to speak, and so men do not get tired of his speaking. He laughs when there is occasion to be joyful, and so men do not get tired of his laughing. He talks when it is consistent with righteousness to do so, and so men do not get tired of his talking. . .'[101]

Certainly, then, between deeds and words, deeds are much preferred. 'Abdu'l-Bahá expounds that 'if we are true Bahá'ís speech is not needed. Our actions will help on the world, will spread civilization, will help the progress of science, and cause the arts to develop.'[102]

Conclusion

To the Chinese, the realization of full humanity is the realization of *jen* which comprises essentially the performance of one's duties towards oneself and towards others. In fulfilling the duties towards oneself and others, one fulfils one's duties towards Heaven since this is in harmony with the Way of *Tao*. To serve man is to walk in Heaven's way. To serve man is to serve God.

Jen is comparable to the spiritual teachings of all the past prophets. *Jen* may be said to be the queen of virtues since all the great educators have taught that the fundamental purpose of human life is to develop divine attributes or what Confucius calls 'humane attitudes', to become more godly and spiritual, to become what the sages call 'a real man'.

The cultivation of *jen*, and the emphasis on the correct position of the root and the branch, can be equated with the emphasis on spiritual qualities preached with the coming of each messenger of God, such as the Buddha, Christ and Bahá'u'lláh. Such teachings appear to be the only solution to the strife and dissension prevailing in the world today.

10

Leading the Life: *Li*

. . . in this new age the Manifest Light hath, in His holy tablets, specifically proclaimed that music, sung or played, is spiritual food for soul and heart. The musician's art is among those worthy of the highest praise, and it moveth the hearts of all who grieve.[1]

'Abdu'l-Bahá

If a man is not human, what has he to do with rituals?
If a man is not human, what has he to do with music?[2]

Confucius

Many Westerners appear to view Confucius as a dried-out pleasure hater, yet the Music Classic is attributed to him and he played the lute. Indeed, Confucius was not opposed to pleasure, advocating, for example, that one should 'use poetry to arouse the good in men, use ritual to give it form and use music to set it in harmonious motion'.[3]

This brings us to the concept of *li* (the Holy). While *jen* is the most important concept, *li* is the most well-known. Like *jen*, *li* was in existence long before Confucius. *Li* is now associated with Confucius because it was he who changed it from an outmoded, outworn code of aristocracy to a fresh set of rules for polite society. As such *li* remains a vital influence to this day, as revealed in the refined manners of the Chinese people.

Li, which used to mean 'sacrifices offered to God' or 'reverence', now means, in addition, rites, ritual ceremonies, rules of propriety, good form, good manners, decency, norms of conduct, natural law, reasons and consciousness of right and wrong. It refers to the most weighty religious ceremonies as well as to the trivialities of daily etiquette. It means the 'norm' of human behaviour in all social circumstances or, as the Chinese would put it, the 'rules of propriety'.[4] Life, ritual and etiquette became important, not for their own sake, but because they symbolized the outward and visible sign of inner goodness. Confucius used the word *li* to stand for the whole complex of conventional and social usage which he endowed with a moral connotation.[5] The whole range of obligations imposed by the highest conception of both courtesy and moral duty were included in *li*.

To Confucius, the *li* was inseparable from righteousness. Both the *li* and the sense of righteousness were products of propriety. The purpose of *li* was to carry out what is right.[6] *Li*, it is said, is the *li*, the respect for Heaven, and the love for one's fellow man. A Chinese is no longer a Chinese if he stops practising the *li*, stops respecting Heaven and loving his fellow man. Ideally, then, to be a Chinese is not so much a matter of race, location, blood, language or religion but of the practice of the right conduct. Similarly, if a barbarian starts to practise the *li*, to respect Heaven and love his fellow man, he stops being a barbarian.

Function of *Li*

There were many functions of *li* as characterized by Confucius. First and foremost, *li* was used to differentiate men from the beasts:

> The parrot can speak, and yet is nothing more than a bird; the ape can speak, and yet is nothing more than a beast. Here now is a man who observes no rules of propriety; is not his heart that of a beast? . . . Therefore, when the sages arose, they framed the rules of propriety in order to teach men, and cause them, by their possession of them, to make a distinction between themselves and brutes.[7]

An emphasis on protocol, ritual or norms in an age of moral decay and political and social disintegration was especially important as it helped emphasize man's distance from the animals. So although *li* may appear rather formal, rigid and irrelevant in the 20th century, it was necessary twenty-five hundred years ago in a feudal anarchical society. *Li* was necessary to inspire men to believe that they were above animals and should behave differently from them. It was used to regulate the feelings and impulses of man.

Second, the ritual principle was used to keep peace and harmony in society. *Li* was used to demarcate the senior from the junior and the superior from the inferior. It served as a means of emphasizing status in society. It was to keep people from being disorderly as well as to motivate them to understand the distinctions between noble and humble, old and young and all the great principles of morality as taught by the sage. Order, according to Confucius, is Heaven's first law.

Third, many ceremonies were created to elevate human feelings, for example, funeral rites, sacrifice and archery. Their purpose was to elevate man's life to dignity, celebration and consecration, and to create order and decency in society. Institutions and ceremonials were devised for every detail and every need of human life and were made beautiful so that man would enjoy them.

Fourth, rites and ceremonies enabled the individual to participate in cosmic renewal as well as to integrate himself within the human community. The performance of rites and ceremonies enabled the identification of the individuals' past and roots, their present status and their future responsibilities. It gave one a sense of participation in universal salvation and cosmic renewal. Ritual enactments gave individuals a personal orientation wherewith to cultivate the moral and spiritual character necessary for one's integration into society.

Recognizing the love of ritual in the Chinese people from the earliest times, Confucius preserved some of the ancient rites and continued the people's preoccupation in the ceremonial system. As observed, he used the principle of ritual for initiation, moral and spiritual discipline, social cohesion and universal salvation.

Spirit not the Form

Strive that your deeds may be cleansed from the dust of self and hypocrisy . . .'[8] *Bahá'u'lláh*

During the time of Confucius, court etiquette was a well-defined area of fixed rules and roles. Even in some of the so-called later Confucian classics we find the most minute directions for behaviour, which tell one exactly where each finger should be placed in picking up a ritual object. But Confucius himself conceived of *li* quite differently. It was the spirit that counted,

119

and he was contemptuous of those who believed that by a mere ostentatious display of costly trappings, they could excel in *li*: 'High office filled by men of narrow views, rituals performed without reverence, the forms of mourning observed without grief – these are things I cannot bear to see!'[9] Sincerity is the essence of ritual.[10]

Once Confucius was asked to summarize the essence of *li*:

> An important question! In matters of ceremony, if one must err on one side or the other, it is better to be too economical rather than vulgarly ostentatious. In funeral and ceremonies of mourning, it is better that the mourners feel true grief, than that they be meticulously correct in every ceremonial detail.[11]

Li is not just the form but also genuine concern. In this sense it is the partner of *jen*. Confucius said that wherever one went into the world, one should treat all those with whom one came into contact as if one was receiving an important guest or an important official of the government. Bearing in mind the careless conduct of the aristocrats of his day, he added that one should deal with the people as if one were 'officiating at a great sacrifice'.[12]

Confucius knew well that *li*, like everything else, had to change with time. The three royal dynasties (Hsia, Shang and Chou) did not have the same *li*, he said.[13] Thus in the *Analects*, he would sometimes change the prescribed forms of propriety in order to adapt to the situation at hand. Thus the Confucian gentleman in mourning for his parents today would not follow the Confucian dictate that for three days no water or other liquid may enter his mouth and that only with the aid of a walking stick is he to rise.[14] This rule was proposed at a time when there was disorder and disintegration in the Chinese family. Today, this rule is antiquated. But even now, most Chinese refrain from party-going or other pleasure-seeking activities during their mourning period.

11

The Life of the Sage

This Man of whom we speak is not every man; we mean the Perfect Man. For the noblest part of the tree is the fruit, which is the reason of its existence.[1] *'Abdu'l-Bahá*

So far we have looked at the essence of Confucian teachings from the angle of two important concepts: *jen* and *li*. There is, however, another perspective which can delve deeply into the heart of traditional Chinese aspirations. According to this perspective (rather than what comprises *jen* or *li*), the basic concern in Confucian teaching is how to become a sage. To attain this goal, one must not only realize *jen* in one's nature but also extend it to society at large, which involves *li*, the rules of propriety.

The sage is a man of perfect personality. There are various stages of 'perfection', what Confucius calls the superior man, the good man and the constant man. 'Constancy' is the prerequisite for the three categories of man. Confucius says that sagehood is an impossibility even though he urges his fellow men to set that standard as an example to emulate.[2]

The sage possesses profound learning and is of lofty character. 'His movements for ages point the way for the world. His acts are for ages a law to the world. His words are for ages an example to the world. Those who are far from him look up to him; and those who are near him are never wearied with him.'[3]

The second part of the *Doctrine of the Mean* pays tribute to the perfect sage:

The perfect sage is able to combine within himself quickness of apprehension, intelligence, insight and wisdom – qualities necessary for leadership; magnanimity, generosity, benignity and gentleness – qualities necessary to embrace all men; strength, originality, firmness and determination – qualities necessary to maintain a firm hold; orderliness, dignity, seriousness, adherence to the Mean and correctness – qualities necessary to be reverent; grace, method, refinement and penetration – qualities necessary to exercise critical judgement. All embracing and extensive as Heaven and deep and unceasingly springing as an abyss! He appears and all people respect him, speaks and all people believe him, acts and all people are pleased with him. How earnest and sincere – he is humanity! How deep and unfathomable – he is abyss! How vast and great – he is Heaven! Who can know him except he who really has quickness of apprehension, intelligence and sageliness, and wisdom, and understands the character of Heaven? He is simple and yet rich in cultural adornment. He is amiable and yet systematically methodical. He is reverent without any movement and truthful without any words.[4]

As one reads the many descriptions of the sage, one recalls irresistibly to mind the Bahá'í equivalent – 'Abdu'l-Bahá, who is said to have lead the perfect moral life. The Governor of 'Akká said of Him:

Most of us here have, I think, a clear picture of Sir 'Abdu'l-Bahá 'Abbás, of his dignified figure, walking thoughtfully in our streets, of his courteous and gracious manner, of his kindness, of his love for little children and flowers, of his generosity and care for the poor and suffering. So gentle was he, and so simple, that in his presence one almost forgot that he was also a great teacher, and that his writings and conversations have been a solace and an inspiration to hundreds and thousands of people in the East and the West.[5]

Descriptions of a sage also abound in the *Mencius*:

A sage is the teacher of a hundred generations. This is true of Po-i and Hui of Liu-hsia [legendary sage kings of ancient China of whom there are no written records]. Therefore, when men now hear the character of Po-i, the corrupt become pure and the weak acquire determination. When they hear the character of Hui of Liu-hsia, the mean become generous and the niggardly become liberal. They exerted themselves a hundred generations ago, and after a hundred generations those who hear of them are aroused. Could such be the case if they had not been sages? And how much more did they affect those who were personally under their inspiring influence?[6]

The influence of the sage in making the corrupt pure, the weak determined, the mean generous and the niggardly liberal is eternal, without limits of time and space. Indeed, the sage has almost supernatural powers where the transformation of men is concerned:[7]

When this great man exercises a transforming influence, he is what is called a sage. How great the way of the sage is! Like the overflowing water, it nourishes all things and rises up to the heights of Heaven.[8]

The Superior Man

Since no one can aspire to be a sage, what then is the superior man (*chün-tzu*)? The superior man here can be translated to mean the virtuous man, the noble man and the gentleman. Men should emulate the conduct typical of a superior man. Confucius also invented the concept of the ignoble, inferior or small man (*xiao ren*) for the purposes of comparison. These contrasting concepts drive home the difference between the superior man, whose behaviour men must try to emulate, and an ignoble man, whose behaviour men must try to avoid. To call a man a *xiao ren* is, in the Chinese tradition, the worst condemnation of him, just as to call a man a *chün-tzu* is the highest praise.

Up to the 6th century BC, the term *chün-tzu* had a significance like the original meaning of the word 'gentleman', that is, a man of good birth. Confucius changed this usage completely. He asserted that any man might be a gentleman if his conduct was noble, unselfish, just and kind. On the other hand, he asserted that no man could be considered a gentleman on the grounds of birth; this was solely a question of conduct and character.

The first mention of the superior man and the ignoble man as a contrast of behavioural patterns comes in the second chapter of the *Analects*: 'A superior man is catholic (universal) and not partisan. An ignoble man is partisan but not universal.'[9]

So begins a series of contrasts. A superior man thinks of virtue; an ignoble man thinks of comfort. A superior man thinks of the sanctions of law; an ignoble man thinks of the favours he can receive. The mind of a superior man is conversant with righteousness; the mind of an ignoble man is conversant with gain.[10] A superior man seems to perfect the admirable qualities of men but does not seek to perfect their bad qualities. An ignoble man does the opposite.[11] The virtue of a superior man is like the wind; the virtue of ignoble man is like grass which will bend when the wind blows across it.[12] A superior man is in harmony with others but not in conformity; an ignoble man is in conformity but not in harmony.[13]

A superior man is easy to serve and difficult to please. If one tries to please him in any way which does not accord with right, he will not be pleased. But in his employment of men, he uses them according to their capacity. An ignoble man is difficult to serve but easy to please. If one tries to please him, though it be not in accord with right, he will be pleased. But in his employment of men, he demands all-round perfection.[14] A superior man has a dignified ease without being arrogant; an ignoble man is arrogant without a dignified ease.[15] A superior man is always composed; an ignoble man is full of distress. There have, alas, been superior men who have not been virtuous from time to time but there never has been an ignoble man who was at the same time virtuous.[16] When a superior man seeks, he seeks within himself; when an ignoble man seeks, he seeks in others.[17] A superior man cannot take part in small matters but can be entrusted with great matters; an ignoble man cannot be entrusted with great matters but can take part in small matters.[18] A superior man is reverently careful in the cultivation of himself, and he cultivates himself so as to give rest to others and to all the people.[19] When he is in a high position, he does not treat his inferiors with contempt. In a low position he does not court the favour of his superiors. He rectifies himself, and seeks nothing from others, so that he has no dissatisfaction. He does not murmur against Heaven nor grumble against men.

We may conclude that whatever a superior man does, an ignoble man will do the opposite; whatever an ignoble man does, a superior man will not do.

The *Analects* also contains a brief summary of the superior man:

> The superior man has nine cares. In seeing he is careful to see clearly, in hearing he is careful to hear distinctly, in his looks he is careful to be kindly, in his manner to be respectful, in his words to be loyal, in his work to be diligent. When in doubt he is careful to ask for information; when angry he has a care for the consequences; and when he sees a chance of gain, he thinks carefully whether the pursuit of it would be consonant with the Right.[20]

We may conclude that the superior man of the Chinese people is quite different from the physical prowess of an Achilles or a Hercules. Chinese heroes are respected and honoured not so much for physical strength but for their loyalty to their sovereign and their acts of righteousness. For example, Kuan Kung was a defeated general who lost his life and yet is revered and worshipped to this day because he stood for loyalty and righteousness. In the Sung dynasty (960–1280 AD) the soldier statesmen and Prime Minister Wen Tien Xiang and a general, Yue Fei, lost their lives but are remembered because of their loyalty to their sovereign and country and because they stood for righteousness.

The Example of the Master

Both Confucius and 'Abdu'l-Bahá were known as 'Master' to their followers. It would be interesting to compare what others have said about them. Shoghi Effendi, the Guardian of the Bahá'í Faith, counselled the American Bahá'ís to remember the conduct of the Master and, in so doing, provided a summary of His qualities:

> Let them call to mind, fearlessly and determinedly, the example and conduct of 'Abdu'l-Bahá while in their midst. Let them remember His courage, His genuine love, His informal and

indiscriminating fellowship. His contempt for and impatience of criticism, tempered by His tact and wisdom. Let them revive and perpetuate the memory of those unforgettable and historic episodes and occasions on which He so strikingly demonstrated His keen sense of justice, His spontaneous sympathy for the down-trodden, His ever-abiding sense of the oneness of the human race, His overflowing love for its members . . .[21]

'Abdu'l-Bahá 'came to be regarded as the embodiment of all the virtues that Bahá'ís long to attain. He was gentle and courteous; he was generous and brave. He combined great wisdom with touching humility; and His love for God and His fellow men knew no bounds. He spent every day of His life serving others and bringing joy into the lives of all around Him. The poor and the sick were His special care, and the orphan looked upon Him as a father. His friends loved Him to the point of adoration, and His enemies could find no blemish in His beautiful character. His station was not that of a Messenger of God, but His life was an example of human perfection.'[22]

Confucius was known to be 'mild and yet dignified, majestic and not fierce, respectful and yet easy and was an example of great self control'.[23] Confucius' own life-style was a living witness to his teachings. He loved fellowship with people in food, drink and good song. He was cheerful yet firm, pleasant yet dignified. A review of the *Analects* shows his great wisdom and knowledge and, at the same time, his humility. He was earnest in constantly improving himself. He had a willingness to listen to inferiors and a readiness to admit mistakes. He was responsive to all human values, patient and tactful in teaching others and indifferent to honours and riches. A spirit of joy and a sense of humour as well as a deep understanding of the rhythm of tension and relaxation are also evident in his writings. All these seem to be inspired by his desire to be perfectly human, to contribute towards the realization of full humanity.[24]

The specificity of the depiction of Confucius' attire, facial expressions, gestures and mannerisms is telling and unequivo-cally conveys the humaneness of the Master: 'Our Master is benign, upright, courteous, temperate and complacent in demeanour.'[25] There is little 'magic' in the way Confucius walked, spoke, ate and taught. He was, as he himself described, an untiring learner and teacher. Nor is there anything mysterious about his personality. However, to his students and to those who followed his teachings for centuries to come, the plainness and simplicity of Confucius' style of life was awe-inspiring. To them, his great strength as an exemplary teacher lay in his simplicity. His conscious choice not to resort to the extraordinary, the powerful, the superhuman or the transcendental to impress the people came to be seen as a sign of real inner strength.

Conclusion

The core of Confucius' philosophy can be looked at from the perspective of *jen*, *li* or of what constitutes a sage as well as a superior man. In addition, the ideal of the sage expounded by the Chinese philosophers bears a striking resemblance to the life led by 'Abdu'l-Bahá, the 'Perfect Exemplar'.

The qualities that Confucius advocated are strongly human-centred and this-worldly. He was essentially a pragmatist. His philosophy was an attempt to achieve harmony between the ideal and the real, between Heaven and man, and always with more emphasis on reality and man. In this respect, he may have overlooked the profound desire of man for life hereafter and for God since he put more emphasis on man's duty on earth than on man's spiritual destiny in relation to God.

However, it would have been impossible for Confucius to have expanded on man's spiritual destiny since to him a revelation was not given. He was only keenly in touch with the vibrations emanating from India or from some other Manifestation of God sent to the great civilization of the people he loved so deeply.

12

Learning and Education

From the Son of Heaven down to the mass of the people, all must consider the cultivation of the person the root of everything besides.[1]
Confucius

More than any other society in the world, China has given status to learning. Traditional Chinese culture stresses vigorous learning in youth and a familiar Chinese proverb reminds the younger generation that a lack of effort in youth will bring grief in old age. A belief in the value of education and in the acquisition of knowledge permeates all strata of Chinese society. A man is not highly regarded or respected unless he is properly educated and cultured.

Confucius' fondness for learning is legendary and to him is attributed China's Socratic tradition. In an effort to promote a love for learning, Confucius himself commented that in a hamlet of ten houses there would most certainly be someone as loyal and true to his word as Confucius was, but no one so fond of learning.[2] He confessed that he had often spent a whole day without food and a whole night without sleep to think and study. Throughout his life, he silently accumulated knowledge and never tired of this task:[3]

At fifteen I set my heart upon learning. At thirty, I had planted my feet firm upon the ground. At forty, I no longer suffered from perplexities. At fifty, I knew what were the biddings of Heaven. At sixty, I heard them with docile ear. At seventy, I could follow the dictates of my own heart for what I desired no longer overstepped the boundaries of right.[4]

Fifteen was the age that Confucius set as the time for the commencement of more profound studies such as the spiritual and ethical. Before that, rudimentary knowledge and technical common sense were to be taught.[5] It may be noted that fifteen is also the age set in the Bahá'í Faith as the age of maturity and independent decision. It symbolically marks the turning of a child into an adult.

In the opinion of Confucius, models which were supremely worth imitating had to be sought in antiquity.[6] This viewpoint is not difficult to understand considering that in the 6th century BC, China was physically isolated from other major civilizations and unaware of any great cultural tradition apart from its own. Therefore, what was of supreme importance in Confucius' eyes was the investigation and transmission of the correct traditions concerning the Golden Age of antiquity. As Confucius always looked back to the past for examples worthy of emulation, it is not surprising that he placed an emphasis on learning.

Confucius' time was a non-technological era without the convenience of mass communication. Thus, the imitation of models was the easiest and simplest form of learning. An important part of the teacher's role was to act as a model himself and to provide an example of what the moral human being should be like.

However, although Confucius looked to the past, he did not blindly imitate it. He organized and clarified the material he studied, developing his own theories from those sources.

The Importance of Education

... the aim of an educator is to so train human souls that their angelic aspect may overcome their animal side.[7] 'Abdu'l-Bahá

The Chinese have always believed that the value of education lies in the fact that it teaches men to differentiate white from black, the beneficial from the harmful, and right from wrong. It gives people the ability to weigh the feasibility of a project. A man is, after all, not born a superior man. He has to be educated. In the *Book of Great Learning*, a man has to be cultivated, 'cut and then filed, chiselled and then ground'. [8] As 'Abdu'l-Bahá puts it, 'Were there no educator, all souls would remain savage, and were it not for the teacher, the children would be ignorant creatures.'[9]

The Chinese believe that it is education which has been responsible for the ascent of mankind and progress in society.

129

The Chinese sages have taught that the moron who is fond of learning is better than an intelligent man who does not exert himself.[10] In addition, diligence is necessary: it has been said that there has never been a person from the ruler and ministers of state down to the ordinary people who has been successful without diligence.[11]

Following Confucius, Mencius taught that man's intrinsic nature is good – that is, he is born good – and that should he commit evil deeds, it is because some time in his life he allowed himself to be corrupted. Thus, education becomes of the utmost importance in the development of character.[12] Mencius said, 'Of all the seeds the best are the five kinds of grain, yet if they are not ripe, they are not equal to lower grades of grain. So the value of benevolence depends entirely on it being brought to maturity.'[13] Only the cultivated or educated man, according to Mencius, could be depended upon to remain virtuous in the face of economic privation. (By education, Mencius seems to have meant moral cultivation.) Education was the only way to raise a cultivated man.

In the Bahá'í writings, education is greatly emphasized and encouraged. As Bahá'u'lláh puts it, 'Knowledge is as wings to man's life, and a ladder for his ascent. Its acquisition is incumbent upon everyone.'[14] Bahá'ís are exhorted to acquire as much education as possible so as to be of useful service to the world of humanity. Education and the arts of civilization, it is said, 'bring honour, prosperity, independence and freedom to a government and its people'.[15] 'Abdu'l-Bahá continually encouraged the establishment of schools for young children throughout Persia, even in the smallest country towns and villages.[16] He felt that this was the most urgent and primary requirement. It was inconceivable, He said, 'that any nation should achieve prosperity and success unless this paramount, this fundamental concern is carried forward'.[17] The failure to educate a child is an unpardonable sin. However, Bahá'í education does not simply refer to the establishment of schools. It covers three aspects of education: material, human and divine, all of which may be subsumed by what Confucius referred to as 'education'.

Material education refers to the needs and cares of the body. Human beings perceive the material world through their senses.

Therefore these senses must be fully developed in order that the reality or essence of man, which is his intelligence and the power of thought, and by which he is distinguished from the animal, manifests itself in the highest degree.

Human education focuses on developing man as a rational thinker, to train him to 'discover the realities of things, comprehend the peculiarities of beings, and penetrate the mysteries of existence'.[18] It trains intellectual skills and focuses on civilization and progress, that is, administration, technical and scientific advancement, industry, charitable works, etc.

Finally, there is divine education, which is concerned with the teachings of the Supreme Ultimate. Its objective is to enable human beings to acquire divine perfections. There is an emphasis here on the training of character and conduct above education in the sciences and arts because knowledge, without a trained character, will only be injurious.

Learning for Application

Nothing in this world can ever be supported by words alone.[19]

Learning is not a memorization of some external set of criteria for human behaviour and blind conformity to that criteria in one's everyday conduct. For Confucius, learning takes place when one is able to enact social norms after having learnt them. A 'transformation' effected in practical action must take place.[20] This tradition can be traced to the *Book of History* in which it is stated: 'It is not difficult to know but difficult to act.'[21] Not only must a person labour assiduously to acquire the knowledge transmitted from ancient times, but even more crucial, he must be able to take it one step further in applying it to present conditions. Confucius said:

If a man can recite three hundred of the Odes and yet when given a government post cannot fulfil it, or when sent out to distant quarters cannot speak for the government without waiting for instructions, then although he knows a lot, what good is it to him?[22]

It is pointless to learn merely for the sake of learning. Application must be the end and learning the means.[23] Learning does not imply bookishness; one is not meant to accumulate facts for their own sake. Knowledge must be gathered for the sake of guiding one's conduct.

In relation to this, the Bahá'í Faith cautions that academic pursuits should not begin and end in words and that one should beware of a philosophy in which the ultimate yield is nothing but words.[24] One's knowledge should not be confined to mere words. Instead, the learned of the day must direct the people to acquire those branches of knowledge which are of use so that both the learned themselves and the generality of mankind may derive benefits therefrom.

This notion of 'practical application' is at the heart of the distinction Confucius draws between 'learning' (*hsueh*) and 'thinking' (*ssu*). Confucius says, 'He who learns but does not think remains in the dark; he who thinks but does not learn will strain himself.'[25]

In the investigation of things, Confucius advocated 'extensive study, accurate inquiry, careful reflection, clear discrimination and earnest practice', methods which may be said to coincide fully with today's scientific research and method where the search for truth and proof is of great importance.

Another interesting feature of the Confucian tradition is the deliberate encouragement of independent thinking and doubt. He wanted to encourage his students to doubt and to raise questions or objections. The best known Confucian dictum here is 'Learning without thinking is labour lost; thinking without learning is perilous'.

Intellectual honesty was also an important part of this tradition. 'Shall I tell you what knowledge is? To hold that you know a thing when you know it, and to hold that you do not know when you really do not know; that is knowledge.'

The Bahá'í correlate is that each individual should make his own independent search after truth. He should not accept authority blindly but use his judgement, independently and fearlessly, to ascertain the truth.

Certainly, learning must aim at practical application. If one possesses extensive knowledge and can neither classify nor apply it, it is like a library with thousands of unclassified and un-catalogued books. Such a library is worthless because it is impossible to find a book one is seeking. In like manner, a man possessing impractical knowledge will be no help to his fellow man.

Moral Education

... education cannot alter the inner essence of a man, but it doth exert tremendous influence, and with this power it can bring forth from the individual whatever perfections and capacities are deposited within him.[26]*'Abdu'l-Bahá*

The whole Confucian enterprise is directed towards the development of the moral individual. The pursuit of knowledge is inseparable from the quest for moral perfection. The ancient Chinese always believed that morality should be the goal of education because it was morality that moved the universe.[27] In the *Book of History* and in *The Mencius* it is reported that the legendary sage-emperor Shun appointed a Minister of Education to give instruction to the people because they were not observing the five relationships (i.e. the duties involved in the relationships between father and son, ruler and subject, husband and wife, elder brother and younger brother, and friend and friend).

Confucius defines an educated man as one 'who treats his betters as betters, wears an air of respect, who in serving mother and father knows how to put his whole strength, who in the service of his prince will lay down his life, [and] who in intercourse with friends is true to his word'.[28] Thus famous men in politics were judged by moral standards, as the famous men in the period of the middle Chou had been judged by Confucius.

The reason for Confucius' emphasis on moral education, rather than technical, as the most basic form of education was his belief that 'no man is an island'. It is impossible for a person to maintain an isolated existence independently of other people. Thus, it is imperative to look into the means of harmonizing relations between men. The natural prerequisite for human conduct is to find how man can fit into his environment and fulfil the

133

requirements of living so as to make possible the common existence of mankind. Confucius' answer was to set down the cultivation of the person as the root of all things.

Confucius believed that society is nothing more than the interaction of people with other people and that the conscience of the individual must forbid him to withdraw from society or to surrender his moral judgement to it. It is wrong to become a recluse or to 'follow the crowd'. The moral man must refrain from conforming with the practice of the majority if it is immoral or harmful. Only education can give a man moral courage. He is not born with it.

Education must cultivate both the intellect as well as the emotions. Today, our education cultivates our intellect but fails signally to discipline the emotions. Educating the will (spirit) is just as important as educating the intellect. Confucius places the will of the indivdiual in a stronger position than that of the commander of an army. In his view, the commander may be taken prisoner by an enemy but the will of an individual can never be captured by anyone.[29] For Confucius, intellectual cultivation was of little worth if it was not accompanied by emotional balance. He suggested that such a balance could be maintained through discipline by means of *li* which would enable a person 'to hold true to his principles through any crisis and in the face of every temptation'.[30]

Moral education has been the supreme aim of all the founders of the great religions. In the Bahá'í Faith, the fundamental importance and limitless possibilities of education are announced in the clearest terms: 'Every child is potentially the light of the world – and at the same time its darkness; wherefore must the question of education be accounted as of primary importance.'[31] The most important education is the love of God and to regard service to humanity as the highest aim of life. Education is to develop the power of the individual to the best advantage for the general good of all. Certainly, then, simply filling the memory with facts has comparatively little effect in producing noble and useful lives.

Therefore, learning in both the Bahá'í and Chinese traditions is not merely understanding facts in the natural order but also knowing how to conduct oneself and how to live a moral life on the basis of that understanding. It is a union of physical, spiritual and mental effort, each complementing the other.

Education for All

> ... all mankind should attain knowledge and acquire an education.[32] 'Abdu'l-Bahá

In his Book of Laws, revealed in 1873, Bahá'u'lláh commands every parent to ensure that both sons and daughters are instructed in reading and writing. Where the parents cannot afford to educate their children, the authorities must provide the means to ensure that the children are educated.[33] The Bahá'í commitment to universal education has resulted in a number of village tutorial schools in the third world and given rise to educational projects such as the Rabbani Vocational Agricultural School in Gwalior, Central India, and the Anís Zunúzí School in Haiti.

For his part, Confucius is credited with being the first man in China to have accepted the principle of education for all – rich or poor, prince or commoner. He was more interested in his pupils' eagerness to learn than in their class status. Very early on Confucius realized that one is a true man insofar as he embodies humanity; and a gentleman is no gentleman if he is not gentle in fact. On the other hand, any commoner may rightly be called a gentleman if he has the qualities of one.

As a consequence, the idea of a nationwide educational system was set before the Chinese long before other people had such a conception. This became a reality by the end of the Han dynasty (c. 220 AD) when the mastery of the Confucian classics became the basis of the nationwide civil service examination. Before Confucius, the privilege of education was always in the hands of a chosen few.

Confucius knew that man will often act unwisely, choosing a more immediate pleasure instead of a greater, deferred one. There is also a tendency for man to act unsocially, preferring often to secure his own happiness even at the expense of others. To correct this, Confucius insisted that there be some degree of universal education. He considered an enlightened citizenry a necessary foundation for the state. Punishment may temporarily compel men to do what they should, but it is, at best, a poor and unreliable substitute for education: 'If one tries to guide the people by means of rules, and keep order by means of punishments, the people will merely seek to avoid the penalties without having any sense of moral obligation. But if one leads them with virtue (both by precept and by example) and depends upon *li* to maintain order, the people will then feel their moral obligation to correct themselves.'[34] Or as Chuang-tzu put it: 'Rewards and punishment are the lowest form of education.'[35]

This finds quite a close parallel with the Bahá'í concept of 'divine civilization', a future civilization much similar to the period of Great Unity (*ta-t'ung*), believed to be the foundation of world peace. In a material civilization people are prevented from doing mischief and harm to society only through the use of force or punishment. In a divine civilization, on the other hand, human beings shy away from committing crimes not because of fear of punishment but because they have acquired the virtues of humankind and seek to commit only those acts which further human progress. To a moral man, the commission of a crime is, in itself, the most severe punishment:

> Divine civilization, however, so traineth every member of society that no one, with the exception of a negligible few, will undertake to commit a crime. There is thus a great difference between the prevention of crime through measures that are violent and retaliatory, and so training the people, and enlightening them, and spiritualizing them, that without any fear of punishment or vengeance to come, they will shun all criminal acts. They will, indeed, look upon the very commission of a crime as a great disgrace and in itself the harshest of punishments.[36]

Thus while the Bahá'í Faith is concerned with educating people through the teachings of the Creator brought forth by Bahá'u'lláh, Confucius assumes the operation of *T'ien* (Heaven) and speaks only of maintaining order through virtue and *li*.

For Confucius, the belief that any man, regardless of his birth, might become a gentleman did not remain only a theory. He undertook to make his students into gentlemen, and he accepted them from the lowest as well as the highest social strata. 'In education', he said, 'there should be no class distinctions.'[37]

From the very poorest upwards – beginning even with the man who could bring no better present than a bundle of dried flesh – none has ever come to me without receiving instruction.[38]

A bundle of dried flesh (dried meat) was an extremely humble offering, but Confucius, who endured poverty in his youth, was willing to teach anyone who showed a genuine willingness and capacity to learn. The principle that education should be readily available to all who seek it follows naturally from the idea that all men are born equal in the sense that every man has the innate capacity to develop sage-like qualities.

The extent to which the humble could achieve greatness through study was always, of course, limited by economic factors, but there were cases of men from very humble backgrounds rising to the very top of the civil service, and there are many edifying accounts from Chinese literature of ambitious scholars studying at night while working to support their widowed mothers by day. Many talented but poor young men received an education through the charity of wealthy relatives or in village schools financed by the more prosperous local farmers. Many combined a life of scholarship with agricultural labour.

It is not surprising, therefore, that there has always been a great respect for teachers in traditional China. Confucius himself was known as the 'most accomplished and highest ancient teacher'. He served as a model and inspiration for countless scholars of the imperial age who often had to undertake half a lifetime of study before they at last succeeded in passing the civil service examinations.[39]

This respect can be seen in the fact that the traditional Chinese relationship between teacher and pupil is a warm one, comparable to that between father and son. While the teacher is alive, the pupil serves him as a high priority; when the teacher dies, the pupil takes a part in the burial ceremonies. When Confucius died, his disciples lamented bitterly, as if they had lost a father. Tzu-kung was so grief-stricken that he built a house at the gravesite and remained there for three years.[40]

Similar stories about the devotion of disciples to their spiritual teachers may be found in every tradition, including the Bahá'í Faith. At the passing of Bahá'u'lláh, a vast number of mourners from diverse backgrounds, religions and nations, officials and leading figures, learned men of government and letters, sent their eulogies and tributes. For a week great numbers of mourners, rich and poor, shared their grief with the bereaved family. One of Bahá'u'lláh's disciples, Nabíl, in his uncontrollable grief, drowned himself in the sea when he heard the news.[41]

The respect that the Chinese had for teachers was destroyed both by the Communist takeover of China in 1949 and by westernization. In political campaigns during the Cultural Revolution, for example, intellectuals were often the target of persecution and teachers suffered at the hands of their pupils. Educators were considered to be part of the 'heavy yoke of tradition' which had stifled, and was still preventing, the material progress of the Chinese people.

Among the overseas Chinese in various parts of Southeast Asia, education has also become 'westernized' to different degrees. It is not an exaggeration to say that for many overseas Chinese living in predominantly capitalist environments, schools and universities are increasingly regarded as mere markets, teachers as storekeepers and learning as a business transaction.

Learning to Rule

Observe carefully how education and the arts of civilization bring honour, prosperity, independence and freedom to a government and its people.[42] 'Abdu'l-Bahá

One of the responsibilities of the universal education advocated by Confucius was to produce the most capable men to administer the country. Only if they are educated can leaders and administrators be chosen for their character, knowledge and wisdom rather than by their birth or wealth.

It should be noted that Confucius did not demand that rulers should vacate their thrones. Indeed, it was not yet time for rule by the people. Rather, he tried to persuade the kings that they should reign but not rule, that they should hand over all administrative authority to ministers chosen for their qualifications. These ministers would be loyal not so much to individuals as to moral principles. This was the best solution for axial China, as voting was unheard of and the common people were uneducated and without political experience. However, such a solution understandably did not win Confucius much favour or approval from the rulers who, characteristically, thought he was eccentric, if not dangerous.[43]

Conclusion

Today, many educators emphasize technique at the expense of morality. Thus it is refreshing to find that the importance of education in the promotion of private and public morality was recognized more than two thousand years ago. The Chinese have always understood that it is only through education and learning that one acquires not only knowledge but, more importantly, culture and ethical and moral character. Confucius taught that it is only through these qualities that one has the capacity and ability to order the family and govern the state. Although the Chinese Communists have tried to erode this traditional value for learning and education, their attempt has, at best, been only partially successful. Investing in education, especially if it is for one's own children, still remains a favourite preoccupation of the Chinese, particularly parents.

Certainly, the love of learning by people long-conditioned by Confucian values has proved to be a source of continuing energy and adaptability. It has given the Chinese tremendous opportunities to work in various professional fields, as evidenced in many parts of the world today. One remembers that after an initial period of profound dislocation, the peoples of East Asia, whose moral and cultural formation was largely shaped by Confucianism, have proven to be, among all those once seen as retarded or underdeveloped, the most able to assimilate Western learning and engage in rapid modernization. In Japan, Korea, island enclaves like Hong Kong, Taiwan, Singapore and other overseas communities, this capability has manifested itself powerfully. It is also noticeable today in university communities in the West, where a large number of East Asians are making their way successfully into higher education and upper level professions.

13

Unity of the Family

When wives and children and their sires are one,
'Tis like the harp and the lute in unison.
When brothers live in concord and peace,
The strain of harmony shall never cease.
The lamp of happy union lights the home,
And bright days follow when the children come.[1]

It is common to regard filial piety as the central theme of the philosophy of Confucius. However, filial piety is only a means to an end – Confucius treated filial piety as the starting point of humanity which, like charity, begins at home. It must be stressed that the original Confucian vision was not bounded by the wall of the family. Confucius' point was simply this: if a man is not a good son at home, neither will he be a model citizen, a trustworthy friend or a true lover of humankind. For Confucius, filial piety is just the first step on the way to universal love.

Unfortunately, later Confucians tended to treat this starting point as the central theme, if not the only vital one. Their focus greatly narrowed the broad vision of Confucius and paved the way for a kind of detestable clannishness, from which China has suffered so much.

A Pragmatic Vision

Mencius held that the root of the empire is in the state, and the root of the state is in the family.[2] He reasoned that before a community or state could be established, there must be a social unit called the family. Therefore, putting one's household in good order is the preliminary stage in demonstrating one's ability to hold public office in such a way as will bring well-being to the state and peace to the empire. The ancient Chinese scriptures regarded the family as the microcosm of the state. This concept

141

was preserved in Imperial China and was utilized by the government, which saw the family and clan as convenient implements of political control.

This concept was logical to Confucius who felt it was not possible or credible for one to teach others if one could not first teach one's own family. There were, he said, unavoidable moral (and later, legally enforced by the government) obligations to one's parents since one's parents and, by logical inference, one's ancestors, are the source of one's life.

Here, Confucius can be said to be more practical than idealistic. His main concern was for the continuity of human life and so he took up first things first. To safeguard the common existence of mankind, it was vital to stress mutual interest, mutual assistance, the importance of not forgetting one's origins and of remembering favours received. This was a time when human relationships were not well defined. There was political and social anarchy. The family unit was disintegrating: children did not know their fathers, mothers were often left destitute and many children were left to fend for themselves. Without moral guidance, the anarchical conditions prevailing in society would continue to be perpetuated.

In addition, owing to the confusion of blood relationships, the ties between brothers and sisters were unclear. The relationship between husband and wife, father and son and between brothers and brothers remained undefined. Under these circumstances, and in a feudal China in what may be called the primitive age of man, the relations between people were naturally based on desire and not on love, and the continuation of life depended on force, not virtue.

In view of this background, Confucius stressed the importance of a loving supportive family community especially during childhood; of hospitality, generosity, integrity and service; and of the inspiration and guidance of following Heaven's way. He argued that this would be the means for the development of higher human qualities. He realized that while desire and force were factors promoting the age of barbarity, only love and virtue could form the foundation of a great civilization.

The Family Unit

Confucius laid great store in the love between husband and wife. A happy family unit, as described in the opening quotation of this chapter, is like the harp and the lute playing in unison. When two persons are living peacefully and lovingly, a single melody is produced like that of the lute and the harp – two distinct instruments making such harmonious music that they cannot be differentiated. Hence, Confucius stressed that the Way of the superior man begins with the relation of husband and wife.

Due to the high level of sexual immorality during his time, Confucius advocated the strict regulation of men's relationships with women as a means of maintaining the social order. Mencius elaborated on this necessity: 'That male and female should dwell together is the greatest of relationships.'[3]

In the context of the anarchical conditions in China at that time, Confucius advocated what may be considered, from the perspective of the present day, a rather rigid hierarchy of human relationships. According to him, there are basically five types of human relationships:

ruler/minister
father/son
elder brother/younger brother,
husband/wife
friend/friend

These are arranged in order of priority and are superior-inferior relationships with the exception of the last one. The order is arranged according to generation, age and sex. This arrangement was intended to provide order for the smooth running of Chinese society and, when properly observed, the relationship hierarchy is intended to prevent conflict within the family. In this ideal family relationship, the ruler has rights and prerogatives over his ministers; likewise, the father over his sons, and so on.

Since disorder in human relationships was the topic of the day, order beginning with the family unit was advocated as the supreme tonic. It must be noted that this was not an original Confucian invention but a revival of something that had worked in the past and had served the Chinese society well. In the *Book of Rites*, the domestic ethic is expressed:

The father is merciful, the son filial; the elder brother is good, the younger brother submissive; the husband is upright, the wife complaisant; the adult is kind, the child obedient.[4]

Mutuality is a basic motif in Confucian ethics. Relationships are based not on the one-dimensional imposition of ideas and powers upon others but on the concepts of mutuality and reciprocity. Thus, mutual love is advocated between those above (fathers) and below (sons), in front (elder brothers) and behind (younger brothers), left (husbands) and right (wives). If this were to be followed, family harmony would ensue and there would be unity, propriety, righteousness and good order.

The regulation of the family was the first step towards peace and mutual benefit for all. As a rule, the internal affairs of the family were to be decided by the wife, while the external affairs were to be the domain of the husband. Where children were concerned, the father was to be strict and the mother kind since it was believed that strictness led to wisdom and kindness consolidated affection. It was hoped that the two together would build a rising generation which would be both wise and affectionate.

This familial hierarchy established by Confucius and elaborated upon and expounded by his principal followers came to permeate all Chinese families. Even Buddhist and Taoist monks and nuns living apart from society are still guided in their conduct largely by this Confucian family-style morality.

The Bahá'í Family

If love and agreement are manifest in a single family, that family will advance, become illumined and spiritual; but if enmity and hatred exist its destruction and dispersion are inevitable.[5]
'Abdu'l-Bahá

Once again, 2500 years later, the bonds between the family members are breaking and it becomes important to stress yet another time that the well-being of the family is highly important for the spiritual and material well-being of society and the world at large.

According to the teachings of Bahá'u'lláh, the family is a sacred institution and of utmost importance in contributing to the usefulness and worthiness of an individual's life. It calls upon all people to honour the sanctity of marriage. Bahá'ís believe that where unity exists in a family, the family makes progress and prospers in the world. Members of the family enjoy comfort and tranquillity. Their positions are assured and they have a feeling of security.[6] The integrity of the family bond must be constantly considered and the rights of the individual members must not be transgressed. Like the Confucian concept, each member has rights and obligations:

> The rights of the son, the father, the mother – none of them must be transgressed, none of them must be arbitrary. Just as the son has certain obligations to his father, the father, likewise, has certain obligations to his son. The mother, the sister and other members of the household have their certain prerogatives. All these rights and prerogatives must be conserved, yet the unity of the family must be sustained. The injury of one shall be considered the injury of all; the comfort of each, the comfort of all; the honour of one the honour of all.[7]

Thus, both the Bahá'í and Chinese traditions emphasize that the unity of the family is the most important element for the progress of any civilization. The disintegration of the family means the disintegration of society and ultimately of life itself.

What is different between the two, however, is the Chinese emphasis on superior/inferior relationships and a precise hierarchical order. In the Bahá'í conception, it is not so much a matter of superior/inferior relationships but rather of mutual cooperation. There is now no need for such clear-cut precision as delegating the external affairs to the man and the internal affairs to the woman because today society is much more educated and sophisticated. Either the man or the woman may take charge of the internal or external affairs depending on their respective abilities and aptitudes or they may be jointly responsible for them. Social rules, Confucius said, must change with the times.[8]

In the Bahá'í Faith, affairs can be managed by consultation or delegated to a certain individual by consensus based on that individual's capacity to handle a specific task.

Men and Women

The world of humanity has two wings – one is women and the other men. Not until both wings are equally developed can the bird fly. Should one wing remain weak, flight is impossible. Not until the world of women becomes equal to the world of men in the acquisition of virtues and perfections, can success and prosperity be attained as they ought to be.[9] *'Abdu'l-Bahá*

The Bahá'í Faith is the only religion that establishes the equality of men and women in its scriptures. All other religions have placed men above women. The Bahá'í Faith acknowledges that woman's lack of progress and proficiency has been due to her lack of educational opportunity and that the happiness of humankind will be realized only when women and men coordinate and advance equally since each is the helper and the complement of the other.[10]

It is not difficult to understand the inferior status to which women were relegated in ancient times. In the past, physical prowess was taken as the only criterion of superiority or preeminence. This, in turn, was perpetuated by force or pressure through ritual, tradition, law, language, custom, education, etiquette and the division of labour. Lacking relatively in physical strength, women were naturally relegated to a subordinate position. They themselves accepted this situation and were not resentful. Being subordinated to a physically stronger male, after all, offered a means of protection from the sexual harassment of other males.

With the pronouncement by Bahá'u'lláh of the equality of the status of women and men in the mid-19th century, the stage was now set for an era where modern conveniences would begin to free much of womankind from the drudgery of housework. It became an era where the law gave women equivalent basic rights such as security, ownership of property and equal treatment before the courts. It became an era where education became increasingly available for both sexes. The technological age has arrived, where physical strength is not prized as much as other skills such as mental agility and creativity.

The Confucian era of China, as in other parts of the world, gave women a status lower than that of men. However, since the Chinese mentality has always been inclined towards moderation, compromise, flexibility, and harmony, women were not as oppressed as one might believe. When the *Book of Rites* prescribed that 'the woman follows the man', it also said that 'Harmony between husband and wife is the happiness of the family and that mutual respect, love and care can be nourished. Everyone should respect one another's opinions. Husband and wife should help each other to better their lives. They should help preserve harmony.[11]

One of the most important conjugal virtues was mutual respect. An ancient saying suggests that 'husband and wife should respect each other like guests'. Without respect, love becomes passion and withers. The relationship between husband and wife was considered to be the very foundation of moral order as well as a reflection of a universal principle – the harmony between Heaven and Earth. Children learn how to respect others from their parents. Without respect, there can be no social order. Thus both husband and wife were taught to fulfil their duty of living in harmony. Without harmony, love and joy in the family, there cannot be social justice or peace.

Although the marriage relationship was of great importance, yet it must be borne in mind that in the Chinese psyche, the love of husband and wife, which can only begin after a person comes of age, cannot compare with the love of parents for their children, which a Chinese saying describes as 'arising out of human nature and, eternally strong, endures from birth until earth'.[12]

Filial Piety

Blessed is he who remembereth his parents when communing with God.[13] *The Báb*

For the sake of societal growth and durability, Confucius shrewdly placed filial piety as the highest of virtues. Thus, in traditional Chinese society, there was no crime greater than unfiliality. Cursing a parent used to be a capital offence.[14] Every child, it was taught, should love, serve and respect his parents.

It is interesting to note the remarkable similarity between the Chinese thought on this subject and the importance which the Bahá'í Faith accords to the obedience of children to their parents. Bahá'u'lláh enjoined 'every son to serve his father'.[15] In fact, He emphasized that it is more meritorious to serve one's parents than to serve Him:

> Beware lest ye commit that which would sadden the hearts of your fathers and mothers. Follow ye the path of Truth which indeed is a straight path. Should anyone give you a choice between the opportunity to render a service to Me and a service to them, choose ye to serve them, and let such service be a path leading you to Me. This is My exhortation and command unto thee. Observe therefore that which thy Lord, the Mighty, the Gracious, hath prescribed unto thee.[16]

To Confucius, there was nothing more important than the favours received by children from their parents. To relegate such favours to oblivion would result in failure to provide for the elderly and for the young in their formative years. It was, again, a theory of mutual help and respect which was to lead to some form of order in the society.

There were other reasons for the concept of filial piety. In an agricultural society, people tended to cluster together. Sometimes as many as three generations (or more) lived together. It was essential to consolidate the relations between one generation and the other. Thus, filial piety took on great importance.

Eventually, the idea arose that failure to have children was the greatest unfiliality because of the problems which arose when there was no younger generation to inherit. As land was traditionally passed on to the male descendants, lack of a son was particularly difficult.

The Nature of Filial Piety

We may wonder what the nature of filial piety was for the Chinese. How should a child serve his parent before he can be called 'filial'. What degree of duty and respect must the child manifest to his parents? Confucius was very clear that it was the sincerity behind one's deeds that was important. The essence was valued above the form. Mere material support without the expression of reverence and affection could not, for him, be called filial piety.

The filial piety of nowadays means the support of one's parents. But dogs and horses likewise are able to do something in the way of support without reverence, what is there to distinguish the one support given from the other?[17]

Mencius also stressed that material support without spiritual consolation could not be called filial piety.[18] Filial piety for Confucius comprised the elimination of all bad habits so as not to injure or humiliate one's parents. It also meant the care of one's own health so as not to cause one's parents any anxiety. Of course, it was necessary for children to remonstrate with their elders if they were wrong but in doing so, they were to adopt a gentle and respectful attitude, so as to influence their parents in such a way that the advice might be accepted.[19] Total and blind obedience to parents was not advocated. Thus, although Confucius saw the virtue of a son shielding his sheep-stealing father, he also taught the son to remonstrate, mildly but persistently, with his erring father.

Filial piety also meant that in the event of marriage, the man should inform his parents. Next to the parent-son relationship is the marriage relationship, which in ancient China was held to be inviolable except in the case of certain prescribed conditions. The dwelling together of the male and female was said to represent the greatest of relationships.[20] Parental consent was thus required in the event of a marriage, as they were naturally anxious to be informed about such a major lifetime commitment on the part of their offspring.[21] Matchmaking was the order of the day. To be filial, then, one should 'behave in such a way that your father and mother have no anxiety about you, except concerning your health'.[22]

In the Bahá'í context, while children are given the freedom to choose their own spouses without the interference of parents, yet consent must be obtained from the natural living parents of the prospective bride and groom once their choice is made. This is to preserve the unity and harmony of the family, the root, as it were, of the whole moral order of society.

The Tutor as Part of the Family

In Confucian ethics, the position of the tutor was particularly respected. In fact, the tutor ranked next to the father's position in the traditional Chinese household. This may sometimes be seen in the simple tablet on the family altar which describes the objects – more or less personified – which are to be worshipped. These are 'Heaven, Earth, Sovereign, Father and Tutor'. It was reasoned that, as parents had given birth to the physical body of the son, it was the teacher who had much to do with formulating the pupil's spiritual and cultural life. Just as one honours one's physical life-giver, so one honours one's cultural life-giver.

Regarding the tutor as part of the family may also be seen as an expansion of the principle of filial piety. Traditionally, the Chinese built kinship ties through marriage. They were also in the habit of establishing clans based on blood relationships. Regional relationships were also built up through the village in which one was born and brought up. In addition, one's ancestors, and still further, tutors and friends were linked together through academic pursuits or mutual attraction or other causes. All these relationships can be said to revolve around the centre of gravity of the practice of filial piety.

Teachers also enjoy a high position in the Bahá'í Faith. The teacher is like the doctor to the child, for in instructing the child, he remedies his faults, gives him learning, and at the same time rears him to have a spiritual nature. In the *Kitáb-i-Aqdas*, teachers are listed among the beneficiaries who stand to inherit a portion of a deceased's estate.[23]

Ancestor Worship

Ancestral worship is a form of reciprocity in which the individual exists by virtue of his descendants and similarly, his ancestors exist only through him. This means that the spiritual well-being of the ancestors are dependent upon their descendants through their prayers and material sacrifices at the altars. Likewise, the descendants are dependent upon their ancestors for spiritual assistance and guidance.

Although Bahá'ís do not worship their ancestors, there are certain similarities between the two religions in this regard. Bahá'ís believe that there is life after death and that in the spiritual world after death there exist souls who have passed away from this world. These souls are able to assist people in the physical world just as living human beings are able to assist souls in their spiritual development:

> Concerning your question whether a soul can receive knowledge of the Truth in the world beyond. Such knowledge is surely possible, and is but a sign of the loving Mercy of the Almighty. We can, through our prayers, help every soul to gradually attain this high station, even if it has failed to reach it in this world. The progress of the soul does not come to an end with death. It rather starts along a new line. Bahá'u'lláh teaches that great and far-reaching possibilities await the soul in the other world. Spiritual progress in that realm is infinite, and no man, while on this earth, can visualize its full power and strength.[24]

Bahá'ís believe that once a soul has departed from this physical world, it will behold in that next world whatever was hidden from it here. It will be able to 'gaze on his fellows and peers, and those in the ranks above him, and those below'.[25] Bahá'ís are encouraged to pray for those who have died in order to assist their spiritual progress.

Confucius did not encourage the practice of ancestor worship but he did not discredit it either. He certainly did not invent it, as is commonly assumed. Ancestor worship is a very ancient practice. Early historical records from the first centuries of the Chou dynasty[26] show the ancestors of the ruling house dwelling 'on high' in some sort of close association with, and in subordinate capacity to, the Supreme Ruler in Heaven. Their power over their descendants seems to derive from this position; that is, they are able to communicate with Heaven to send down blessings or calamities. From the earliest times there was the assumption that the dead and living were dependent upon each other – the dead depend on the living for sacrifices (prayers and offering of food) and the living depend on the dead for blessings.

In addition, archaeological evidence shows that funeral services at the time of the Shang dynasty were lavish and involved the interment of horses, carriages, vessels, as well as wives. The more important the person, the more people were buried along with him. This was done on the grounds that the departed would need them in the other world. Also, he had to be kept happy, for his powers to inflict punishments or grant favours increased after death.

We may compare this with the present-day practice of the burning of 'hell money' (money that is bought to give to the dead), paper houses, cars, etc. by the Chinese in Taiwan, Hong Kong and Singapore. These paper replicas of day-to-day objects are today bought in special shops. There is little basic difference between these practices and those of their Shang ancestors. There is a strong belief that the dead exist and have to be accorded their due respects.

This basic Chinese idea is not unlike the Bahá'í belief that 'the progress of man's spirit in the divine world, after the severance of its connection with the body of dust, is through the bounty and grace of the Lord alone, or through the intercession and the sincere prayers of other human souls, or through the charities and important good works which are performed in its name'.[27] The difference is that for the Bahá'ís there are only heartfelt remembrances and prayers whereas Chinese ancestor worship has evolved into an elaborate ceremony not unlike that of a formal religion.

Conclusion

It has often been said that the secret of Chinese strength lies in the family. However, it must be noted that in the last half-century, Western culture and Western education has contributed to the dissolution of the traditional Chinese large-scale family. The stringent criteria surrounding the practice of filial piety has also been diluted.

Nevertheless, most Chinese families still maintain reverential service to their elders as the Heaven-ordained obligation of all children. In virtually all Chinese households, for example, elderly parents live with their married son or daughter in harmony. Sending one's parents to a home for the aged or allowing them to live on their own is still uncommon, although it has become usual in Western society.

14

Unity of the State

> It behoveth every king to be as bountiful as the sun, which
> fostereth the growth of all beings, and giveth to each its due . . .[1]
>
> *Bahá'u'lláh*

The governing of a state by an enlightened ruler has always been
the basic criterion for ensuring the peace and harmony of the
state and for enabling the normal orderly working of life. The
political theories of both Confucius and Lao-tzu were critical
reactions to the political climate of their time. What was this
political climate that provoked such a response?

Pre-axial Political China

Although there is evidence of advanced civilization in China in
very early times, actual recorded history only began with the
Shang dynasty in the 14th century BC. Archaeological discoveries
confirm the existence of sophisticated works of art during this
period. The Shang dynasty, however, ended with the invasion by
the more primitive Chou people who, according to tradition,
established the Chou dynasty in 1122 BC.

Not having the means to administer all of the conquered
territories as one central state, the Chou rulers delegated
administrative power to friendly chiefs and nobles, providing
parcels of land in exchange for the cooperation of the newly-
endowed landowner. This worked quite well and there was a
period of relative peace and security which came later to be
regarded as the 'golden period' in China's early history.

However, as time went on, it was recognized by the chiefs of the
districts that the Chou kings did not really have the strength to
control all the conquered land, even through the device of
feudalism. Not surprisingly, unrest gradually pervaded the
countryside and civil wars became more and more frequent.

Things reached such a state that by 770 BC the kings were controlled by the coalition of feudal lords who happened to be in power at the time. Power was constantly shifting hands, and war and strife were common. Violence and intrigue characterized the political scene and the price of this instability was unimaginable levels of poverty, suffering and death. This was the situation for two centuries prior to the births of Confucius and Lao-tzu.

The teachings of Confucius and Lao-tzu initiated a period of enlightenment. Because of them, the 6th century is considered a watershed in Chinese history since it marked the coming of a new era – what may be called the Confucian era. It was a watershed because old values and institutions were doomed to give place to the new – an evolutionary process which could not be stopped by any person. There have been other watersheds in world history but these have usually been brought about by a divine Messenger such as the Buddha, Christ or Muḥammad. In the unique case of China, the teacher did not have a divine mission; he was only a very exceptional sage who himself denied that he was even that.

The Rectification of Names

A well-ordered society can only be possible through 'the rectification of names'. This refers to the idea that things in actual fact should be made to accord with the implications attached to them by their names.

Once a disciple asked Confucius what he would do first if he were to rule a state, whereupon Confucius replied, 'The one thing needed first is the rectification of names.'[2] On another occasion, one of the dukes of the kingdom asked Confucius the first principle of government. 'Let the ruler be ruler, the minister minister, the father father, and the son son,' he replied.[3]

In other words, every name contains certain implications which constitute the essence of the class of things to which this name applies. Such things, therefore, should agree with this ideal essence. The essence of a ruler is what the ruler ideally ought to be. If a ruler acts according to the way of a ruler, he is then truly a ruler, in fact as well as in name; there is an agreement between name and actuality. But if he does not conform to this ideal, he is no ruler, even though he may popularly be regarded as such.

Every name in the social relationship implies certain responsibilities and duties. Ruler, minister, father, son and friend are all the names of such social relationships, and the individuals bearing these names must fulfil their responsibilities and duties accordingly.

If the sovereign is no longer a sovereign, and the minister no longer a minister; if the father is no longer a father, and the son no longer a son, shall I have a chance to eat the food I have?[4]

Confucius further stated that 'if a prince has rendered himself upright, he will have no difficulty in governing the people. But if he cannot rectify himself, how can he hope to rectify the people?'[5] Everybody must behave as his 'name' or 'title' implies. The rectification of names is thus the key to a stable and happy society. It is the only means of preventing anarchy, strife and unhappiness. On this premise, Confucius rests his theory of kingship and the state.

Duties of the Ruler

A ruler who governs his state by virtue is like the north polar star which remains in its place while all the other stars revolve around it.[6] *Confucius*

... belittle not the rank of such rulers as administer justice amidst you.[7] *Bahá'u'lláh*

The traditional role of the ruler was based on the ancient ideal of the benevolent ruler entrusted with the Mandate of Heaven. Since the Mandate of Heaven was given to him, the ruler should first and foremost revere Heaven. Reverence for Heaven could be shown through ceremonies and sacrifices, which are not, according to Confucius, as efficacious as a sincere love for man. A ruler worships Heaven by being kind to the people he rules. To be kind or loving to the people is to show Heaven how seriously or sincerely it is revered.[8]

The first and foremost duty of the prince, then, was to cultivate his personality, for it was only when he himself was morally perfect that he could win over the people's hearts.[9] It was impressed on the ruler that virtue preceded strength and right preceded might. Possessing virtue would give the ruler the people. Possessing the people would give him the territory and with the territory he would be able to accumulate wealth. Virtue was thus the root and wealth the result. In other words, the spiritual condition of human existence (virtue) should precede its material condition (wealth). Their position and relationship should not be reversed nor their sequence confused.[10]

Confucius was far-sighted enough to realize that while wealth is indispensable, it cannot be regarded as the root; and that while strength cannot be ignored, it certainly cannot be relied upon as the long-term factor; that while technique is essential to human life, true wisdom consists of knowing what virtue is and possessing the courage to practise it.[11] 'Virtue was the root, wealth was the branch.'

Interestingly enough, 'Abdu'l-Bahá used the same metaphors of 'root' and 'branch' to illustrate almost the same concepts: 'Then it is clear that the honour and exaltation of man must be something more than material riches. Material comforts are only a branch, but the root of the exaltation is the good attributes and virtues which are the adornments of his reality.'[12]

The ruler was also urged to adopt *yin* values. In the *Tao-te ching*, Lao-tzu exhorted the ruler to 'know the masculine but keep to the feminine' as well as 'to know the white (*yang*) but keep to the black (*yin*)'.[13] *Yin* qualities are commonly associated with the female role. The ruler was urged to be 'weak' in order to be 'strong', as shown in the image of the infant, whose helplessness can dominate the whole family.[14] The Taoist notion here foreshadows the words of Jesus five hundred years later: 'Blessed are the meek, for they shall inherit the earth.'[15] Such words of wisdom are restated in the Bahá'í scriptures which remind us that through meekness, man is elevated to the heaven of power while 'pride abaseth him to the depths of wretchedness and degradation'.[16]

In addition, the duties of a ruler also took into account the economics of expenditure.[17]

To lead a country of a thousand chariots, the ruler must attend reverentially to business and be of good faith. He must practise economy in expenditure and love all men, and employ the people in accordance with the seasons.[18]

In this regard, rulers were told to imitate the sage kings of antiquity:

The ruler of antiquity was concerned about the hardships of his subjects to the extent that if there were people starving in his state, at each meal he would have only one single dish, and if there were people freezing in winter he would not attire himself in fur garments. Only when the harvest was good and the people had plenty would he then set up the bells and drums and display the shields and axes, and with ruler and subject, superior and subordinate, all enjoying these together, there was no sorrowful person left in the whole state.[19]

In relation to economics, the Bahá'í Faith advocates the amelioration of the condition of the poor and the altering of the economic structure throughout the world so as to be more egalitarian. 'Abdu'l-Bahá envisages a world with no extremely rich and no extremely poor people, a world with progressive taxes and supplementary income to provide relief to the needy.[20] He also boldly advocated joint ownership of firms by employees and employers with the workers enjoying part of the profits in addition to their salaries.[21]

The Role of Education

Confucius' major concern can be said to be a universal one – that political power should be wielded by men of wisdom and virtue. This was also Plato's ideal, and it remains the greatest wish of our world today. Here, Confucius emphasized the role of education in producing such rulers.

He stated that the government should be administered by the most capable men in the country if the welfare and happiness of the people were to be achieved. Capable administrators were to be found not by birth, wealth or position but through character, knowledge and proper education.[22] He even asserted that one of his disciples, who was not the heir of a ruling house, might properly occupy a throne should he have the required knowledge and wisdom.[23] Education thus became at one with political activity and progress.

Confucius was also so advanced in his thinking that he specifically repudiated the ideal of feudal loyalty to individuals, insisting that his disciples must instead remain true to moral principles.[24] The administrators of a country, he taught, should also be loyal to principles rather than just to the particular ruler who had appointed them to their positions.

It must be noted that government by virtue and moral magnetism was not a completely new idea in China as the country had had a republican episode much earlier. In 2500 BC Emperor Yao chose Shuen to be his successor in preference to his own son Tan-chu. Emperor Shuen, in his turn, chose Yu to be his successor in preference to his own son, Shang-chiun. Confucius admired these two selfless emperors more than any other ruler and he often made reference to them in his teachings.

Government for the People

Confucius often referred to the golden period in which the ancients ruled the world and which exemplified for him an age of enlightened government where the interests of the people were taken care of.

> Of old, when the emperor would hold court, the high ministers would proffer honest admonition, the learned scholars would chant the odes, the music masters would sing their criticisms, the common people would communicate their opinions, the court historians would chronicle errors in judgement and the court chefs would reduce the number of dishes at meals, but still this was not considered enough. Thus Yao set up a drum for those offering bold admonition, Shun established a notice board for criticisms, T'ang instituted an independent judicial authority, and King Wu provided a small drum to forewarn him against rashness. Before an error could show itself there was already a safeguard against it.[25]

The importance of retaining the confidence of the people was recognized very early by the Chinese sages:

> Tzu-kung asked about government. The Master said; 'Enough food, enough weapons, and the confidence of the people.' Tzu-kung said: 'Suppose you definitely had no alternative but to give up one of these three, which would you relinquish first?' The Master said: 'Weapons.' Tzu-kung said: 'Suppose you definitely had no alternative but to give up one of the remaining two, which would you relinquish first?' The Master said: 'Food. From of old, death has come to all men, but a people without confidence in its rulers will not stand.'[26]

Again, the political importance of the people was not a new idea in axial China. In the *Book of History*, we read that 'Heaven sees and hears as the people see and hear'. Moreover, the doctrine of the Mandate of Heaven justified rebellion to get rid of a tyrannical ruler. If a wayward ruler should turn a deaf ear to the warnings and admonitions in the ancient texts of what would befall a ruler should he be unjust or 'misbehave', not only would his forceful removal be permitted, but he by whose hands this act is done would be regarded as a vassal of God as well as a saviour of man.[27]

This can be said to be the most articulate expression of the democratic ideal in Chinese political thought. The right of the sovereign rested on a trust – a divine trust. Heaven or God is involved in this scheme and revolution becomes part and parcel of the restoration of good and balance.

Mencius also said that, first, high ministers of the royal house could dethrone a ruler; second, that others not belonging to the royal house could banish him; third, that a sovereign who acted like a robber and a ruffian was a 'mere fellow' whom anyone could put to death; and fourth, that a ruler who could not support the people would return his charge to them. By this Mencius meant to exhort the reigning princes to remember that their role was to love and enrich their people.[28]

While Confucius himself had nothing to say about the confidence of the people being won by consulting them and taking their opinions into acocunt,[29] Mencius went so far as to say that the views of the people should be canvassed concerning cases of promotion, dismissal or crimes meriting the death penalty,[30] and that 'the people are the most important element in a nation; the spirits of the land and grain are the next; and the sovereign is the lightest'.[31]

We find that Mencius' enthusiasm for political democracy comes from this deep-seated faith in moral democracy. Such enthusiasm is indeed remarkable when we realize that the individual common man of the time was just emerging out of the tenant slavery of a feudalistic society and had hardly shaken off its vestiges.[32]

The Bahá'í View

God grant that the light of unity may envelop the whole earth, and that the seal 'the Kingdom is God's' may be stamped upon the brow of all its peoples.[33] *Bahá'u'lláh*

Today, the concept of an individual ruler, however enlightened, wielding absolute power like that of Yao and Shun is grossly outdated. Confucius would not have disagreed with this view since it was he who said that reforms should be relevant to the needs of the age. He himself modified many of the ancient practices to suit the conditions of his time. Humankind has passed through the stages of forming the tribe, the city state and the nation. The theory of national sovereignty has been largely undermined by the fact of economic interdependence. The face of the planet has been radically changed by mass communication. The world is, in effect, one country. The time is now appropriate for the establishment of the Great Unity, as foretold in the ancient Chinese and Bahá'í scriptures.

'A world federal system,' said Shoghi Effendi, 'ruling the whole earth and exercising unchallengable authority over its unimaginably vast resources, blending and embodying the ideals of both the East and the West, liberated from the curse of war and its miseries, and bent on the exploitation of all the available sources of energy on the surface of the planet, a system in which Force is made the servant of Justice, whose life is sustained by the

161

universal recognition of one God and by its allegiance to one common Revelation – such is the goal towards which humanity, impelled by the unifying forces of life, is moving.'[34]

The Bahá'í notion of world government means that the different races of the world will meet as equals. Each nation will be represented in a world parliament which will be concerned with the prosperity of all nations and the happiness of all humankind. The world government will preserve the autonomy of each nation and safeguard the personal freedom of the individual, but it will require the governments of the world to give up the right to hold armaments except for those necessary to maintain internal order, to impose certain taxes, and to wage war.

A uniform system of currency, weights and measures will be established; the extremes of wealth and poverty will be eliminated. The use of an international language for easier communication will be promoted and an educational system providing basic needs will be developed. A supreme tribunal will be created with representatives from all nations giving judgement on any international disagreement. Following the traditional Chinese conception of government, the world government will be staffed by people whose executive talents will be imbued with moral principles.

Unlike the Chinese system, however, and in accordance with the spirit of the age, the Bahá'í Faith calls for elected representatives rather than a selection based on educational or intellectual merit judged by some external criteria. In 1875, when there was a debate over government reforms both in the Ottoman Empire and Iran, 'Abdu'l-Bahá wrote:

In the present writer's view, it would be preferable if the election of nonpermanent members of consultative assemblies in sovereign states should be dependent on the will and choice of the people. For elected representatives will on this account be somewhat inclined to exercise justice, lest their reputation suffer and they fall into disfavour with the public.[35]

The Bahá'í Faith embodies a straight-forward commitment to certain elements of political democracy such as the right to vote and the holding of elections – a radical change from the traditions of the major religions of the past. Within the Bahá'í religious institutions themselves – which are designed to coexist with secular government institutions for at least some time – democratic elections are practised. As the religion spreads, particularly in the third world, it inevitably socializes its members towards more democratic methods of self-government, thus helping to spread an appreciation of participatory rights.

Participatory rights also include freedom of speech, freedom of assembly, and freedom of the press, all of which are necessary for the creation of an informed public opinion. 'Abdu'l-Bahá urged the publication of beneficial articles and books establishing the present-day requirement of the people, and whatever would contribute to the happiness and advancement of society.[36]

Bahá'ís are told to seek the advice of others in their personal and business lives and to reach decisions affecting their communities through consultation in a group. The solution of all problems, it is said, depends on the sincere meeting for discussion of all parties to the question, and their willingness to abide by the decisions so made.

For Confucius, 'democracy' was not so much political elections or group consultation as the emphasis on the worth of man, the dignity of the individual, the primacy of *jen* among all the virtues, the good sense of the common man, and the perfectibility of humankind as a whole. It was a call for selflessness, a spirit of toleration, a willingness to live together with persons who hold different religious and political ideas from oneself.

Conclusion

The Bahá'í Faith and the traditional Chinese religion are much in agreement in their vision of the importance of a just and virtuous government. They agree in principle that virtue rather than wealth should be the root of all governmental endeavours. While Confucius advocated government by a virtuous ruler who would unite the warring factions and bring feudalism to an end, Bahá'u'lláh advocated a world government which would unite the warring states and bring nationalism and discord to an end. While the task of the Chinese rulers was to establish peace in the kingdom, the central task of rulers today is to establish peace in the world. Like the Chinese religion, the Bahá'í Faith focuses on and outlines a plan for social salvation and not just personal salvation. This sets the two religions apart from other major religions which focus mainly on personal salvation.

15

The Winter of Chinese Religion

> Buddha ... established a new religion, and Confucius renewed
> morals and ancient virtues, but their institutions have been
> entirely destroyed. The beliefs and rites of the Buddhists and
> Confucians have not continued in accordance with their funda-
> mental teachings.[1] 'Abdu'l-Bahá

As with all things, the passage of time eats away at the once
pristine messages of the great spiritual leaders, inexorably
disarraying their character and fragmenting their meaning.
Confucius' call for a rare humanism and for moral considerations
could not, therefore, long survive in its pure form.

Confucianism, just like all religions, underwent many trans-
formations in the course of its long history. By the time of its
official and general acceptance, it was far removed from its
source, Confucius himself.

In the first place, regarding the authenticity of the writings of
Confucius, it must be remembered that the Confucian sacred
texts – the five classics – took their definitive shape only in the
second century BC during the Han dynasty (206 BC–8 AD). Indeed,
several texts reconstructed after the burning of the books in the
Ch'in dynasty (221–206 BC) must have undergone significant
changes in the hands of the Han editors.

Next, Confucian moral values have often been politicized to
serve an oppressive authoritarian regime. The politicization of
Confucian symbols in the form of an authoritarian ideology of
control (not unlike the history of the Catholic church) has long
been dominant in Chinese political history. The fact that
Confucius was venerated by the state was not so much due to his
greatness but to the fact that he had become the mortal whose
interpretation of the past was the most congenial to the crown.
But the state did not take his teachings *in toto*: they only
emphasized things which they thought were relevant such as
values and protocol which kept the people subservient.

The virtue of loyalty to the state, for example, was naturally exploited by the autocratic regime in Imperial China. A spurious composition known as the *Book of Loyalty*, a forgery of the late T'ang or early Sung, was widely accepted as a genuine work of antiquity in the Sung and later periods. It taught blind and undeviating loyalty to the ruler. In the later empire, as the state became increasingly despotic, the concept of loyalty became transformed into that of unquestioning subservience, and the support of Confucius himself was claimed for the view that ministers owed absolute loyalty to ruler and dynasty.

The Deification of Confucius

The first development that significantly marked the deviation and deterioration of the Confucian ideal was the development of the worship of Confucius as a god, a development that would have horrified the sage since during his lifetime he had himself rejected even the lesser honour of sagehood.

This came about because of the growth of his prestige after his death, despite brief periods when the ruling class grew disenchanted with him and relegated him to his original position of teacher.[2] In the century after his death, Confucius had come to be considered as *the* teacher, superior to all others. As the centuries passed, he was elevated to a higher plane. By the first century BC, five hundred years later, Confucius was regarded as even more than a human being. According to many people of that time, he was a living god among men – a divine being who knew that after his time there would someday come the Han dynasty (206 BC – 220 AD) and who therefore set forth a political ideal which would be complete enough for the men of Han to realize. By the 2nd century AD, Confucius may be said to have reached the height of his glory. According to many Confucianists of that time, Confucius had actually been appointed by Heaven to begin a new dynasty that would follow that of Chou.[3]

Indeed, Confucius was so venerated in the later Han dynasty that regular worship of him was conducted in government schools. Later, in the T'ang dynasty (618–907 AD), temples to the Master were erected throughout the empire. In these temples the chief disciples and distinguished Confucians of later ages were also honoured. Above the altar were the words, 'The teacher of 10,000 generations' and only scholars could take part in the sacrifices. As the patron deity of scholars and officials, Confucius became an important figure and his role comparable with those of the deities of the various crafts, which were commonly worshipped by practitioners of those crafts at their guild meetings.[4]

By the 17th century, the diverse elements of the Confucian tradition had been merged into a rather unwieldly official cult. According to an official list of those to whom imperial worship was due in the 17th century, there were three classes of worthies. First came the Empress Earth, the imperial ancestors, the guardian spirits of the land and the harvest. Second came the sun, the moon, the emperors of the preceding dynasties, the patrons of agriculture and the spirits of the earth, the planet Jupiter, whose revolution around the sun regulated the Chinese calendar, and Confucius.[5] Third, came the patron saints of medicine, war and literature, the North Star, the god of Beijing, the god of artillery, the god of the soil, the patron saint of the mechanical arts, the god of the furnace, the god of the granary, the god of the doors and many official patriots.[6]

This list illustrates how Confucius' teachings were subsequently altered. Confucius taught that one should follow only Heaven's way and should not worship spirits. Yet the lists show influences of ancestor veneration, veneration of the deities of the earth, veneration of the patron gods or saints or particular clans. Some of the deities in this list are very ancient, going back to the Shang and Chou dynasties, at the very beginning of Chinese history. Confucius, we note, was listed among the remnants of all the superstitious beliefs that had accumulated over the centuries.

By the time of the Ch'ing dynasty (1644–1911), a whole series of elaborate rituals began to accompany the official veneration of the deities. There was an intensification of the theory that Confucius was divinely appointed to be a king.[7] Rituals now began to take quite a different connotation from the original *li* propounded by Confucius. They were performed for the sake of performance – the original motivation for them apparently forgotten. Form rather than spirit became a major, if not vital, consideration – the government paid serious attention to the instruction of its officials in the particulars of worshipping the cult figures of the different ranks. The official was, besides undertaking a host of multifarious duties, to bathe, fast, prostrate to various deities and make thanksgiving offerings of incense, lighted candles, gems, fruits, cooked foods, salted vegetables, etc.

With the establishment of the Chinese Republic in 1912, Confucius' reputation fell until he came to be regarded as something less than the teacher. Today, most Chinese would say that he was primarily a teacher, and certainly a great one, but far from being the only teacher.[8]

Polytheism

The meaning is that the Buddhists and Confucianists now worship images and statues. They are entirely heedless of the Oneness of God and believe in imaginary gods like the ancient Greeks. But in the beginning it was not so; there were different principles and other ordinances.'[9] 'Abdu'l-Bahá

It must be noted that the coming of Confucius did not entirely destroy the shamanistic religious practices that operated in the pre-axial period. As the popular Chinese folk novel *Monkey* shows, other ancient attitudes have continued well into the present.[10] Indeed, the primitive animism of the peasant that originated in the fear of the formidable power of nature remained quite intact under the shadow of the Confucian humanistic tradition. This is not to say that the peasants were indifferent to the Confucian ideal. In fact, they were imbued with the Confucian ethic, which, at least after the Christian era, became widely disseminated through proverbs and moral axioms, the tales of the story teller and the rustic sage.[11] It was simply that the old and the new were kept together; at certain times Confucianism took ascendancy, and at other times, the superstitious practices prevailed.

Since neither Confucius nor Lao-tzu claimed to be divine teachers, there was no intrinsic compulsion to their message. Their message brought enlightenment and something similar to a 'new' religious dispensation. But the people remained free to continue in their superstitious practices without the fear of divine wrath. They had a choice to believe what the sages taught of the Supreme Ultimate or they could retain their animistic practices. The sages exhorted them to be wise but they did not have the weight of divine authority to impel the masses to change their ways. Thus, the masses imbibed the teachings of the sages while retaining some of their superstitious practices.

The polytheistic ideas of gods and spirits prevailed. These ideas became less popular as Confucianism spread, but after some time polytheistic ideas came to the forefront again. Popular cults also continually grew up and new divinities were worshipped: gods from India and Tibet, deified heroes who died in national struggles and figures from local cults whose reputation spread from district to district in China. Through the centuries, scholar administrators did not check or even try to turn the peasants from the superstitious activities surrounding their ancient and primitive belief in gods and spirits. Already corrupted by the distortion of the original Confucian concepts themselves, these administrators also retained some of the primitive ideas and superstitions in their own religious practices.

Nevertheless, it must be noted that although such popular beliefs, magic, animism, superstitions, etc., were common and widespread, they have never been important in the making of the Chinese ideal. The Chinese ideal has always been linked to the humanistic philosophy of Confucius.

Today, popular deities among the Chinese peasants are those that can bring earthly blessings, prosperity and help their worshippers solve problems. The local god of the soil, for instance, is more frequently worshipped and sacrificed to than the god of Heaven because the former is so closely related to people's lives.

The traditional Chinese home – which is fast disappearing from Taiwan, Hong Kong and Singapore – is a complex centre of religious worship. Upon entering one sees paper 'door gods' (names of deities inscribed on paper), either painted in colourful portraits or written in Chinese characters, posted on the doors to protect the house and its family members against possible invasion by evil spirits. Near the floor or on the floor is an altar to T'u-ti, the earth god, who protects the family against destructive influences and who ensures that the members of the family behave themselves with religious and social propriety. T'ien-kuan, the Heavenly Official, is usually stationed in the courtyard, while the wealth gods, who bring well-being and prosperity to the family, are in the hall or the main room. On or near the cooking stove is Tsao-shen, the kitchen god, who at the end of the year makes an annual report to the Jade Emperor, the supreme god in Heaven, regarding the conduct of the family and its members, a report which would result in either reward or punishment. Some families also have an altar for the goddess of mercy, or another deity, as a special patron of the family's well-being.

Although the Chinese hold the concept of *T'ien* (Heaven) deep in their hearts, through the long years of disassociation from their original spiritual heritage, they have continued to worship an organic or hierarchical pantheon of gods – which includes the worship of a Supreme God and his assemblage of divine beings, natural forces and deified cultural heroes and ancestors – which actually resembles the hierarchy of government officials in the Chinese traditional feudal system. In popular belief, after great men die, they turn into deities because of the contributions they have made in their lifetimes. A conspicuous example is the popular deity Kuan Kung, a good and just general known for his loyalty to the throne.

The pure essence of religious truth which Confucius and Lao-tzu tried to instil are now all but forgotten. Religious ceremonies are regarded by the vast majority of people as magic rather than merely pure form. The masses are fatalistic, believing that spirits have direct control over their fortunes and misfortunes. Thus they are impelled to go to various deities primarily to seek blessings such as children, wealth and long life. Heaven and Hell became a reality with the coming of Buddhism and the masses came to believe in 33 Buddhist heavens, 81 Taoist heavens and 18 Buddhist hells.[12]

This is a far cry from the aspirations of a true Confucian who would keep spirits at a distance, emphasizing instead harmonious socialization with his fellow men. In worship, he also has only thanks to give and no favours to seek. He honours only Heaven, his ancestors and his teachers rather than a myriad of spirits and deities. Heaven for him is not a 'place' but a way of being at one with the *Tao*. There is no Hell – evil is a result of a deviation from the goodness of one's original nature.

The Misrepresentation of Filial Piety

The family unit is important to the Confucian because it is the basis of social harmony for the whole community. The Confucian, after fulfilling his love for his family, should extend it to the country as a whole and even to the world at large. This concept was not understood in its full significance by the masses and, in actual practise, many Chinese who followed Confucian principles restricted their love only to members of the family and possibly to friends.

Through the passage of time, it became convenient for the great majority to interpret filial piety as something concerned solely with the family rather than society and the country as a whole. In this respect it may be observed that although the Chinese can be said to be a friendly, warm and gregarious people, they are short on social concern. They do not appear to be as public-spirited and law abiding as their Western counterparts. There is a story among the Chinese that should burglars break into one's house, it would be easier to get neighbours to respond to a cry of 'fire, fire, fire' rather than to 'burglars, burglars, help!' If one called 'burglars', the neighbours would just lock their doors even more tightly; while with a fire, their own interests would also be at stake, so the neighbours would run to extinguish the fire.

In time the concept of filial piety was used to condone private revenge. Reverential service to elders came to be narrowly interpreted and linked to the revenge theme. The Confucian adage of forgiveness was forgotten. It became a 'duty' for a son to avenge the blood of his father killed by another. Thus began a continuous line of revenge upon revenge as epitomized in popular Chinese sword fighting movies. Mencius was often quoted out of context as condoning private revenge. He said, for instance, that 'if you kill your neighbour's father, then your neighbour would kill your father'.[13] The conflict between law and moral ideas, between the interests of the family and that of the state, was one of the burning questions throughout the history of China until about a century ago when people began gradually to realize that private revenge was wrong from the moral point of view.

However, one must be fair to Mencius and judge him in the context of his time rather than through 20th century eyes. Private revenge was indirectly condoned during a time when one could not depend on the law to rectify a wrong, especially when the judicial arm was not well-developed or reliable. In the Old Testament itself there is the injunction of 'an eye for an eye and a tooth for a tooth'. Today, private revenge is certainly considered to be wrong, and there is now a well-developed judicial apparatus as well as appeal bodies and various organizations to mediate in conflicts.

Such misrepresentations exist because of blind devotion and attachment to the letter of the ancient scriptures without considering the context or the essence of what was actually written.

Ancestor Worship

Confucius did not rule out the possibility of the existence of spiritual beings although he cautioned that one should not be preoccupied with them. Certainly, he taught that one should serve one's fellow man rather than the world of spirits. Nevertheless, he did not discourage the practice of the veneration of the dead. He emphasized that such veneration should be a form of respect for one's ancestors rather than the seeking of favours.

This practice was based on a belief in the continued existence of the dead in the form of souls and the further assumption of mutual dependence between the souls and the living. Belief in the souls of the dead, their power to influence the living morally and physically, and the need for perpetual sacrifice by the descendants became a part of classical theology. Thus, in many a traditional Chinese household lamps radiating a dim glow perpetually burn before ancestral tablets. Incense and candles are periodically offered to the tablets and religious ceremonies performed, which suggests that the symbols of the dead continue to occupy a place in family life.

However, the simple respect and reverence that Confucius encouraged turned into the serious formality of a 'family religion'. The tragedy is, for many Chinese, that the primary obligation of religious life became merely such acts of commemorative reverence. An excessive amount of time and resources was spent on these acts, so much so that before the Communist takeover ancestral temples were among the best-endowed religious establishments in the country. At times, professional priests were hired to participate in some of the rituals, although they did not officiate at the worship.

Practices predominant in the pre-axial period also reemerged in full force in the modern era to play a part in ancestor worship. Ancient functionaries such as mediums and shamans were frequently employed to call on a personal spirit for enlightenment. The shaman would then convey the message to his employer. Susceptible individuals believed that spirits with lights and messages or the spirits of departed ancestors spoke through a medium in a trance. If one did not revere them and give them gifts of food, the ancestor spirits could turn nasty.

It also came to be believed that the ancestor spirits lived in a spiritual equivalent of the human world, where they needed such things as food, clothing and money. Thus, pious children would burn paper money and send assistance to their departed parents.

On the whole, ancestor worship has degenerated to the extent that it has ceased to be observed solely as an occasion of love, memory and piety. It has become a ceremony where protection from evil spirits is sought and favours are asked in pursuit of worldly goals.

The Question of Women

After Confucius, filial piety came to be associated primarily with the continuation of the bloodline so that the line of one's ancestors might be extended. It also came to mean 'carrying on and paving the way for the future', and being responsible for continuing the national life and culture of one's country rather than loving and having reverence for one's parents as a first step towards love for all humankind.

To ensure a continuous line of descendants, good physical health became of great importance in the choice of a spouse. Marriage thus became a relationship forged by considerations other than instinctive desire. Approval of one's future spouse was to be sought from parents, not so much out of a sense of love and consideration but because it was important that the marriage gain the support of the older generation and the generation that had already passed away. The children of the union were likewise regarded as essential to the completion of the couple's filial responsibilities, as is indicated by a saying of Mencius which became proverbial: 'There are three ways in which one may be unfilial, of which the worst is to have no heir.'[14] Women were therefore put under enormous pressure to fulfil this primary obligation of bringing forth a male offspring. The spiritual basis for parental consent (a means of preserving family unity and harmony, a concept also found in the Bahá'í Faith) was lost; in its place was put a utilitarian motive.

Gradually, the mutual respect due to the wife because she was essentially a human being, similar to man – the indispensable complementary component of *yang* – was forgotten. Mutual respect was accorded to her only after she became a mother and fulfilled the function of continuing the family line. Her role was the transmitter of the ancestor's life. Accordingly, it became customary for the husband to divorce the wife or take on one or more concubines should she fail to produce a male descendant.

Unfortunately, such a narrow vision of filial piety continues to exist especially among the older generation and in the vast countryside of China. Thus, Chinese peasants are still known to kill their daughters under the one-child policy of the Chinese government. They are, it seems, fulfilling their duty as filial descendants of their ancestors. There are also reports that female babies and infants in some Asian countries are often neglected, resulting in a higher mortality rate for them; for example, a male child who is ill might get immediate medical attention while the family might wait a while if the sick child is female.

The inferior status of Chinese women has been ascribed to Confucius. Indeed, he did advocate that women should follow men as part of his recommendation to establish some form of order in society. However, it must be noted that in the same breath Confucius also advocated that the subject should follow the ruler; the son, the father; and the younger brother, the older brother. The inferior status of women in traditional China must be understood in the overall context of culturally defined roles for every member of the society as a means of maintaining order and harmony.

Doubtless Confucius would take a different stand today. It is obvious that the disintegration of patriarchy is in sight and that such a position can no longer be justified. The context in which Confucius justified this practice no longer exists. The feminist movement is one of the strongest cultural currents of our time and will have a profound effect on humanity's evolution.

Eclecticism

Having adapted itself to a variety of political and social situations over 25 centuries, Confucianism has become very close to a form of eclecticism, occasionally verging on a total disintegration of its inner identity.[15] It is Confucian, Taoist and Buddhist at the same time. There is a folk saying that the Chinese is a Confucian when everything is going well, a Taoist when things are falling apart and a Buddhist as he approaches death. It has further been said that 'the average Chinese wears a Confucian crown, so to speak, a Taoist robe, and Buddhist sandals.'[16] It is easy for a Chinese to say that he is both a Taoist (a lover of nature), a Confucian (who is serious about his duties) and a Buddhist (deeply aware of the transience of life) at the same time.

Only at the elite level were Confucianism, Taoism and Buddhism mutually exclusive; that is to say, it was usually only a Confucian official, a Taoist priest, or a Buddhist monk who identified with his religion. Proof of this is manifest in folk temples in Hong Kong and Singapore where one sees statues of Confucius, Lao-tzu and the Buddha set up alongside those of traditional Chinese immortals as objects of veneration. This practice has been termed the 'syncretic' nature of Chinese religion.

To be sympathetic, we may say that this syncretism is due to the harmonizing tendency of the Chinese – that is, the belief that every element should work together to contribute to the public good without opposing each other. This has some similarity to the Bahá'í belief that as there is only one God and all of the revealed religions come from Him then all religions teach the same

175

spiritual truth and a true believer sees truth in all. The Chinese position would be fine if people followed the original teachings of each religion as they would contain the same essence. In practice, however, the Chinese religion is an uneasy blend of social traditions and practices that are modifications and appendages of the original teachings of each founder.

The Taoist Winter

The Taoist religion is a case in point. The Taoist religion today is an invention hardly connected with the spiritual insights of Lao-tzu as portrayed in the *Tao-te ching*. Thus, it has become essential to distinguish between what has been called the 'Taoist philosophy' (the original teachings) and the 'Taoist religion' (the later practices). Taoism has changed to such an extent that the teachings of original Taoism and Taoism today are not only different but even contradictory.[17]

The practice of Taoism today is not so much associated with the philosophy of the *Tao-te ching* but more with the rites and rituals which are observed by a good Taoist as established by its advocate, Chang Tao-ling, towards the end of the 2nd century AD. Taoism today may be more rightly called Tao Chiao, a religious Taoism. Through the centuries, religious Taoism began to shape many of the popular beliefs, customs and festivals. However, it is associated today not so much with the *Tao-te ching* as with all sorts of mysteries, superstitions, gods and idols, miracles and magic. There is a hierarchy of gods, including mythical figures as well as other divine beings. The religious Taoists formed a 'church' and, through the centuries, generated a massive literature complete with ritualistic and alchemical lore. They became embroiled in politics and sponsored violent revolutionary groups. Religious Taoism also developed regimes of meditation, which are coupled with a complicated roster of gods presiding over particular organs of the body and functions. It resembles in many ways the folk religion still found in Korea and Japan, which is dominated by shamanic beliefs and practices. (Not surprisingly, it has contributed to the rather popular opinion that there are probably more superstitions in China than in any other civilized country in the world.)

It is perhaps with regard to this development that 'Abdu'l-Bahá referred to the 'despondent hearts of the Chinese' and their 'depressed souls'[18] as well as to the fact that the belief and rites of the Chinese religion have not continued in accordance with their fundamental teachings.[19] Whatever has survived of Taoism (or for that matter, Confucianism) today may be appropriately labelled as 'a body without a soul'.[20]

In view of this association of later Taoism with magic and fortune-telling and the occult in general, it is well to emphasize that the Taoism of Lao-tzu is not less iconoclastic than other prophetic faiths. The *I Ching*, a work now popular among Westerners, reflects a mixture of wisdom and divination that characterized the Chou dynasty during which Lao-tzu lived, but its conventionality and superstition are not *Tao* but what *Tao* is against. The notion that nature can be magically manipulated to further personal interests is foreign to Lao-tzu:

As to foreknowledge,
It is a blossomy path
And the beginning of folly.[21]

Today, there is a decline of folk religion among the Chinese but this is especially true of Taoism, which underlies the religion of the masses. There may still be temples, shrines, idols and priests but the real spirit of the religion is dead, and its vitality is fast disappearing.

The Buddhist Winter

The coming of Buddhism to China from the first century AD took place more than five hundred years after the passing of the Buddha. By then, unfortunately, Buddhism had already divided into fourteen different schools of thought as to what the original meaning and purpose of the Master's teaching was, and other schools soon crystallized. It was also greatly influenced by Hindu practices and rituals of those times. Hinduism had begun to encroach upon the pristine purity of the Buddha's teaching stifling that simplicity of belief and conduct from which early Buddhism derived its life and vigour.[22]

Another complication is that there is nothing reliable concerning the teachings of Buddha which can be accurately dated earlier than 250 years after His passing. In addition, just as there has been little information regarding the author of the Taoist scripture, in the same way we have very little information regarding the authors of the Pali and Sanskrit Buddhist scriptures – outside the fact that the Buddha did not write them.

Of the many varieties of Buddhism available at that time, two were most dominant: the Hinayana (Theravada) and the Mahayana. The more dominant Hinayana variety did not succeed in gaining a foothold in China. Theravada (or 'path of the elders'), as called by its present day adherents, remained relatively faithful to what it considered the true tradition of Buddha's teachings. It was, however, unpopular because principles such as the rejection of life's pleasures, the pursuit of salvation through asceticism as practised by the Theravada group were all foreign to the Chinese. To abandon one's duty to serve one's parents, to deny oneself the honour and pleasure of having descendants to honour and serve one were completely alien, not to say difficult. What was favoured was what later came to be called the Mahayana (or 'the means of salvation available to a large number of people') version. The Mahayana was more amenable to the Chinese psyche since it emphasized the transformation of one's relationship with the world and attitude towards life. Holding the dual virtues of wisdom and compassion, Mahayanists stressed that one must rise above worldly ills and pleasures (wisdom), yet at the same time remain involved in the world to the extent necessary for salvation. A cardinal tenet of the Mahayana which is not found in the Theravada and which is parallel to the Bahá'í view of prophethood is that the Buddha is not just a human teacher but an eternal phenomenon that manifests itself on earth at intervals of time for the salvation of mankind.

In time, in addition to the ones existing in India, nine major Buddhist schools developed in China of which the most notable may be said to be the Ch'an school (or Zen in Japan), the Kosa school (which followed the realist school of Theravada Buddhism) and the Pure Land school which developed faith and devotion to the Buddha Amitabha of the Pure Land.

Buddhism became quickly sinicized on entry into China. It coalesced with the Confucian and Taoist traditions to form a complex multi-religious ethos within which all three traditions were more or less comfortably encompassed. The first translation of Buddhist sutras into Chinese – namely those dealing with such topics as breath control and mystical concentration – utilized a Taoist vocabulary to make the Buddhist faith intelligible to the Chinese. In fact, it became widely believed that Lao-tzu had been reborn in India as the Buddha, and many Chinese emperors worshipped Lao-tzu and the Buddha on the same altar. In addition, Buddhism became deeply coloured by magical practices, making it compatible with popular folk Taoism. Indeed, after the Han period, in the north of China, Buddhist monks were often used by non-Chinese emperors for their political-military counsel as well as for their skill in magic.

True to the Chinese spirit, Chinese Buddhism developed a rather practical 'this worldly' character. Its members engaged in gardening, and thus did not beg for the food they ate, and they practised cultural pursuits, for example painting, sculpturing, ceramics and poetry as supplements to meditation. They looked within the world, especially the natural world, for inspiration and they discovered that ordinary life situations could produce profound spiritual insights. The Buddhist religion became very much like the native Chinese religion. Thus, it was not the wandering mendicant of the Indian religions who became the standard ideal for monks in China; rather, it was the figure engaged in ordinary tasks – cooking, eating, digging, planting or chopping wood – who became popular in Chinese monastic lore.

In their turn, Chinese intellectuals who were Confucianists and Taoists reduced, added and modified the teachings of the Buddha. This modification reduced Buddhism to a variant of religious Taoism. Only the features which were agreeable or adaptable to Chinese religion and culture were received. A number of new ideas had to be explained and this was done by 'matching ideas' in Taoism. For example, *tathatā* (thusness, ultimate reality) became equated with the Taoist term 'original non-being' (*pen-wu*, pure being) and the Buddha came to be called a sage.

In time, Taoism and Buddhism became closely merged. This was because, when Buddhism entered China, Taoism had already been engaged in a search for a concept of immortality for centuries but had neither organization nor creed. Thus, Buddhism came to emphasize Taoist tendencies towards belief in immortality while Taoism, by stages, began to copy the structural and operational aspects of Buddhism.

We may summarize that the Buddhism that reached China was not the original doctrine which the Buddha preached but a semblance of it. It became ever more remote from its Indian roots with the modifications imposed by the Chinese intellectuals. In fact, through the centuries, Buddhism was so intertwined with later Confucianism and Taoism that it became quite indistinguishable from them.[23] For example, Buddha and Bodhisattvas (enlightened beings) joined the ranks of divine beings for whom people made offerings, constructed images and held birthday celebrations. Certain ones, such as the Buddha A-mi-t'o-fo (to use the Chinese name of Amitabha) and the Bodhi-satta Kuan Yin (Guan-yin) assumed positions of supreme importance within Chinese folk religion.

In addition, Buddhist 'heavens and hells' described in the Buddhist scriptures became part of the Chinese conception of the hereafter and the performance of Buddhist rituals became an accepted part of the ceremonies usually held for deceased Chinese. Even more important than this, however, was the fact that the doctrine of *karma* and reincarnation added a new dimension to the way the Chinese thought about ancestors and the afterlife. It became a part of the theory of ancestor worship.

Conclusion

It is apparent that the Chinese religion, revitalized in the axial period, once again became associated with gods and sacrifices rather than the humanitarian virtues of *jen* and *li*, with nepotism and revenge rather than filial piety, with formality rather than morality, with superstitions rather than ethics, with magical practices and beliefs and the world of spirits and gods rather than with Heaven and the *Tao*.

Towards the end of the 19th century, 'Abdu'l-Bahá, who had a high opinion of the spiritual capacity of the Chinese people had sadly to concede that the Chinese were currently 'the most rejected of men' because of their worship of idols. 'The Europeans', by contrast, He said, 'are at least "Peoples of the Book" and believers in God'.[24]

Religions may continue to rise and fall as they have done in the past. Taoism, Confucianism and Buddhism have had their spring, summer and autumn, and are obviously now in their winter. After more than 2500 years, they have lost their 'uncarved pristine nature' about which Lao-tzu first spoke and have become encrusted with layers of thoughts and practices not their own. This situation was predicted by Lao-tzu:

Things overgrown fall into decay.
That is not-*Tao*,
And what is not-*Tao* soon ends.[25]

16

Conclusion

... and their cycle is completed.[1] *'Abdu'l-Bahá*, speaking of the Buddha and Confucius

Confucius was the most outstanding as well as the most representative of all the great personages in Chinese history. 'There has never been', said Mencius, 'any other man as great as Confucius.'[2] No Chinese can be said to be free of the deep impact of the sage's thought and the sage's virtue. Confucius was one of the world's greatest thinkers and educators.

He was also the great synthesizer because he had absorbed the essence of all that was good from the many teachers and sage kings before him. He read all that was to be read in his time; he examined, summarized, organized and improved on them, and turned them into a systematic philosophy for living. Because his teachings contained the essence of spiritual truths, they remain alive despite the passing of 25 centuries. Confucius taught a unique humanism based on great faith in man as the meeting point of what is transcendent and what is immanent.[3] If we take seriously the process of learning to be human, the Confucian persuasion, far from being a static adherence to a predetermined pattern, signifies an unceasing spiritual self-transformation.

For over two millennia, the axial ideas and beliefs we have described prevailed with amazing stability and consistency. It is these ethics which even today we meet all over East Asia.

Contributions

Confucius' most important contributions may be summarized to include the following:

1. *Heaven's Way*. Although Confucius did not regard hmself as a religious leader or the founder of a new religion, he taught the Way of Heaven as the right way. He clarified the real meaning

182

of human life. His emphasis on the importance of a faith in Heaven and the adherence to Heaven's Way was so powerful that many Chinese in subsequent centuries began to venerate him as a god.

2. *Clarification of the meaning of man.* He conceived 'man' as the highest expression of Heaven's work. To be human was to participate in Heaven's work. He advocated the love for one's fellow men through the concept of *jen* and *li*. He wanted people to belong to some 'bigger self' such as the family, the community, the state or the world.

He encouraged the attitude of rationalism as a means of turning the people away from their preoccupation with phenomenon such as ghosts, spirits, miracles or supernatural aid. He succeeded in tilting the balance and brought forth a semblance of enlightenment to the Chinese court that lasted for centuries.

3. *Rights and obligations.* The values in the Chinese ethical system largely influenced by Confucius were not absolute values, but reciprocal obligations. A subject had to be loyal to his ruler but the ruler, on his side, had to be considerate and benevolent. A son had to be filial to his father but the father had to be loving and kind. Through centuries of such teachings, it may be said that the Chinese developed a deep sense of obligation.

4. *Ethical orientation of politics.* Morality was the key to the ills of the world and politics was to be the extension of ethics. In the traditional Chinese educational system, every scholar had to set his final goal at securing peace in the world or, when limited by circumstances, at governing his state well. To cultivate one's self and regulate one's family were just preliminary steps towards rendering good services to one's own fellow-countrymen and/or all the men of all the countries in the world. A political career was not to be looked upon as a climb to power and wealth but rather as a dedication and a 'thankless task' of making the state or the world better.

Politics was never regarded as the 'science or the art of government'. It was, according to Confucius, a synonym of the word *cheng*, to rectify. To engage in politics was to 'rectify' whatever needed to be rectified. It included the tasks of righting the wrongs suffered by the people and correcting the mistakes of the ruler and his advisor, and so on.

5. *Family unity.* The Chinese conceive of the state as an enlarged family. The unity of the family is conducive to the well-being of society. This idea has been firmly implanted through the centuries and is apparent in the strong sense of family unity which is the hallmark of Chinese society today. The Chinese family is often marked by a large measure of family consultation and cooperation and is not run simply by the imposition of dictatorial authority.

6. *Promotion of education.* Prior to Confucius, schools were all run by the government for the benefit of the sons of the nobles. Confucius was the first educator in China who ran a private college open to all without consideration of social status, class, nationality or race. Tuition fees were symbolic – usually bundles of smoked meat. The institution was a full-fledged college which taught not only the six arts[4] but also moral education. This democratization contributed to the eventual extermination of feudalism. Thanks to Confucius, teachers are highly respected and praised and have a highly esteemed position in traditional Chinese society.

7. *Innovation in writing.* Prior to Confucius, there were virtually no authors among the common people. The only books were those written by the officials of the government in the form of documents, manuals, calendars, etc. Confucius compiled over 300 poems and tunes in an anthology known as the *Book of Songs* (*Shih-ching*) and he also selected a hundred historical documents to form the *Book of History* (*Shu-ching*). He gave many lectures on the *li* and the notes taken by his disciples on this subject passed into the hands of their disciples, to result finally in a collective work known as the *Collection of Rituals* (*Li Chi*).[5]

Certainly it is not difficult to concur with these verses written in the 11th century AD on the ceiling of a postal station by an anonymous traveller.

It would have been an eternal night for all of us,
if Heaven did not give birth to Confucius.[6]

As for Lao-tzu, his greatest contribution was his brilliant and timeless exposition of the great *Tao*. We recall his exposition of the great *Tao* as absolute and unknowable as well as immanent and transcendent. Through the subtly enchanting verses of the *Tao-te ching*, hearts are stirred by the promise of immortality and the gems of wisdom related to living the *Tao* way – a way of life that promises the greatest happiness and fulfilment.

Lao-tzu's naturalism and simplicity, inward calm, optimism of bodily and spiritual health as well as his scepticism of doctrinaire programmes have remained ever potent.

Certainly, then, one reason for 'Abdu'l-Bahá's optimism and faith in the spiritual capacity of the Chinese people is the ability of China's two major sages to have tapped the wisdom of China's past and of the Buddha. The Chinese people are the inheritors of a spiritual heritage buried deep in their past – a heritage which has contributed significantly to their great civilization.

'Abdu'l-Bahá's remark remains no longer an enigma as one observes the original Chinese religion: a religion of reason, a religion of the heart, morality without a church, social order without priests and good conduct without supernatural sacrament. Dogma is not needed because no one knows God and it is simply arrogance to decide what attributes He should have.

Priesthood is not needed because all have the same duty of extending the divine love to all creation. Temples are not needed because the whole universe is the temple of God. A religious person is not one who is always in prayer, receiving sacraments or performing rituals, but one who lives a good life with love and consideration for his fellow men.[7]

Unfortunately, it is today a spiritual heritage that has become encrusted with a nature not its own and is more adhered to and remembered for its forms rather than its essence. Certainly, it has long ceased to serve a revitalizing or inspiring influence. In terms of the arts and sciences, China is now one of the most backward countries of the world.

Criticisms

We may wonder why, despite its many notable contributions, the Confucian name does not have universal connotations, of purity, spirituality or 'progress'. Why did leading 20th century writers criticize Confucius as a pedlar of ritual and a trickster who duped rulers with his moralistic nonsense? Why did Mao Tse-tung, who was influenced by Confucian classics and Buddhism, repudiate them both and denounce religion?[8] In fact, today the word Confucianism is an anachronism and an embarrassment to many Chinese.

This disenchantment with China's leading sage must be understood in the light of the closing decades of the Ch'ing dynasty, where those who pressed for change were largely prompted by the painful realization that no matter how great and glorious China's traditional culture might be, it crumbled not only before Western powers, but also before its hitherto insignificant neighbour, Japan.

In the eyes of the revolutionaries who wanted to leave the past behind because of the humiliation of China in the Opium War and in its war with Japan, it was Confucius who was to blame for the rigid and hierarchical society which brought about these defeats. When the young wanted to assert themselves, they pointed the finger of scorn at Confucian subordination of children to their parents. When women's rights were at issue, reformers blamed Confucian literature for the fact that the traditional female role was first and foremost to bear children for the perpetuation of the family life, which many now regard with scepticism and disfavour.

Confucianism has had too many bad associations. Two thousand years ago, emperors began to use it (in distorted form) as a cloak for despotism. We have also seen how the virtue of loyalty was distorted to mean blind loyalty to the sovereign as well as how filial piety came to mean only the perpetuation of a line of male heirs.

Moreover, during the past century, conservatives who tried to block all change rallied more frequently under the banner of Confucianism. After the Chinese Republic fell apart in 1949, some of the most notorious warlords posed as particularly pious Confucians. When the Japanese occupied much of China between 1931 and 1945, they tried to revive Confucianism to make it more palatable to the Chinese. Not surprisingly, the men who founded the Chinese Communist Party were outspokenly hostile to the Chinese tradition.

There have been three other major charges against Confucianism. The first has already been mentioned – the inferior status of women. The injunction that women obey their husbands and sons as a means of maintaining harmony in the household and in society is now outdated. One could add to the dismal picture such practices as female infanticide and the sale of daughters in difficult times.

Chinese society, like most other societies, had, long before Confucius, been patriarchal and patrilineal. The hierarchical structure is evidenced by comments in the *I Ching*: 'The wife must always be guided by the will of the master of the house, be he father, husband or grown son. Her place is within the house.'[9]

Confucius had very little to say about the question of women's rights, as the equality of men and women was just not an 'issue' in his time.[10] What he did say was of little credit to him in terms of present-day thinking.[11] We do know, however, that the Confucian *li* has been universalized to apply to all human relations, irrespective of rank or status, and that *jen* refers to loving all and embracing all with benevolence. Women are not mentioned specifically but this may be due to the fact that women are included in the Chinese concept of *jen* or 'person'. 'Man' is used generically for human beings. Since the Chinese languages do not make this gender distinction, only the context can determine whether *jen* refers to a particular sex or to humankind in general.

However, Confucius did not leave women out of his vision of mass education. Several chapters of *Collection of Rituals* are concerned with the subject of the education of women.[12] These notes were taken by Confucius' disciples at his lectures. Although Confucius did not lecture directly to women, he did direct his comments to the future husbands and fathers of women, following the conventions of the day.[13] Throughout his lectures there was not a single word which implied disrespect for women. Rather, the opposite is true: he emphasized again and again that husbands ought to treat their wives as equals, in the sense of *jen*, and allow them to have privacy.

187

Another charge is that of the emphasis on elitism. The revolt against elitism has been the main reason for the Chinese Communists sending intellectuals 'downwards' and recruiting members of the least advantaged groups as university students.[14] Documentary evidence frequently quoted is Mencius' distinction between those who labour with their mental strength and those who labour with their physical strength. Since the distinction is thought to have implied the supremacy of the mental labourers, it is concluded that there has been a strong bias against working people in the Mencian tradition of Confucianism.

An appeal to context must again be made. Mencius made the remark in his debate with a physiocrat. What he intended to do there was simply to point out that it is neither possible nor desirable to have every person involved in agricultural production. He stressed the functional necessity of a division of labour and argued that the scholars or intellectuals could justify their existence and usefulness without making a direct reference to productivity. Scholars also perform equally significant duties such as government service and education.[15]

In addition, since Mencius did affirm on another occasion that the people are more important than the king and that the people have the right to rebel against tyrannical rulers, he was certainly not an enemy of the people by conscious choice.[16]

The third major charge against Confucianism may be said to concern the Confucian stress on virtue at the expense of economics. Those who marvelled at the wonders of Western science and technology saw a China helpless against the military might of the West and considered Confucius' opposition to specialization and his concentration on virtues as detrimental to the study of science and the external world.

This charge is too sweeping, for Confucius did not overlook the importance of material life and the abundance of material production. He had remarked, 'Let the producers be many and the consumers few. Let there be activity in their production and economy in the expenditure, and the wealth will be sufficient.'[17]

In addition, China's contributions to the natural sciences in earlier times were by no means meagre. Needham records that there was rather good science done in early Confucian China. The

Chinese invented gunpowder and cannons, the mechanical clock, the magnetic compass and printing. In addition, they recorded sun spots, and developed methods of harnessing horses and boring wells, and developed watermills, ships, refining steel, suspension bridges, rubber, immunology and many other things. The Chinese contribution to present-day biology, chemistry, astronomy and physics cannot be ignored.

However, after the Sung dynasty (960–1279), scholars were inclined to stress the mind while neglecting matter. They did this because they lacked a clear understanding of the true significance of the principles inherent in the *Doctrine of the Mean* and the *Tao-te ching*. They did not adhere to the policy of moderation and balance.

They failed to heed the words of their sages and indulged in a deceptive pride that led them to believe that they were self-sufficient. Gone was the humility so apparent in the lives of their great sages. The Chinese success in sciences and the arts and their achievement of a relatively high level of mortality and literacy led to pride and self complacency. This pride was bolstered by the fact that neighbouring peoples looked up to China (until the 19th century) as the source of civilization. Thus, although it is natural for people to take pride in their own culture, this tendency was stronger in China than in many other parts of the world.

There were other reasons besides pride and a lack of moderation for China's scientific backwardness, which lead to her sub-colony status for almost a century. For example, bad government, foreign aggression, a weak military and civil uprisings contributed to this state of affairs. The blame for China's backwardness cannot be put solely on the Confucian emphasis on virtue at the expense of economics.

Besides these three major charges against Confucianism, there were others which cropped up from time to time. Filial piety, for example, came under attack for being a factory for the manufacture of obedient subjects. Confucian mores such as elaborate funeral rites came to be looked upon as unnecessary and cumbersome rituals for contemporary living.

Certainly, in the face of a number of criticisms, of which the above are only a sample, and widespread disenchantment, most of which is the result of an incomplete understanding of the essence of the sages' teachings as well as the human tendency to find a scapegoat for misfortunes, it is difficult for the great Chinese spiritual, religious, cultural and political traditions to regain credibility. The past appears to be too muddled and tangled to uncover whatever remains of the speckles of gold dust among the refuse that has accumulated all around it. It is no longer possible to live with the derogatory associations connected with Confucianism that have collected over the centuries, unless they can be understood as such.

The Future

With the downfall of the traditional Chinese religion, there is now a spiritual vacuum in China. The traditional naturalism and animism have been replaced by science, and the *yin-yang* cosmology has been replaced by that sense of alienation from nature so well known in the modern West. No satisfactory substitute has been provided to furnish this spiritual vacuum with hope. Chinese intellectuals, and young people in particular, are looking for something to fill the huge gap in their lives. They are unsure of whether an ideal standard of justice and ethics can exist.

China appears to be a civilization divorced from its ideals. It is inevitable that a civilization without ideals will end in self destruction. A lack of faith in the ultimate can only lead to a rising crescendo of profligacy and lawlessness. People, being out of control, will become, as Mencius cautioned, like wild beasts. Acts of spirit and ethics are vital if human society is to survive. History shows no record of any civilization that has not been sustained by the power of some moral code derived from the teachings of a great religion. History is, after all, the story of religion.[18]

Whatever must fill this spiritual vacuum in the future cannot realistically bypass the challenge of the most profound and pervasive articulation of 'Chineseness' in the past. In the Chinese worldview, the past and future are always interrelated. The adoption of the sayings and writings of Chairman Mao as the repository of truth, for instance, has its parallel in the strict orthodoxy based on the Confucian classics. The emphasis on model workers and model communes reminds us of the Confucianist emphasis on the use of models for training. Similarly, just as there has always been a preference for generalists rather than technicians, so the Communists stress that it is better to be 'red' than 'expert', since nothing worthwhile can be achieved except on the basis of right thinking.

Certainly, it is difficult to dispose of a past that has been there for so long. In addition, because Confucianism is essentially a spiritual creed which expounds certain eternal truths, its fate can never be sealed. The sayings of Confucius, when rediscovered in their original purity, will appeal like new wine. The emphasis on the personal realization of the human heart and its extension to the entire universe remains forever vital. When reexamined, the broad humanity of Confucianism, its practical wisdom and the universality of its teachings will once again be discovered. If so, its spiritual values in art, literature, history and philosophy may again assert a shaping influence on creative minds throughout China.

It must also be noted that, although the Chinese people have abandoned certain Confucian religious practices and given up many Confucian social, political and educational institutions, they have not discarded the fundamental doctrines of Confucianism. Respect for parents, for example, is not questioned, although parental authority in marriage has long been challenged. The official sacrifice to Heaven has been terminated, but most Chinese still believe in Heaven. What has fallen is institutional Confucianism; but the original Confucius never advocated institutionalization, so its loss is not a great blow.

Nevertheless, although strains of the teachings of the ancients linger in the Chinese psyche, there is also a profound feeling, not far away from disappointment and despair, that their cultural heritage is irrelevant to present-day society and to present-day needs and is incapable of contributing to its moral fabric. This is where the Bahá'í Faith can play a part by lifting the 'despondent hearts' and 'depressed souls' of the Chinese that they may once again become inflamed with the freshness and grace of a faith in Heaven and the Great *Tao*.[19]

The Bahá'í Faith continues the Chinese search for the ultimate reality, the meaning of life, the way of cosmic harmony comprising the love of the environment and the love for all humankind. By reiterating basically similar values and beliefs, the Bahá'í Faith rejuvenates the worthiness of Chinese traditional culture, belief and self-confidence. In many ways, the Bahá'í Faith is remarkably compatible with the Chinese humanistic tradition. The Chinese religion (as with the other great religions) and the Bahá'í Faith share many fundamental spiritual and ethical principles.

For example, the Chinese sages realized that Truth is Truth wherever and whenever it may appear. The purposes and principles are the same whenever men translate into practice their comprehension of the Way of Heaven. The only difference here is in point of time and space. The Mahayana version of Buddhism, which forms an intricate part of the Chinese religion, also confirms this approach.

In addition, the Chinese concept of *Tao* and Heaven parallels the concept of God in the Bahá'í Faith (and the other major religions). Both religions recognize a higher invisible power and advocate sacrifice and obedience to that power. Both Bahá'u'lláh and Confucius (as well as Lao-tzu and other Chinese sages) were always conscious of the influence and presence of an ultimate power and expressed this consciousness openly in their teachings. Both stand in awe of the ultimate source of creativity which, according to them, works incessantly in the universe and the human world. Both had a mission and were in regular contact with this ultimate source. For Confucius, this supreme ultimate was the God of his ancestors – a God who is compatible with Bahá'í monotheism, eternal from the beginning and eternal to the time which has no end.

Both the Chinese religion and the Bahá'í Faith are also concerned not only with individual salvation but also social salvation. Confucius' message, like that of Bahá'u'lláh, encompasses the inner constitution of every individual as well as the outer constitution of the state. Where the state is concerned, there is a call for the moral and political reestablishment of a benevolent government, capable of promoting social order and harmony both in the family and in the state. There is an emphasis on justice and virtue as the foundation of government rather than economics or wealth. While the government of Confucius' day was told to establish peace in the nation, the governments of today have been told by Bahá'u'lláh to establish peace in the world.

Where the individual is concerned, both the Chinese religion and the Bahá'í Faith believe in the perfectability and educability of human beings, as well as their potential for evil, if they are not educated. Both stress the basic goodness of human nature, explaining evil as a deflection from the good and a perversion of the natural. There is, for example, no clear equivalent of 'sin' in the Chinese language (the closest term is *tsui* but it has a double significance, meaning crime as well as sin). Both religions challenge man to be a human being who, in their view, is the noblest being in the whole of creation. In relation to this ideal of the human being, both emphasize the role of education in the refinement of human nature. The Confucian and Bahá'í writings also stress that it is only through education and learning that one acquires not only knowledge but, more importantly, culture and ethical and moral character. 'Abdu'l-Bahá may thus be said to echo the essence of Confucius and Mencius on education when He says, 'Through cultivation, the crooked branch becomes straight; the acid, bitter fruit ... becomes sweet and delicious ...' He continues, 'Through education, savage nations become civilized ... animals become domesticated.[20]

Indeed, the main ethical principles of Confucianism – *jen* (humanity), *chung* (faithfulness), and *shu* (altruism) compare very well with those of the Bahá'í Faith. It must be noted, however, that these teachings are not original, having always been available to humanity. These are the eternal truths found in all the major religions, although called by different terms in different cultures in different times. They teach human beings the best way in which they can live with one another. They are the foundation for effective human relationships. Confucius called for a sense of justice and fairness, a spirit of tolerance, a readiness to compromise, coupled with a firm determination to enforce the observance of those virtues against the teachings of egoists. For him, love is to *love* mankind and wisdom is to *know* mankind. Similarly, the Bahá'í Faith calls for a human dignity characterized by forbearance, mercy, compassion and loving kindness.[21] The following quotation from the Bahá'í scriptures may be said to echo much of the ethical teachings of the foremost sage of the Chinese religion:

Be generous in prosperity, and thankful in adversity. Be worthy of the trust of thy neighbour, and look upon him with a bright and friendly face. Be a treasure to the poor, an admonisher to the rich, an answerer of the cry of the needy, a preserver of the sanctity of thy pledge. Be fair in thy judgement, and guarded in thy speech. Be unjust to no man, and show all meekness to all men. Be as a lamp unto them that walk in darkness, a joy to the sorrowful, a sea for the thirsty, a haven for the distressed, an upholder and defender of the victim of oppression. Let integrity and uprightness distinguish all thine acts.[22]

The ethical teachings of both Confucius and Bahá'u'lláh culminate in the love of one's fellow human being. To serve man is to serve God. This belief makes it impossible for the followers of such religions to become recluses since it is important to live and work together with all peoples of the earth according to the principles laid down by the sage or the manifestation. Nor is it acceptable for the adherents of either religion to 'follow the crowd' since they are to exercise justice and fairness by seeing with their own eyes and not through the eyes of others. An emphasis on love and service to mankind also means a turning away from a study of, or preoccupation with, the supernatural. Human destiny is to be mastered in reverence for God and Heaven and without anxiety about ghosts and spirits.

Having love for one's fellow human being is not without a consideration for fairness and justice. On the subject of the love for one's enemy and of returning kindness for injury, Confucius says, 'What then will you return kindness with? Injury should be returned with correctness; kindness should be returned with kindness.'[23] Similarly, Bahá'u'lláh puts justice above forgiveness although He also stresses the element of mercy in the exercise of justice.

Perhaps most fascinating of all is the fact that both the Chinese religion and the Bahá'í Faith look forward to a future united and peaceful world. The Bahá'í description of the time of the Most Great Peace echoes the Chinese description of society in the time of the Great Unity (ta-t'ung). Confucius believed that if his teachings were followed, they would lay the foundation for a utopian world where everyone would abide by the Great *Tao*. Similarly, Bahá'u'lláh told His followers that if the world recognized His station and attempted to follow His teachings, the era of the Most Great Peace, as foretold in all the scriptures of the world, would come to pass. Both great educators looked upon political problems in terms of human relationships and prescribed their solutions accordingly.

Finally, the Chinese religion and the Bahá'í Faith share not only some spiritual and ethical principles but there are also similarities in the lives of their chief proponents. While Bahá'u-'lláh appeared 2,500 years after Confucius and while Persia and China observed different customs, there are many interesting parallels. Both were teachers of the Way. One was an educator, the other a professed prophet of God. Accounts of their births were entwined with legends. Like Confucius, Bahá'u'lláh was said to be marvellously precocious. However, we know nothing certain about the former's boyhood. Both created a new paradigm for the troubled world in which they found themselves. Both were born during a time of great social, political, economic and moral chaos.[24] Both were subjected to periods of arduous wandering – Confucius wandered around trying to find a prince who could use his teachings and Bahá'u'lláh was banished from one place to another. Neither advocated nor followed the ascetic life but both worked, ate and drank and were criticized by the pious. Neither was a metaphysician speculating about God; both were more concerned with the practical following of the message.

The essential question both faced was how men could live in peace. Confucius' response to that question contributed to the much-needed political and social stability of China for centuries. Bahá'u'lláh's contribution has yet to be accepted by the gener-ality of mankind and its value remains to be assessed. Just as the 6th century BC of Confucius and Lao-tzu is viewed as the axial period of Chinese history, it remains for the future to view the 19th century of the Báb and Bahá'u'lláh as the axial period in world history. Whether Bahá'u'lláh will be as historically influential for the world as Confucius was for China is left to be seen.

Nevertheless, just as there are similarities, there are also, of course, differences, between the Chinese religion and the Bahá'í Faith. However, these seem to be structural and superficial compared to the similarities which typify the essence of these religions. In view of the wide panorama of world religious traditions, if one emphasizes the essence, there is but one religion and all the great educators have taught it; if one emphasizes structure, authority, clergy or other institutional elements that often develop after the passing of the founder, then there will be at once obvious structural differences. Thus if one observes the monastic and ritualistic practices of the Chinese religion today, it is inconceivable that it could share any similarities with the Bahá'í Faith. On the other hand, if one looks to the original scriptures, parallels not apparent at first at once appear.

Perhaps the only worthwhile difference between the Chinese religion and the Bahá'í Faith to warrant discussion is the differing stations of Confucius and Bahá'u'lláh. While Confucius admitted that he was an ordinary man, bookish, and in love with learning, Bahá'u'lláh claimed unequivocally to be the latest manifestation of God endowed with innate knowledge. In other words, while Confucius was inspired by books from the Golden Age of China with its perfectly virtuous semi-divine rulers, who threw a lasting spell on him, Bahá'u'lláh was unschooled and received his insights directly from a higher invisible source. Unlike Confucius, Bahá'u'lláh claimed to fulfil the prophecies of all the past religions regarding the coming of a 'redeemer' in this portentous age. Further, unlike Confucius, Bahá'u'lláh had a forerunner who told of His coming – the Báb.

Thus, while the Bahá'í Faith is established as a revealed religion brought by a prophet-messenger, the Chinese religion is not. The Chinese religion is a unique instance of a religion without revelation, a religion with the sage as a central figure rather than a prophet. While the Bahá'í Faith stresses belief in God *and* in the ideal human relationship, the Chinese religion assumes a belief in God and stresses primarily human relationships. The Chinese religion is not so much concerned with prophetic calling as with the teaching of wisdom.

However, while the Bahá'í Faith is young and vibrant, the Confucian doctrine is old and withered. After Confucius, a reunited China reached a peak probably equivalent, or nearly equivalent, to the era of the sage kings in ancient Chinese history. However, through the centuries, Confucianism has petrified into a system of nepotism, pride and rigid patterns of behaviour and with it has come the inevitable downfall of Chinese civilization. The original spiritual teachings on which it rests remain forever vital but they are obscured by customs and rituals which have become obsolete and meaningless. A new system of social reforms based on the same eternal truths must take its place. Then, and only then, can there be once again an upsurge in the vitality of the once great Chinese civilization.

The Chinese intellectual heritage teaches us that the only constant in our universe is change. Long before Confucius, the *I Ching* expounded:

After a time of decay comes the turning point. The powerful light that has been banished returns. There is movement, but it is not brought about by force ... The movement is natural, arising spontaneously. For this reason the transformation of the old becomes easy. The old is discarded and the new is introduced. Both measures accord with the time; therefore no harm results.[25]

The Bahá'í Faith complements this idea: 'When the season of winter has had its effect, again the spiritual springtime returns, and a new cycle appears.'[26]

China is now at a turning point in all aspects of its culture. This is a moment of great anticipation. Certain fundamentals that lie deep in the psyche of the great masses of the Chinese people are waiting to be awakened.

Appendix 1

Chart of Chinese History

(Dates and entries before 841 BC are traditional)

Sage kings (3rd millennium BC) Little more than mythical figures. Stories about them are probably idealized inventions of a much later period. Nevertheless, often referred to by Confucius and Lao-tzu in their accounts.

> *2852–2697 BC* Cultural heroes such as Fu Hsi, inventor of writing, fishing, trapping; Shen Nung, inventor of agriculture, commerce; and the Yellow Emperor.

> *2357–2205 BC* The Sage kings referred to as Yao, Shun and Yu, the last being the virtuous founder of the Hsia dynasty.

Hsia (2205–1765 BC) Historical evidence of first Chinese dynasty founded by Yu, and terminated by Chieh.

Shang (1766–1123 BC) Their excavated capital in Northern Honan Province yielded an abundance of inscriptions carved on bone and tortoise shell. These remain today the major remnants of written records of ancient Eastern Asia.

Chou (1122–256 BC) A brilliant historical record; known as the Golden Age of Chinese philosophy. The dynasty begins with King Wen who was succeeded by King Wu. These two kings were often mentioned by Confucius as a model of virtue. By the time of Confucius (551–479 BC) and Lao-tzu (6th century BC) as well as a host of other philosophers who followed in their footsteps, the dynasty had declined and there was political chaos.

Ch'in (221–206 BC) Ch'in Shih Huang Ti unifies China and builds the Great Wall to defend it from the northern nomads. The Confucian books and other ancient literature are destroyed in the 'Burning of the Books' in 213 BC, part of Ch'in Shih Huang Ti's attempt to wipe out opposition.

198

Former Han (206 BC – AD 9) Much of the old literature is recovered and restored and Confucianism becomes the dominant philosophy and heart of the educational system.

Later Han (25–220) Buddhism is introduced into China.

Sui (581–618) China is reunified after four centuries of division, for most of which time North China has been split between various non-Chinese states. Known also as the high watermark of Chinese cultural achievement.

T'ang (618–907) Buddhism is at the height of its influence but Confucian influence is strong and predominant as the revived civil service grows in importance.

Sung (960–1279) This is the heyday of Neo-Confucian philosophy, and a period of great technological and industrial progress.

Yüan (1279–1368) China is ruled by the Mongols and Confucianism suffers a setback with the suspension of the examinations for several decades. The Mongols contribute little to Chinese philosophy.

Ming (1368–1644) This is a conservative and autocratic regime.

Ch'ing (1644–1912) China is governed by the Manchus, whose rulers adopt Confucian culture to show themselves worthy of the Mandate of Heaven. Examinations dominated by Confucian classics are abolished in 1905.

Birth of the Chinese Republic (1912–49) Dr Sun Yat-sen establishes the Chinese Republic. Confucianism suffers a great setback and is vehemently criticized as outdated.

The Communist Regime (from 1949) Mao Tse-tung takes over the country. A Marxist view of religion prevails. Religion is seen at best as a useless excrescence of primitive or bourgeois society, and at most as the instrument used by feudalistic oppressors, foreign imperialists and counter-revolutionaries to subvert and exploit the Chinese masses.

Appendix 2

Figures often mentioned in the Text

'Abdu'l-Bahá (1844–1921)

This is a title which means 'servant of the Glory'. 'Abdu'l-Bahá is the eldest son of Bahá'u'lláh and the Perfect Exemplar and infallible interpreter of His teachings. Together with that of Bahá'u'lláh and the Báb, His writings comprise the Bahá'í sacred literature. As He grew into manhood, 'Abdu'l-Bahá came to be regarded as the embodiment of all the virtues that Bahá'ís long to attain. His life was considered an example of human perfection.

The Báb (1819–50)

This is a title meaning 'the Gate'. The Báb proclaimed Himself as the Qá'im, the expected twelfth Imám of the Islamic Faith. He is the founder of the Bábí religion and one of the three central figures of the Bahá'í Faith. He declared His central mission to be the proclamation of another Messenger of God, far greater than Himself. Bahá'ís believe this Messenger to be Bahá'u'lláh. The Báb's message created a great commotion and aroused the prejudice and hatred of the clergy. Many thousands of His followers were tortured to death; and He Himself, after being made to suffer innumerable persecutions during the six years of His ministry, was publicly executed when He was 30 years of age.

Bahá'u'lláh (1817–92)

This is a title meaning 'the Glory of God'. Bahá'u'lláh proclaimed Himself a Manifestation of God and the prophet for the age. He is the founder of the Bahá'í Faith. His teachings are believed to initiate a new religious dispensation for this era. Bahá'ís believe Bahá'u'lláh to be the latest in a series of past and future divine Manifestations that includes Jesus, Muḥammad, Zoroaster and the Buddha. He revealed more than a hundred works including the *Kitáb-i-Aqdas* (The Most Holy Book), the repository of laws; the *Kitáb-i-Íqán* (The Book of Certitude), an exposition of essential teachings on the nature of God and religion; the *Hidden Words*, a collection of brief utterances aimed at the education of man's soul; *The Seven Valleys*, a mystic treatise; *Epistle to the Son of the Wolf*, His last major work; as well as innumerable prayers, meditations, exhortations and epistles.

Chuang-tzu (no dates)

Known also as Master Chuang, he was a native of Meng and lived at the same time as King Hui (370–319 BC) of Liang which makes him a contemporary of Mencius. He wrote a work of around 10,000 words or more which was 'mostly in the form of a fable'. His main exposition is on the *Tao* as the universal way of things, the all-pervading principle of all that exists. The only way to salvation, for Chuang-tzu, is to identify oneself with the orderly process of all being, the *Tao*. Death is nothing to fear, for man lives as long as his essence, the *Tao*, lives; and the *Tao* is eternal.

Confucius (c. 551–479 BC)

Confucius is the latinized rendering of the Chinese K'ung Fu-tze. Kung was his surname while Fu-tze means 'the master'. Confucius and Mencius are the only Chinese with latinized names. He taught that *jen*, the ideal relationship among human beings, is the perfect virtue of man and that man's actions should be controlled by *li*, the rules of priopriety. The *junzi* or ideal man is one who practises *jen* in accordance with *li*: consequently, he treasures and seeks the *Tao*, the Right Way.

Lao-tzu (c. 600 BC)

Lao-tzu is revered as the founder of the Taoist school and as the author of the *Tao-te ching*. Most Confucian scholars agree that it is impossible to say whether Lao-tzu ever lived. Despite its brevity and relative simplicity, the *Tao-te ching* is often quoted and alluded to in the literature of the period and many emperors and statesmen in historical China advocated its doctrine. Lao-tzu is famous for his exposition of *Tao*, the universal principle underlying everything, the supreme, ultimate pattern, and the principle of growth. He advocated that the *Tao* man must hide his power and appear soft and weak, for he who shows his power is without power; and the soft overcomes the weak.

Mencius (371–289 BC)

Mencius is the latinized form of the Chinese Meng-tzu (or Mengzi – Hanyu Pinyin). He wrote the book called after him in the 4th century BC. His fame is based on the doctrine that man is endowed by Heaven and his nature tends towards good as naturally as water flows down hill. As proof, Mencius cited the natural love of children for their parents, man's universal sense of right and wrong, and the spontaneous alarm one experiences when one sees a small child in danger. His other major contribution is his theory of what makes an ideal ruler, and here he advocates moral leadership and adequate social welfare.

Mo-tzu (c. 479–381 BC)

Mo-tzu is the founder of Mohism (also spelled Moism) in the 5th century BC. Mo-tzu taught the necessity for individual piety and submission to the will of Heaven. He deemphasized the Confucian focus on rites and rituals. He advocated 'universal love' rather than 'filial love', believing that a love without distinction was far superior. He also taught that aggressive war should never be practised since it is never politically, morally or economically advantageous. His ideas were popular only from the 5th to the 3rd century BC.

Shoghi Effendi

Shoghi Effendi is the grandson of 'Abdu'l-Bahá who was appointed by 'Abdu'l-Bahá in His Will and Testament as

Guardian of the Cause of Bahá'u'lláh. During the 36 years of his ministry the Bahá'ís, working under his direction and in close collaboration with each other, established their administrative institutions throughout the world on a foundation strong enough for them to work together efficiently and harmoniously.

Appendix 3

Important Chinese Sources

The most important sources of Chinese philosophy are the thirteen classics. Their authority in China can be compared to that of the Bible in the West. Besides this, there is the *Tao-te ching* which has equal if not more importance in Chinese thought. The *Chuang-tzu, Hsun-tzu* and the writings of the hundred schools are equally of great influence in the making of the Chinese mentality.

Below is a brief account of the thirteen Confucian classics (this summary owes much to Chih, *Chinese Humanism*):

1. **Shu-ching (Shu-king)** *(Book of History or Book of Historical Documents)*   Scholars do not agree on its date and authenticity. Some believe that only the documents of Chou (1111–249 BC) are authentic and the rest are forgeries of later periods. Others believe that only the earlier chapters were not contemporary. Still others believe that the documents are all trustworthy because of the confirmation from the Oracle Bones, and that an account which puts Chinese history as starting in 2145 BC is sufficiently authentic.

2. **Shih-ching** *(Book of Poetry, Book of Odes* or *Book of Songs)*   This is a collection of poems compiled by Confucius. Some of them are from the Shang (1751–1121 BC) while most are from early Chou times (1111 BC).

3. *I Ching (Book of Changes)*   This work is attributed to the legendary Emperor Fu Hsi (2953–2838 BC), who is said to have constructed the eight diagrams. The 64 hexagrams are attributed to King Wen of the Chou dynasty (1111 BC).

4–6. **Li-chi** *(Collection of Rituals)*   This is one of the books of rituals and belongs to the Chou dynasty. The other two are *Chou-li (Rituals of the Chou Dynasty)* and *I-li (Manual of Ceremonies)*. Although they belong to the Chou dynasty, they were compiled by the Han scholars, around the 1st century BC.

7. **Chun-chiu** (*The Annals of Spring and Autumn*)   This work is attributed to Confucius himself and is a brief chronicle compiled from the Annals of the State of Lu.

8. **Lun-Yu** (*The Analects of Confucius*)   This is by far the most important classic. It is a collection of the sayings of Confucius and is the first of four books that Chinese children had to memorize in the old days.

9. **Mencius**   This is a collection of the works of Mencius. He is the most important disciple of Confucius, although he lived a hundred years later.

10, 11. **Ta-hsueh** (*The Great Learning*) and **Chung Yung** (*The Doctrine of the Mean*)   These are taken from the *Li-chi* and represent the mature thought of Confucius.

12. **Hsiao-ching** (*The Book of Filial Piety*)   This book records a conversation between Confucius and his disciple Tseng-tzu. It is the commentary on a work by an emperor of the T'ang dynasty. The many other commentaries on it have made this small treatise very influential in Chinese social life.

13. **Erh-ya** (*Dictionary*).

Bibliography

In writing this book I have been very conscious that space has allowed me to include only a relatively small number of the sayings of Confucius, Lao-tzu and other Chinese sages such as Mencius and Chuang-tzu. The translations of the *Analects* to which I have most commonly referred are Legge, Waley and Chan. The translation of the *Tao-te ching* is by Maurer. The translations of *Mencius* are Legge and Lau, while the translation of *Chuang-tzu* is by Giles.

'Abdu'l-Bahá. *Foundations of World Unity*. Wilmette, Illinois: Bahá'í Publishing Trust, 1971.
—— *Paris Talks*. Oakham: Bahá'í Publishing Trust, 1979.
—— *The Promulgation of Universal Peace*. Wilmette, Illinois: Bahá'í Publishing Trust, 1982.
—— *The Secret of Divine Civilization*. Translated by Marzieh Gail. Wilmette, Illinois: Bahá'í Publishing Trust, 1957.
—— *Selections from the Writings of 'Abdu'l-Bahá*. Translated by a Committee at the Bahá'í World Centre and by Marzieh Gail. Haifa: Bahá'í World Centre, 1978.
—— *Some Answered Questions*. Translated by Laura Clifford Barney. Wilmette, Illinois: Bahá'í Publishing Trust, rev. edn. 1981.
—— *Tablets of Abdul-Baha Abbas*. New York: Bahá'í Publishing Committee, 1909–16.
Ames, Roger T. *The Art of Rulership: A Study in Ancient Chinese Political Thought*. Honolulu: University of Hawaii Press, 1983.
Ashvaghosha. *The Awakening of Faith*. Translated by D.T. Suzuki. Chicago: Open Court, 1900.
The Báb, *Selections from the Writings of the Báb*. Translated by Habib Taherzadeh with the assistance of a committee at the Bahá'í World Centre. Haifa: Bahá'í World Centre, 1976.
Bahá'í World Faith: Selected Writings of Bahá'u'lláh and 'Abdu'l-Bahá. Wilmette, Illinois: Bahá'í Publishing Trust, 1976.
Bahá'u'lláh. *Epistle to the Son of the Wolf*. Wilmette, Illinois: Bahá'í Publishing Trust, 1976.

—— *Gleanings from the Writings of Bahá'u'lláh*. Wilmette, Illinois: Bahá'í Publishing Trust, 1983.

—— *Kitáb-i-Aqdas*. Haifa: Bahá'í World Centre, 1992.

—— *Kitáb-i-Íqán*. Wilmette, Illinois: Bahá'í Publishing Trust, 1989.

—— *Tablets of Bahá'u'lláh revealed after the Kitáb-i-Aqdas*. Haifa: Bahá'í World Centre, 1974.

Balyuzi, H.M. *Bahá'u'lláh, The King of Glory*. Oxford: George Ronald, 1980.

Berling, J.A. *The Syncretic Religion of Lin Chao-en*. New York: Columbia University Press, 1980.

Capra, Fritjof. *The Turning Point: Science, Society and the Rising Culture*. London: Fontana, 1983.

Chan, Wing-tsit. 'The Historic Chinese Contribution to Religious Pluralism', in Edward J. Jurji, *Religious Pluralism and World Community*. Leiden, Netherlands: E.J. Brill, 1968.

—— (ed.) *A Source Book in Chinese Philosophy*, 1963.

Chang, Chi-yun. *Confucianism: A Modern Interpretation*. Los Angeles: The Partridge Bookstore, 1980.

Chen, Li Fu. *The Confucian Way*. London: KPI Ltd., 1986.

Chih, Andrew, *Chinese Humanism: A Religion beyond Religion*. Taiwan: Fu Jen Catholic University Press, 1981.

Chiu, Milton M. *The Tao of Chinese Religion*. Boston: University Press of America Inc., 1984.

Chu Kuang Ch'ien. *Chinese Thoughts*. Canton: Union Insurance Society of Canton, Ltd., no date.

A Compilation on China. Prepared by the Research Department of the Universal House of Justice. Haifa: Bahá'í World Centre, 1986.

Creel, H.G. *The Birth of China*. London; Jonathan Cape, 1936.

—— *Chinese Thought. From Confucius to Mao Tze-tung*. Chicago: The University of Chicago Press, 1953.

Das, Bhagavan. *Essential Unity of All Religions*. Madras: The Theosophical Publishing House, 1955.

Dawson, Raymond. *Confucius*. Oxford: Oxford University Press, 1981.

Faizi, Gloria. *The Bahá'í Faith*. No publisher. 1971.

Family Life. Compilation of the Universal House of Justice. Oakham: Bahá'í Publishing Trust, 1982.

Fozdar, J.K. *The God of Buddha*. New York: Asia Publishing House, 1973.

Fung Yu-Lan. *A Short History of Chinese Philosophy*. New York: The Free Press, Collier Macmillan, 1948.

Giles, H.A. *Chuang Tzu: Mystic, Moralist and Social Reformer*. London: George Allen and Unwin, 1989.

Giles, Lionel. *The Book of Mencius*. London: John Murray, 1942.

Hornby, Helen (comp.). *Lights of Guidance*. New Delhi: Bahá'í Publishing Trust, rev. edn. 1988.

Huxley, Julian. *Religion without Revelation*. London: M. Parrish, rev. edn. 1959.

Ispiring the Heart: Selected Writings of the Báb, Bahá'u'lláh and 'Abdu'l-Bahá. London: Bahá'í Publishing Trust.

Jaspers, K. *The Origin and Goal of History*. New Haven, Connecticut: Yale University Press, 1953.

Joachim, Christian. *Chinese Religions*. New Jersey: Prentice Hall, 1986.

Koller, John M. *Oriental Philosophies*, New York: Charles Scribner Sons, 1970.

Lau, D.C. *Lao Tzu: Tao Te Ching*. Harmondsworth: Penguin, 1963.

—— *Mencius*. Harmondsworth: Penguin, 1970.

Legge, J. *The Chinese Classics*. 5 vols. Hong Kong: Hong Kong University Press, 1960.

—— *The Four Books: Confucian Analects, The Book of Great Learning, The Doctrine of the Mean and The Works of Mencius*. New York: Paragon Books Reprint Corp., 1966.

—— *The Shoo King*. Hong Kong: Henry Fowde, 1965.

Liu, Shu-hsien. *The Contemporary Significance and Religious Importance of Confucianism*. Singapore: The Institute of East Asian Philosophy, 1986.

Living the Life: A Compilation. London Bahá'í Publishing Trust, 1974.

Magill, F.N. (ed.) *Masterpieces of World Philosophy in Summary Form*. New York: Harper and Row, 1961.

Maurer, Herrymon. *Tao – The Way of the Ways*. London: Wildwood House, 1982.

Mei, Yi-pao (trans.). *The Ethical and Political Works of Motse*. London, 1929.

Moore, Charles A. *The Chinese Mind*. Honolulu: The University Press of Hawaii, 1967.

Needham, J. *Science and Civilization in China*. Cambridge: Cambridge University Press, 1956.

Nivison, D.S. and Wright, A.F. *Confucianism in Action*. Stanford: Stanford University Press, 1959.

Pattern of Bahá'í Life. London: Bahá'í Publishing Trust.

Payne, Robert. *Mao Tze-tung, Ruler of Red China*. New York: Penguin, 1950.

Ro, Young-Chan. 'The Significance of the Confucian Texts as "Scripture" in the Confucian Tradition'. *Journal of Chinese Philosophy*. 15, 1988, pp. 269–87.

Rost, H.T.D. *The Golden Rule: A Universal Ethic*. Oxford: George Ronald, 1986.

Scharlemann, R.P. (ed.) *Paul Tillich: Writings on Religion*. Berlin: De Gruyter – Evangelisches Verlagswerk GmbH, 1988.

Shoghi Effendi. *World Order of Bahá'u'lláh*. Wilmette, Illinois: Bahá'í Publishing Trust, 1980.

Sih, Paul K.T. (ed.). *Chinese Humanism and Christian Spirituality. Essays of John C.H. Wu*. New York: St John's University Press, 1965.

Star of the West. Oxford: George Ronald, rpt. 1978.

Tang Chun-i. 'The Development of Ideas of Spiritual Value in Chinese Philosophy'. In Moore (ed.), 1967.

Teillard de Chardin, Pierre. *The Divine Milieu*. London: Harper and Row, 1960.

Thompson, L.G. *Chinese Religion: An Introduction*. California: Wadsworth, 1969.

Townshend, George. *'Abdu'l-Bahá, The Master*. Oxford: George Ronald, 1987.

Toynbee, Arnold J. *A Study of History*. London: Oxford University Press, 1934.

Waley, Arthur (trans.). *The Analects of Confucius*. New York: Vintage Books, 1971.

—— *Monkey*. New York: Grove Press, 1958.

—— *The Nine Songs: A Study of Shamanism in Ancient China*. London: George Allen and Unwin, 1955.

Watts, A. *Tao, The Watercourse Way*. London: Penguin, 1979.

Wei, Harry. *The Guiding Light of Lao Tzu*. Illinois: Theosophical Publishing House, 1982.

White, Robert A. 'Spiritual Foundations for an Ecologically Suitable Society'. *Journal of Bahá'í Studies*, 2.1. 1989.

Whitehead, A.N. *Religion in the Making*. Cambridge: Cambridge University Press, 1926.

Yang, C.K. *Religion in Chinese Society*. Los Angeles: University of California Press, 1961.

Yong, Choon Kim. *Oriental Thought: An Introduction to the Philosophical and Religious Thought of Asia*. Toronto: Helix Books, Rowman and Allenhald, 1973.

Notes and References

Preface

1. 'Abdu'l-Bahá, cited in *Star of the West*, vol. 13, p. 185. The original text of 'Abdu'l-Bahá's words is not available.
2. Shoghi Effendi, letter to the Bahá'ís of the East, 23 January 1923.
3. Shoghi Effendi, letters to individual believers, 26 January 1923. Compilation on China, 1986.
4. Thompson, *Chinese Religion*, 1969, 1979, p. 1.
5. When the word is used for Taoism or Buddhism, it may be any of these three. When it is used for Confucianism, it often means culture and moral education rather than religion. A follower of Confucian doctrines includes religion as an element but is not a follower of an organized institutional religion.
6. 'Abdu'l-Bahá, *Paris Talks*, p. 21.

1. An Introduction to China

1. Jaspers, *Origin*, 1953, pp. 1–2. Jaspers believes that God's acts of revelation represent the decisive dividing lines in a civilization.
2. Surely there was an earlier axial period, but information about it has been lost in antiquity. Our history thus begins from the 6th century BC.
3. From the oracle bones (inscribed bone and tortoise shell) of the Shang period (1766–1123 BC) found in the archaeological site in Northern Honan, one can deduce that the Chinese of that period were preoccupied with the world of the supernatural.
4. Waley, *Nine Songs*.
5. For a more detailed account, see Creel, *Birth of China*.
6. There may have been instances where human sacrifices may have been offered by the king, but these were probably

enemies or captives. The first Ch'in emperor had buried with him all those who constructed his underground mausoleum as well as the childless ladies of his harem. The impressive, life-size terracotta army of men and horses have recently been recovered from their burial place by archaeologists.

7. Waley, *Nine Songs*.

8. *T'ien* (Heaven) is a less anthropomorphic term and refers to a cosmic and moral power (order, being) that possesses intelligence and will and impartially directs the fate of all human beings. *Shang-ti* (Lord) can be translated as 'Supreme Lord of all deities and spirits' and understood more anthropomorphically. It is often associated with the ruling house.

9. See Appendix 1.

10. See chapter 15.

11. Dawson, *Confucius*.

12. 'Abdu'l-Bahá, *Japan*, p. 36.

13. My focus is on the original teachings of Confucius, rather than its later development, and on how its essential insights compare with those of other religions. Space does not permit me to discuss the various types of Confucianism such as Sung Neo-Confucianism and Han Confucianism.

14. See Appendix 1 for chart of Chinese history.

15. Confucius, *Analects* 17:22.

16. This was also the fate of most of the great sages, e.g. Lao-tzu, Mencius, Mo-tzu and Chuang-tzu. They were considered heretics and 'odd' during their lifetimes. Their fame was often posthumous.

17. Creel, *Chinese Thought*.

2. A Chinese Religion

1. Confucius, *Analects*, 14:8.

2. See the work of Legge and Giles, well-known Western Sinologues.

3. The term *T'ien* had denoted the Supreme God for centuries. It was written like 'a man with a big head' on the oracle bones of the Shang period and on the bronze ritual vessels of the early Chou period. It was sometime later that *T'ien* acquired the meaning of 'sky'. It retained its old meaning of 'God' while being used concurrently as 'sky'. A new word for God – *ti* –

came into use, as if to fill a need after *T'ien* came to mean 'sky'. Sometimes another word, *shang*, was put with *ti* to mean 'God above'. The reason for adding this character was because some earthly rulers began to call themselves *ti*. Ti Hsin, the last ruler of the Shang, was a notorious example of such self-appointed gods-on-earth.

4. Bahá'u'lláh, *Tablets*, p. 146.
5. Confucius, *Analects*, 8:19.
6. ibid. 3:13.
7. ibid. 2:4.
8. Quoted in Liu, *Confucianism*, p. 13.
9. Confucius, *Analects*, 14:37.
10. The Virtue (*te*) is not virtue in the sense of moral rectitude but rather 'virtuality' in the sense of having the possession of force or power. *Te* is manifest in, for example, the miraculous fruition of plants and the unconscious circulation of blood.
11. Confucius, *Analects*, 9:5.
12. ibid.
13. Sih, *Chinese Humanism*, p. 8.
14. Legge, *Mencius*, bk. 6, pt. 1, ch. 6, art. 8.
15. Chan, *Source Book*, p. 78.
16. This was also the fate of his most famous disciple, Mencius. See chapter 8.
17. Cited in Chan, *Doctrine of the Mean*, p. 311.
18. Confucius, *Analects*, 14:37.
19. ibid.
20. ibid. 3:12.
21. For other examples of Confucius referring to the transcendental power of Heaven, see *Analects*, 2:4, 3:12, 3:13, 6:26, 7:22, 7:34, 8:19, 9:5.
22. *Mencius*, A:4. This may be said to be an unequivocal condemnation of human sacrifice, even when performed symbolically.
23. Quoted in Chang, *Confucianism*, p. 335.
24. Confucius, *Analects*, 6:26.
25. It is possible to state that, unlike Confucius, the Buddha did have a speculative metaphysical idea of Nirvana and Buddhahood.
26. See, for example, the work of Legge and Giles.
27. Confucius, *Analects*, 6:20.

28. The problem of Confucius' relationship to religion has been a difficult one for scholars in the past as well as in the present.
29. With the influence of the West in the 19th century, Confucian scholars began to discuss this issue.
30. If one terms Confucianism a 'philosophy', then that philosophy is comparable to the place of religion in other civilizations. In traditional China, if a man were educated at all, the first education he received was philosophy. Philosophy (or religion) may be said to be every educated man's concern. When children went to school, the *Four Books*, which consist of the *Confucian Analects*, *The Book of Mencius*, *The Great Learning* and *The Doctrine of the Mean* were the first they were taught to read. Sometimes, when the children were just beginning to learn the characters, they were given a sort of textbook to read. This was known as the *Three Characters Classic* and was so called because each sentence in the book consisted of three characters arranged so that when recited they produced a rhythmic effect and thus helped the children to memorize them more easily. This book was in reality a primer, and the very first statement in it is that 'the nature of man is originally good', one of the fundamental ideas of Mencius.
31. See, for example, the work of Derk Bodde.
32. See, for example, the work of Lin Yu-tang, Wing-tsit Chan, Fung Yu-lan and Francis L.K. Hsu who deny that Confucianism is a religion.
33. Confucius, *Analects*, 5:12.
34. Liu, *Confucianism*, 2:4, p. 13.
35. Confucius, *Analects*, 11:11.
36. Scholars today, however, are much more objective in the discussion of the 'religion' of Confucius and there are now about equal numbers rallied on both sides of the issue as to whether Confucianism is a religion or a philosophy. This is in sharp contrast to thirty and more years ago, when almost every scholar was convinced of the agnostic nature of the Confucian doctrine.
37. Scharlemann, *Paul Tillich*, p. 231.
38. Whitehead, *Religion*, p. 16.
39. Yang, *Chinese Society*, p. 1.
40. Huxley, *Religion without Revelation*, p. 1.
41. de Chardin, *The Divine Milieu*, pp. 122, 141.

42. Confucius, *Analects*, 15:23.
43. Matt. 7:12.

3. The Great *Tao*

1. Lao-tzu, *Tao-te ching*, ch. 25.
2. Chang, *Confucianism*, p. 312.
3. Down the centuries, Taoism strengthened the metaphysical aspect of Confucianism. Later, during the Sung dynasty (960–1279 AD), it contributed to the emergence of Neo-Confucianism.
4. See, for example, *Webster's New Collegiate Dictionary*, *Random House Dictionary* and *The Concise Oxford Dictionary*.
5. See Chiu, *The Tao*, p. 403.
6. See Wei, *Guiding Light*, p. 5.
7. ibid.
8. The influence of the *Tao-te ching* has been circumscribed, however, by the fact that even the best translation failed to do it justice. The subtle rhythms, pictorial images and tonal values which pervade the original are largely untranslatable yet are the very qualities which not only awaken man's intuition but act as a stimulus to produce a mesmerizing effect on his heart and mind.

   English translations of the *Tao-te ching* include Stephen Mitchell, *Tao Te Ching*, London: Macmillan, 1988; C. Poynton, *The Great Sinderesis: A Translation of the Tao Te Ching*, Adelaide: The Hassell Press, 1949; I. Mears, *Tao Teh King*, London: Fletcher and Sons, Ltd., Norwich, 1922, rpt. 1971; R.G. Herricks, *Lao Tzu – Te-Tao Ching*, New York: Ballentine Books, 1989; and A. Crowley, *Tao Teh King*, London: Askin Publishers Ltd., 1976.
9. Needham's treatise on the 'Fundamental Ideas of Chinese Science' in chapter 13, vol. 2 of his book provides valuable reading for the understanding of yin-yang and the Five Elements.
10. Sih, *Chinese Humanism*, p. 53.
11. The following account of Lao-tzu is attributed to his early biography, *Ssu-ma Ch'ien*. However, it has mixed fact with fantasy: it lists some titles of Lao-tzu and names a few places which he may have frequented, but it also contains some quite fantastic and absurd speculations.

12. The book can be divided into two parts: the first part deals with the metaphysical – what it says about the ultimate reality (chapters 1–37); and the second is about the practical – how to live in this world (chapters 38–81).

13. The earliest historical work containing an account of such a meeting is the *Shih-ching*. In the *Chuang-tzu* there is an account of a meeting and the censure of Confucius by Lao-tzu. In the *Li chi*, a Confucian work compiled in the 1st century BC, we have four instances of Confucius recalling what he learned about the rites from Lao-tzu. See Lau, *Lao Tzu*, p. 14, and Appendix 3 entitled 'Important Chinese Sources'.

14. Lau, *Lao Tzu*, p. 48.

15. Quoted in ibid., p. 8.

16. See Chih, *Chinese Humanism*, p. 37.

17. ibid. p. 39.

18. See Giles, *Chuang Tzu*, chapters 2 and 6 for his exposition of the relativity of knowledge and the futility of argument on this subject.

19. Bahá'u'lláh, *Gleanings*, pp. 3–4.

20. Lao-tzu, *Tao-te ching*, ch. 14.

21. ibid. ch. 22, 24, *passim*.

22. Bhaktivedanta Swami, *Bhagavad Gita as It Is*, text 13, p. 149; text 21, p. 157; text 24, p. 199.

23. Chih, *Chinese Humanism*, p. 36.

24. *Doctrine of the Mean*, passage 13.

25. Bahá'u'lláh, *Gleanings*, p. 63.

26. ibid. p. 151.

27. The dates for Chuang-tzu are unknown. All we can say is that he was a younger contemporary of Mencius (371–289 BC).

28. Chuang-tzu was to Lao-tzu what Mencius was to Confucius.

29. One notes that Chuang-tzu's book, together with the *Tao-te ching*, has been a source of inspiration to Chinese scholars and poets through the centuries. Although it deals with roughly the same subject, it is ten times larger than the *Tao-te ching*.

30. Giles, *Chuang Tzu*, p. 76.

31. ibid. p. 132.

32. For a compilation of many names and titles of Bahá'u'lláh, see Rabbani, *The Desire of the World*.

33. Bahá'u'lláh says something similar: 'Thou art the All-Bountiful, the overflowing showers of Whose mercy have

rained down upon high and low alike, and the splendours of
Whose grace have been shed over both the obedient and the
rebellious.' *Prayers and Meditations*, p. 250. See also Matt.
5:44–5.

34. Lao-tzu, *Tao-te ching*, ch. 49. 'For virtue is good' and 'For
virtue is faithful' are probably not correctly translated.
Although the word for Virtue (*Te*) is used here, it is actually 'to
obtain' (also *Te* but written differently in modern usage).
Alternative translations for these lines would be 'That is how
goodness is obtained' and 'That is how faithfulness is obtained'.

35. Lao-tzu, *Tao-te ching*, ch. 79. Here it is interesting to note that
the otherwise impersonal and 'remote' *Tao* gives way to a
personified conception of activity and differentiation.

36. *Book of Rites*, xxvi.

37. 'Abdu'l-Bahá, *Foundations*, p. 41.

38. Bahá'u'lláh, *Gleanings*, p. 107.

39. *Book of Changes*, II, the Kuen Hexagram.

40. Some popular traditional Chinese proverbs warned about the
foolhardy preoccupation with material things: 'While living,
one vainly spends life in acquiring the things of this world; but
at death, one goes empty-handed'; 'God is vain, silver is vain,
death you cannot retain them'; and 'Man's life is an empty
bubble' (that is, unreal).

41. The Báb, *Selections*, p. 78.

42. 'The Home Sayings of Confucius', quoted in Chih, *Chinese
Humanism*, p. 415.

43. Confucius, *Analects*, 11:

44. Lao-tzu, *Tao-te ching*, ch. 50. See also chs. 16, 52.

45. See, for example, Bahá'u'lláh, *Gleanings*, pp. 132, 162, 328 and
'Abdu'l-Bahá, *Some Answered Questions*, pp. 326, 337.

46. Giles, *Chuang Tzu*, ch. 2, p. 16.

47. 'Abdu'l-Bahá, *Tablets*, p. 202.

48. Giles, *Chuang Tzu*, ch. 22, p. 29.

49. For Chuang-tzu, spiritual life begins with abandoning the
world so as to free oneself from its entanglements. This gives
one peace of mind and enables one to practise asceticism
quietly and persistently until one is born to a new life. This
brings one near the goal. The rebirth, resulting from giving up
the world and leisures of life, restores one to one's original
vitality as a human being and prepares one for the mysterious

process of transformation which lifts one up to the heavenly plane. Chuang-tzu may be called a God-intoxicated man. However, it is likely that in later years he came more and more to assimilate the spirit of moderation propounded by Confucius, just as Confucius in his later years came very close to the spirit of Lao-tzu.

50. 'Abdu'l-Bahá, in *Bahá'í World Faith*, p. 264.
51. Bahá'u'lláh, *Gleanings*, p. 345.
52. Some Confucians are agnostic and sceptical about the concept of immortality. Prominent Confucians who believed in the concept of immortality were Mencius, Lu Xiang-shan and Wang Yang-ming.
53. Bahá'u'lláh, *Gleanings*, p. 160.
54. Mencius 2A:2 in Chan, *Source Book*, p. 62.
55. In fact, it was not the Taoists alone in ancient China who envisaged such an immortal life. The *Book of Ch'u Tz'u* or *The Songs of the South* and *The Mythology of Mountain and Seas* (Shan Hai Ching) also contained many records of the immortals and mythic or spiritual beings who lived beyond the realm of human beings.
56. Quoted in Yang, *Chinese Society*, p. 249.
57. ibid.
58. Legge, *Mencius*, bk. 1, pt. 2, ch. 16.
59. 'Abdu'l-Bahá, *Some Answered Questions*, p. 244.
60. Giles, *Chuang Tzu*, p. 61.
61. Lao-tzu, *Tao-te ching*, ch. 21.
62. ibid. ch. 60.
63. Bahá'u'lláh, *Gleanings*, pp. 5, 38.
64. Lao-tzu, *Tao-te ching*, ch. 51.
65. ibid. ch. 25.
66. ibid. ch. 53.
67. One notes that the imagery of the fountain is also used in the Bahá'í scriptures: 'the fountain of spiritual outpourings' ('Abdu'l-Bahá, *Selections*, p. 27), 'the fountain of the light of wisdom and understanding' (Bahá'u'lláh, *Gleanings*, p. 289), 'the fountains of soft-flowing water' (Bahá'u'lláh, *Tablets*, p. 97).
68. 'Abdu'l-Bahá, *Selections*, p. 110.
69. Bahá'u'lláh, *Kitáb-i-Íqán*, p. 248.
70. Lao-tzu, *Tao-te ching*, see chs. 10, 15.

71. ibid. ch. 48.
72. ibid. ch. 11.
73. This is a far cry from our current Faustian way of thinking or the scientific method of controlling nature through understanding it, conceptualizing it, cutting it down to human size and subjecting it to the operation of the intellect.
74. Bahá'u'lláh, *Kitáb-i-Íqán*, p. 70; *Epistle*, p. 98.
75. Bahá'u'lláh, *Tablets*, pp. 142, 235–6.
76. Lao-tzu, *Tao-te ching*, ch. 47.
77. ibid. p. 81.
78. Unfortunately, these very lines of Lao-tzu have often been misunderstood by scholars as showing a sort of negative and passive attitude and a philosophy of withdrawal. See, for instance, Yong, *Oriental Thought*, p. 69.

4. Sage or Prophet?

1. 'Abdu'l-Bahá, *Paris Talks*, p. 32.
2. Legge, *Mencius*, bk. 4, ch. 2, art. 1.
3. Confucius, *Analects*, 7:1.
4. This seems to suggest that Confucius was absolutely serious about the rites performed in sacrifices to the ancestors and to Heaven. The *Book of Rites*, which features Confucius as an expert on ritual, did provide detailed instructions for marriage, funerals, ancestor worship and for the celebration of other important religious occasions.
5. Yen Yuan asked how to administer a state. Confucius replied: 'Use the calendar of Hsia, ride about in the state carriage of Yin, wear the ceremonial cap of Chou, and as for music there are the Shao dances (of Shun). Ban the sounds of Cheng music and keep sycophants at arm's length because the sounds of Cheng are wanton and sycophants are dangerous.' Quoted in Ames, *Rulership*, p. 5.
6. Hitting the Mark in Everyday (*Chung-yung*). Quoted in Ames, *Rulership*, p. 4.
7. Ames, *Rulership*, p. 5.
8. The Báb, *Selections*, p. 78.
9. The Báb said something similar. See p. 32.
10. Quoted in Sih, *Chinese Humanism*, p. 9.
11. See Maurer, *Tao*, p. 4.

12. Lao-tzu, *Tao-te ching*, ch. 67.
13. ibid. ch. 53.
14. Jesus, for example, quotes Isaiah: 'You will hear and hear and never understand. You will see and see and never perceive.' Matt. 13:14.
15. Lao-tzu, *Tao-te ching*, ch. 70. See also ch. 78.
16. ibid. ch. 70.
17. ibid. ch. 64.
18. Bahá'u'lláh, *Gleanings*, pp. 79–80.
19. Lao-tzu, *Tao-te ching*, ch. 74.
20. ibid. ch. 67.
21. ibid. ch. 73.
22. ibid. ch. 77.
23. ibid. ch. 72.
24. Confucius, *Analects*, 15:8.
25. ibid. 8:7.
26. ibid. 19:1.
27. ibid. 14:23.
28. Chan, *Mencius*, 7B:38, p. 24.
29. Das, *Essential Unity of All Religions*, p. 398.
30. Confucius, *Analects*, 7:1.
31. ibid. 7:19.
32. ibid.
33. ibid. 7:37.
34. ibid. 7:26.
35. Shoghi Effendi, in Hornby, *Lights of Guidance*, no. 1685, p. 501.
36. ibid. no. 1694, p. 502.
37. 'Abdu'l-Bahá, *Tablets*, p. 470.
38. 'Abdu'l-Bahá, *Promulgation*, p. 346.
39. But then this may be because of the literary genre that has little to do with Semitic tradition but a great deal to do with Confucius and even the ancient Chinese tradition: this is the religious type of the *sage* and the literary genre of *wisdom literature*. It is not without reason that Confucius received the title of 'greatest sage and first teacher', that his grave and temple in Qufu, shantung, became a site of pilgrimage for Chinese scholars, or that his birthday is still celebrated as Teacher's Day in Taiwan.
40. Bahá'u'lláh, *Tablets*, p. 145.

41. Sih, *Chinese Humanism*, p. 53.
42. Shoghi Effendi, in Hornby, *Lights of Guidance*, no. 1696, p. 503.
43. Mencius, commenting on two lines which he quoted from an ancient ode, 'Erring in nothing, forgetful of nothing, observing and following the old statutes.' In Legge, *Classics*, bk. 4, pt. 1, ch. 1, art. 4.
44. *Mencius*, bk. vii, pt. 11, ch. 38. See also Appendix 1,'Chart of Chinese History'.
45. The Shang oracle bones found in the archaeological site in northern Honan province comprised thousands of pieces of inscribed bone and tortoise shell and made it possible to reconstruct much of Shang life. We also have a number of books rewritten just after the Shang period which have been copied and recopied and come down to the present time in what is substantially their original form. Books of early Chou show a familiarity with names and the history of the Shang kings. This meant that the writers of these books knew Shang books which had perished.
46. Reference to the ancients is made throughout the Four Books of Confucius.

5. Unity of Nature

1. Chuang-tzu, cited in Creel, *Chinese Thought*, p. 90.
2. 'Abdu'l-Bahá, *Foundations*, p. 39.
3. See chapter 9 for a fuller exposition of the concept of *jen*.
4. Chih, *Chinese Humanism*, p. 63.
5. 'Abdu'l-Bahá, *Foundations*, pp. 88–9.
6. The phenomenon of *yin* and *yang* was recorded in the *Book of Changes*. It is known that Confucius studied it thoroughly, especially in the last years of his life.
7. Another aspect of nature was the mixture of the proportions of the five vital forces (water, fire, wood, metal and earth) at any given time. They were the qualities that activated nature, that gave particular things and events their character. Together the yin-yang theory and the theory of the five vital forces formed the first Chinese explanations of nature.
8. If we replace the word 'spirit' with the word 'mind', the statement is equally true.

9. Chang, *Confucianism*, pp. 320–1.
10. Capra, *Turning Point*, p. 117.
11. See Confucius' discussion of evil speakers in Giles, *Chuang Tzu*, chapter 4.
12. Lau, *Lao Tzu*, chapter 25.
13. ibid. chapters 25 and 48.
14. ibid. chapter 58.
15. Bahá'u'lláh, *Hidden Words*, Persian 51.
16. Lau, *Lao Tzu*, chapter 23.
17. ibid. chapter 43.
18. ibid. chapter 42.
19. ibid. chapter 41.
20. ibid. chapter 36.
21. 'Abdu'l-Bahá, *Selections*, p. 291.
22. See Capra, *Turning Point*, p. 117 for a further discussion.
23. See Watts, *Watercourse Way*, p. 29.
24. Ashvaghosha, *Awakening of Faith*, p. 55.
25. Chang Tsai (1020–1077), an inscription on the Western wall of his lecture hall, cited in Chan, *Source Book*, p. 497.
26. According to 'Abdu'l-Bahá, absolute equality in fortunes, honours, commerce, agriculture and industry would end in disorder and universal disappointment. See 'Abdu'l-Bahá, *Some Answered Questions*, p. 274.
27. ibid. 178–9.
28. Bahá'u'lláh, *Gleanings*, p. 140. See also 1 Cor. 12:12.
29. 'Abdu'l-Bahá, *Paris Talks*, p. 139.
30. 'Abdu'l-Bahá, cited in *Bahá'í World*, vol. 2.
31. Lau, *Lao Tzu*, chapter 29.
32. Genesis 1:28.
33. See, for example, the writings of Mencius.
34. Bahá'u'lláh, *Tablets*, p. 67–8.
35. Confucius, *Analects*, 11:11, 10:2.
36. 'Doctrine of the Mean', cited in Chih, *Chinese Humanism*, p. 46.
37. Cited in Giles, *Book of Mencius*, VIIB 25.
38. Chih, *Chinese Humanism*, p. 46.
39. 'Abdu'l-Bahá, *Promulgation*, p. 270.
40. This is not meant to imply that in the Bahá'í Faith people living in this world are encouraged to contact people who have passed into the spiritual world. 'Abdu'l-Bahá 'very strongly

warned the believers against using "psychic forces" '. (*Lights of Guidance*, no. 1756).

6. Unity of Religion

1. Lau, *Lao Tzu*, chapter 1.
2. Bahá'u'lláh, *Gleanings*, p. 136.
3. Berling, *Syncretic Religion*, pp. 20–3.
4. Quoted in Chan, *Religious Pluralism*, p. 122.
5. ibid.
6. The Báb, *Selections*, p. 125.
7. How much the Chinese – particularly the peasants – have been changed by the Communist ideology remains to be seen.
8. Poem on the three religions, in the Tao-hsuan. Cited in Chan, *Religious Pluralism*, p. 123.
9. ibid.
10. Cited in Chiu, *Tao of Chinese Religion*, p. 385.
11. *The Book of Changes*, cited in Legge, *The Four Books*, pt. 2, ch. 5.
12. Berling, *Syncretic Religion*, p. 9.
13. Chan, *Religious Pluralism*, p. 122.
14. See ibid. p. 116.
15. Tang, 'The Development of Ideas' in Moore, *Chinese Mind*, p. 199.
16. In later classical Chinese writings under the influence of Buddhism, the concept of sagehood has been elaborated to mean 'the enlightenment that transforms a person into a Buddha'. It became none other than the awakening which Mencius said the sage achieves for himself and helps others to achieve. Although this conception was not exactly similar to the Confucian aspiration, it nevertheless promoted an attitude of religious tolerance and fellowship.
17. The universality of the Buddha nature came to its full expression in the *Lotus Sutra* or the *Saddharma-pundarika*.
18. Chiu, *Tao of Chinese Religion*, p. 387.
19. ibid.
20. This can be taken for the vast majority of the Chinese. Chinese Muslims and Christians have been alone in not sharing the tolerant attitudes that were otherwise universal among their countrymen.

7. The Great Unity

1. 'Abdu'l-Bahá, *Promulgation*, p. 31.
2. Chan, *Source Book*, p. 497.
3. See Toynbee, *Study of History*.
4. 'Abdu'l-Bahá, *Paris Talks*, p. 140.
5. Confucius, *Analects*, 12:5.
6. In his writings Sun seems to aspire to be Confucius' spiritual successor, although he was himself a Christian.
7. Li-Chi, cited in Chiu, *Tao of Chinese Religion*, p. 389. It has been said that these ideals have been wrongly attributed to Confucius and actually smack of Taoist and Mohist persuasions. Nevertheless, they would well represent the kind of society in which universal love (*jen*) completely prevails.
8. If one reads the *Great Learning* (*Ta-hsueh*) or the *Evolution of Rites* (*Li Yun*), one realizes that the Confucian approach is comprehensive and holistic in character where sociopolitical problems are concerned. See Chan, *Source Book*, pp. 84–94.
9. Mei, *Works of Motse*, pp. 79–80.
10. These ideas are taken from chapter 15 of ibid.
11. This is an account written by the great ancient Chinese historian Ssu-ma Ch'ien in his *Shih Chi*.
12. Chan, *Source Book*, pp. 732–4.
13. Cited in Koller, *Oriental Philosophies*, p. 342.
14. Bahá'u'lláh, *Gleanings*, p. 249.
15. 'Abdu'l-Bahá, *Some Answered Questions*, pp. 63–4,

8. The Nature of Man

1. 'Abdu'l-Bahá, *Some Answered Questions*, p. 195.
2. Confucius, *Analects*, 6:17.
3. *Chung-yung*, chapter 20, section 5. For a fuller exposition of the concept of *jen*, see chapter 9.
4. Words of Xun Zi (298–238 BC).
5. Giles, *Chuang Tzu*, p. 82. Here Chuang-tzu is talking about Confucius.
6. See Bahá'u'lláh, *Gleanings*, p. 188.
7. 'Abdu'l-Bahá, *Some Answered Questions*, p. 235.
8. Hsun-tzu's (3rd century BC) ideas also belong to the Confucian tradition but did not become part of the mainstream of

Confucian thought as did Mencius' concepts. The primary reason for this may be that Hsun-tzu took a view directly opposite that of Mencius concerning man's original nature and assumed an authoritative political philosophy which in a sense gave birth to totalitarian legalism later. In opposition to Mencius' theory of the original goodness of human nature, Hsun-tzu advocated that the original nature of man was evil.

9. It must be noted that Confucius did not comment on this very much, probably because it was, for him, an issue too obvious and invisible. Instead, he devoted much of his attention to more tangible and practical matters. Although Confucius did not dogmatically advocate that human nature was originally good, he implied it when he taught his students about the sincerity of man. Since man is capable of cultivating his virtue himself, it logically follows that he has at the very least the innate potential of goodness.

10. Confucius did not deny that sex is a joy to man and he would agree that by nature man desires sex. He would, however, argue strongly that since we share this joy with animals, it is not characteristically human. There is another kind of joy which is uniquely human and of intrinsic value – the joy of morality.

11. Legge, *Mencius*, bk. 6, pt. 1, ch. 14, art. 2.

12. ibid. art. 6e.

13. 'Abdu'l-Bahá, *Promulgation*, p. 294.

14. 'Abdu'l-Bahá, *Paris Talks*, p. 113.

15. 'Abdu'l-Bahá, *Some Answered Questions*, p. 235.

16. Lau, *Mencius*, 6b.2.

17. Legge, *Mencius*, bk. 2, pt. 1, ch. 4, art. 1–2.

18. Giles, *Mencius*, p. 49.

19. 'Abdu'l-Bahá, *Promulgation*, p. 182.

20. Confucius, *Analects*, 17:2.

21. Quoted in Dawson, *Confucius*, p. 44.

22. Confucius, *Analects*, 12:5.

23. Legge, *Mencius*, bk. 6, pt. 1, ch. 6, arts. 1–7.

24. ibid. ch. 19.

25. ibid. ch. 8, arts. 1–2. See also chapter 5 for an account of the non-existence of a positive evil.

26. Legge, *Mencius*, bk. 2, pt. 1, ch. 2, art. 11.

27. Mencius was to Confucius what Plato was to Socrates.

28. The whole description is to be found in Plato, *The Republic*, bk. vi.
29. Legge, *Mencius*, bk. 2, pt. 1, ch. 2, arts. 12–14.
30. Bahá'u'lláh, *Gleanings*, p. 214.
31. Legge, *Mencius*, bk. 4, pt. 1, ch. 4, art. 3.
32. Lau, *Mencius*, 8A:1.
33. Both Confucius and Mencius lived in unfavourable times. The rulers of the various states were not unaware of their abilities but they would not employ them for any length of time.
34. Legge, *Mencius*, bk. 6, pt. 2, ch. 15, art. 2.
35. 'Abdu'l-Bahá, *Paris Talks*, p. 178.
36. Confucius, *Analects*, 12:1.
37. ibid. 6:21.
38. ibid. 12:22.
39. ibid. 17:6.
40. 'Abdu'l-Bahá, *Secret*, p. 67.
41. Confucius, *Analects*, 4:17.
42. See also *Analects*, 2:3.
43. ibid.
44. Quoted in Chen, *Confucian Way*, p. 246.
45. See Bahá'u'lláh, *Tablets*, p. 63.
46. 'Abdu'l-Bahá, *Selections*, pp. 132–3.
47. ibid.

9. Leading the Life: *Jen*

1. Bahá'u'lláh, *Tablets*, p. 60.
2. Confucius, *Analects*, 16:11.
3. Chang, *Confucianism*, p. 73. Others disagree and say it was benevolence.
4. See ibid. p. 76.
5. 'Abdu'l-Bahá, *Some Answered Questions*, p. 178.
6. Bahá'u'lláh, *Hidden Words*, Arabic 29.
7. Confucius, *Analects*, 15:23, 6:28.
8. Quoted in Chen, *Confucian Way*, p. 356.
9. Matthew 7:12.
10. Mahabharata, cited in Das, *Essential Unity*, p. 398.
11. Bahá'u'lláh, *Hidden Words*, Arabic 30.
12. Bahá'u'lláh, *Tablets*, p. 69.
13. Confucius, *Analects*, 11:15.

14. Sih in *Chinese Humanism* remarks that Confucius was serious and yet he had a charming sense of humour. He was too moral to be moralistic, too pure to be puritanical, too practical to be a mere utilitarian and too consistently moderate to be immoderate even in the virtue of moderation. Confucius was not a man to go by half measures. His golden mean is not a compromise but harmony.

15. Lao-tzu, *Tao-te ching*, ch. 48.

16. ibid. ch. 58.

17. Bahá'u'lláh, *Tablets*, p. 69.

18. Bahá'u'lláh, *Gleanings*, p. 216.

19. Confucius, *Analects*, 8:2.

20. 'Abdu'l-Bahá, quoted in *Pattern of Bahá'í Life*, p. 42.

21. Lao-tzu, *Tao-te ching*, ch. 18.

22. ibid. ch. 75.

23. ibid. ch. 53.

24. Bahá'u'lláh, *Tablets*, p. 23.

25. Lao-tzu, *Tao-te ching*, chs. 31, 36.

26. ibid. ch. 22.

27. Creel, *Chinese Thought*, p. 26.

28. See, for example, Psalms 5:12.

29. Legge, *Doctrine of the Mean*, ch. 1.

30. Confucius, *Analects*, 1:4.

31. ibid. 15:14.

32. Bahá'u'lláh, *Hidden Words*, Arabic 27.

33. Bahá'u'lláh, *Gleanings*, p. 297.

34. Confucius, *Analects*, 16:10.

35. ibid. 7:15.

36. ibid. 4:5.

37. Such high standards are understandably difficult to follow. Chinese businessmen, for example, are known to indulge in illegal economic practices and to justify this by differentiating between what they generally call 'common morality' and 'business morality'. In other words, for life there is a 'higher' set of rules of honesty, while for business dealings there is a 'lower' set. This is, however, an invention of men to suit their greed and is un-Confucian in nature. A notable example today is the emphasis on cost-saving and high profit as business aims at the expense of polluting the environment and causing harm to public health. The businessman would not generally be

concerned with environmental cleanliness, particularly if his competitors were not equally concerned.

38. Some of the Chinese scholars after the Sung period were in the habit of decrying all gain. They misunderstood what Confucius said about a gentleman's reluctance to take a gain.
39. Confucius, *Analects*, 4:16.
40. See ibid. 14:13 and 19:1 on honesty.
41. This Confucian downgrading of material wealth has prejudiced the Chinese against commerce and money-making. Thus, in the traditional Chinese hierarchy, merchants were at the lowest rung of the social ladder, below scholars, peasants and aristocrats. But with the present ascendancy and importance of commerce, successful merchant princes are calling the tune in many areas of social activity.
42. Bahá'u'lláh, *Hidden Words*, Persian 50.
43. Bahá'u'lláh, *Gleanings*, p. 103.
44. Matthew 16:26.
45. Lao-tzu, *Tao-te ching*, chs. 46 and 44.
46. Bahá'u'lláh, *Hidden Words*, Arabic 56.
47. Quoted in Chen, *Confucian Way*, p. 591.
48. 'Abdu'l-Bahá, *Secret of Divine Civilization*, pp. 24–5.
49. Bahá'u'lláh, *Tablets*, p. 64.
50. Lao-tzu, *Tao-te ching*, ch. 7.
51. ibid. ch. 81.
52. ibid. ch. 8.
53. ibid. ch. 9.
54. ibid. ch. 22.
55. ibid. ch. 66.
56. ibid. ch. 24.
57. ibid. ch. 78.
58. Matthew 5:5.
59. Lao-tzu, *Tao-te ching*, ch. 78. We may note that the last four lines also portray the idea of bearing the guilt of the people on one's own shoulder. This is reminiscent of the sacrifice of the life of the prophet for the people who refuse to recognize him.
60. See Chih, *Chinese Humanism*, pp. 324–5.
61. Confucius, *Analects*, 7:32–3.
62. Chan, *Doctrine of the Mean*, 13, p. 101.
63. See, for example, the essays of John Wu in Sih, *Chinese Humanism*, p. 7.

64. Confucius, *Analects*, 7:18.
65. ibid. 14:8.
66. Bahá'u'lláh, *Tablets*, p. 26.
67. Giles, *Mencius*, pp. 79–80.
68. Chu Kuang Ch'ien, 'On Activity', *Chinese Thoughts*. See also Confucius, *Analects* 12:3 and 18:22 on the avoidance of idleness.
69. Bahá'u'lláh, *Hidden Words*, Arabic 27.
70. ibid. Arabic 26.
71. Confucius, *Analects*, 17:24.
72. Legge, *Mencius*, bk. 4, pt. 2, ch. 9.
73. Confucius, *Analects*, 14:26.
74. ibid. 15:14.
75. ibid. 17:13.
76. Bahá'u'lláh, *Tablets*, pp. 219–20.
77. Confucius, *Analects*, 7:26.
78. ibid. 5:22.
79. Lao-tzu, *Tao-te ching*, ch. 3. This is different from Confucius, who would 'Requite a grievance with justice'.
80. ibid. ch. 62.
81. ibid. chs. 72–3.
82. Bahá'u'lláh, *Epistle*, p. 13.
83. Bahá'u'lláh, *Gleanings*, p. 210.
84. The Báb, *Selections*, p. 45.
85. Bahá'u'lláh, *Hidden Words*, Persian 5.
86. Lao-tzu, *Tao-te ching*, ch. 56.
87. Bahá'u'lláh, *Gleanings*, p. 265.
88. Bahá'u'lláh, *Hidden Words*, Persian 5.
89. Lao-tzu, *Tao-te ching*, ch. 81.
90. ibid. ch. 22.
91. ibid. ch. 2. For *Tao*, the empty centre is also the centre of man's multiform personality, with its unfathomable ability to explore unconsciously whole fields of activity that the conscious mind overlooks, and to let courses of action merge through rumination about facts rather than through conceptualization of them.
92. ibid. ch. 18.
93. Confucius, *Analects*, 13:27.
94. ibid. 1:3.
95. ibid. 15:40.
96. ibid. 2:13.

97. ibid. 4:24.
98. ibid. 4:22.
99. ibid. 14.21.
100. ibid. 5:9.
101. ibid. 14:14.
102. 'Abdu'l-Bahá, *Paris Talks*, p. 80.

10. Leading the Life: *Li*

1. 'Abdu'l-Bahá, Selections, p. 112.
2. Confucius, *Analects*, 3:3.
3. But the pleasure he advocated was a very sedate kind of pleasure.
4. *Li* furnishes the means of determining (the observances towards) relatives as near or remote; of settling points which may cause suspicion or doubt; of distinguishing where there should be agreement, and where difference; and of making clear what is right and what is wrong. To cultivate one's person and fulfil one's words is called good conduct.
5. There is a religious basis for such proper social behaviour. The ideogram with which *li* is written comprises two parts. The first is a signific indicating communication with the supernatural, and the second is an additional element which was originally a pictograph of a sacrificial vessel containing some object.
6. 'Notes on the *Li*' and *Tso-chuan*, Year 28 of Hsi Kung. Quoted in Chang, *Confucianism*, p. 83.
7. Legge, *Li Chi*, bk. 1, i, pp. 62 ff.
8. Bahá'u'lláh, *Hidden Words*, Persian 69.
9. Confucius, *Analects*, 3:26.
10. See also Giles, *Chuang Tzu*, p. 134.
11. Confucius, *Analects*, 3:4.
12. ibid. 12:2.
13. Quoted in Chang, *Confucianism*, p. 19.
14. This was practised in memory and gratitude of the first three years of the infant's life when he was in the arms of his parents.

11. The Life of the Sage

1. 'Abdu'l-Bahá. *Some Answered Questions*, pp. 196–7.
2. Confucius, *Analects*, 7:25.

3. 'Doctrine of the Mean', cited in Chen, *Confucian Way*, p. 251.
4. 'Doctrine of the Mean', cited in Chih, *Chinese Humanism*, p. 404.
5. Quoted in Townshend, *'Abdu'l-Bahá, The Master*, p. 18.
6. Legge, *Mencius*, bk. 7, pt. 2, ch. 15.
7. ibid. ch. 25; *Doctrine of the Mean*, ch. 27.
8. *Doctrine of the Mean*, 51. We may note a similar idea of Chuang-tzu's: 'The mind of the sage being in repose becomes the mirror of the universe, the speculum of all creation.' Giles, *Chuang Tzu*, p. 131.
9. Confucius, *Analects*, 2:14.
10. ibid. 4:16.
11. ibid. 12:16.
12. ibid. 12:19.
13. ibid. 13:23.
14. ibid. 13:25.
15. ibid. 13:26.
16. ibid. 14:7.
17. ibid. 15:20.
18. ibid. 15:33.
19. ibid. 14:45.
20. ibid. 16:10.
21. Shoghi Effendi, *Advent*, p. 34.
22. Faizi, *Bahá'í Faith*, pp. 18–19.
23. Confucius, *Analects*, 7:37.
24. See also the essay of John Wu in Sih, *Chinese Humanism*.
25. Confucius, *Analects*, 19:9.

12. Learning and Education

1. Confucius, quoted in Legge, *Book of Great Learning*.
2. Confucius, *Analects*, 5:27.
3. ibid. 7:2.
4. ibid. 2:4.
5. ibid.
6. See, e.g. ibid, 7:1, 2:11.
7. 'Abdu'l-Bahá, *Some Answered Questions*, p. 235.
8. Legge, *Book of Great Learning*, ch. 3.
9. 'Abdu'l-Bahá, *Selections*, p. 126.
10. Hsiu-wu, *Striving with Effort*, Book 19, quoted in Ames, *Rulership*, p. 20.

11. ibid.
12. Mencius 6A:7, quoted in Chan, *Source Book*, p. 55. It is to Mencius' credit that he took up and developed much that was merely suggested or implicit in the sayings of Confucius. He believed that 'all things are complete within us'. In other words, man's inborn nature is not only perfect but is also a sort of microcosm which represents or contains the essence of all things. From this, he argued that 'he who completely knows his own nature, knows Heaven'. See Legge, *Mencius*, bk. 7, pt. 1, ch. 4, art. 1 and bk. 7, pt. 1, ch. 1, art. 1.
13. Legge, *Mencius*, bk. 6, pt. 1, ch. 19.
14. Bahá'u'lláh, *Tablets*, p. 51.
15. 'Abdu'l-Bahá, *Secret*, p. 111.
16. ibid.
17. ibid. p. 109.
18. 'Abdu'l-Bahá, *Some Answered Questions*, p. 217.
19. ibid. p. 58.
20. The relationship between knowledge and action continued to be stressed by the great Chinese philosophers after Confucius. Chu Hsi said, 'Knowledge and action always require each other. It is like a person who cannot walk without legs although he has eyes, and cannot see without eyes although he has legs. With respect to order, knowledge comes first, and, with respect to importance, action is more important.' There is also Wang Yang-ming's famous doctrine of the unity of action and knowledge: 'Knowledge is the crystallization of the will to act, and action is the task of carrying out that knowledge; knowledge is the beginning of action, and action is the completion of knowledge.'
21. See Legge, *Shoo King*, p. 258. See also Appendix 3, 'Important Chinese Sources'.
22. Confucius, quoted in Ames, *Rulership*, p. 52.
23. Confucius, *Analects*, 1:1.
24. Bahá'u'lláh, *Tablets*, pp. 51–2.
25. Confucius, quoted in Ames, *Rulership*, p. 5.
26. 'Abdu'l-Bahá, *Selections*, p. 132.
27. Up to the 19th century it was still widely believed that such moral training was the cure for the ills which had beset the country, so it was urged that colleges be established in troubled provinces to educate the people in Confucian principles.

28. Confucius, *Analects*, 1:7.
29. ibid. 9:25. 'The commander of the forces of a large State may be carried off, but the will of even a common man cannot be taken from him.'
30. ibid. 6:25, 4:5.
31. 'Abdu'l-Bahá, *Selections*, p. 130.
32. 'Abdu'l-Bahá, *Bahá'í World Faith*, p. 247.
33. ibid. p. 290.
34. Confucius, *Analects*, 2:3.
35. Giles, *Chuang Tzu*, p. 134.
36. 'Abdu'l-Bahá, *Selections*, pp. 132–3.
37. Confucius, *Analects*, 15:38.
38. ibid. 7:7.
39. Even those who were successful in the examinations had to continue with their studies in order to keep fresh the qualities of character which the classics had instilled into them; and emperors who had undergone a rigorous Confucian training before ascending the throne continued to keep scholars at court to expound the classics to them.
40. See Chen, *Confucian Way*, p. 349.
41. Balyuzi, *King of Glory*, p. 428.
42. 'Abdu'l-Bahá, *Secret*, p. 111.
43. See Chen, *Confucian Way*, p. 349.

13. Unity of the Family

1. *Book of Songs*, quoted in Chan, *Source Book*, p. 102.
2. Legge, *Mencius*, 4A.5.
3. ibid. bk. 5, pt. 1, ch. 2.
4. *Li Chi*, 'Li Yun', quoted in Chih, *Chinese Humanism*.
5. 'Abdu'l-Bahá, *Promulgation*, p. 144–5.
6. 'Abdu'l-Bahá, *Selections*, p. 279.
7. 'Abdu'l-Bahá, *Promulgation*, p. 168.
8. See ch. 10, section 'Spirit not the Form'.
9. 'Abdu'l-Bahá, *Selections*, p. 302.
10. 'Abdu'l-Bahá, *Promulgation*, p. 182.
11. *Book of Rites*, quoted in Chih, *Chinese Humanism*, p. 345.
12. Legge, *Doctrine of the Mean*, ch. 12. Confucius was probably trying to emphasize the moral duty of the parents to look after their children and, simultaneously, the duty of the children to

look after their parents at a time when there was no state-run social security system.

13. The Báb, *Selections*, p. 94.
14. See Thompson, *Chinese Religion*, p. 40.
15. Bahá'u'lláh, cited in *Family Life*, p. 1.
16. ibid. p. 2.
17. Confucius, *Analects*, 2:7.
18. Legge, *Mencius*, bk. 4, pt. 1, ch. 19.
19. Confucius, *Analects*, 4:18.
20. A remark attributed to Mencius.
21. Legge, *Mencius*, bk. 5, pt. 1, ch. 2.
22. Confucius, *Analects*, 2:89.
23. See Bahá'u'lláh, *The Kitáb-i-Aqdas*, p. 26. See also 'Abdu'l-Bahá, *Selections*, p. 130.
24. Shoghi Effendi, cited in Hornby, *Lights of Guidance*, no. 683.
25. 'Abdu'l-Bahá, *Selections*, p. 171.
26. That is, the *Shu-ching* (Book of History) and *Shih ching* (Book of Poetry).
27. 'Abdu'l-Bahá, *Some Answered Questions*, p. 240.

14. Unity of the State

1. Bahá'u'lláh, *Gleanings*, p. 236.
2. Confucius, *Analects*, 13:3.
3. ibid. 12:11.
4. ibid.
5. ibid. 13.
6. ibid. 2:1.
7. Bahá'u'lláh, *Tablets*, p. 139.
8. See Chang, *Confucianism*, p. 321.
9. Confucius listed nine basic duties of the prince. Among these are the cultivation of virtue, rewarding men of worth, showing affection to his kinsmen, respecting great ministers, treating with consideration all officials, taking fatherly care of the common people, promoting the hundred crafts and being friendly to neighbouring princes.
10. See Chen, *Confucian Way*, p. 591.
11. ibid. p. 592.
12. 'Abdu'l-Bahá, *Some Answered Questions*, p. 79.
13. Lao-tzu, *Tao-te ching*, ch. 28.
14. See chapter 9, section on Moderation.

15. Matthew 5:5.
16. Bahá'u'lláh, *Tablets*, p. 64.
17. 'Economy of Expenditure' is the name of a section of the *Mo-tzu* in which Mo-tzu takes a most utilitarian view of production and will not allow anything decorative in the manufacture of clothing, houses, weapons, boats or vehicles. However, Confucius would have probably considered this a little too extreme. It is certainly out of sympathy with Confucian support of culture (*wen*).
18. Lao-tzu, *Tao-te ching*, 1:5.
19. Ames, *Rulership*, p. 25.
20. 'Abdu'l-Bahá, *Promulgation*, p. 217.
21. 'Abdu'l-Bahá, *Foundations*, pp. 43–4.
22. Once when Confucius was asked about the suitability of three of his disciples for government administration (there was no mention of occupying a throne – it would have been unwise and improper to ask such a question), Confucius explained very concisely the one strength of each of the three disciples which qualified them to govern. One was 'decisive', the other had 'understanding' and the third had 'many talents'.
23. Confucius, *Analects*, 6:6.
24. Creel, *Birth of China*, p. 43.
25. Ames, *Rulership*, p. 24.
26. Confucius, *Analects* 12:7.
27. See *Mencius* 1B.3 and other passages.
28. Chen, *Confucian Way*, p. 587.
29. Compared with Mencius who, reflecting the social turmoil of a later era, envisaged a more active role for the people, Confucius looked upon the people as a largely passive force – as indeed they were until the 20th century. Although the winning of their confidence was essential to the government, they were to be moulded and influenced rather than consulted.
30. Lau, *Mencius*, 1b.7.
31. ibid. VIIB 14.
32. It may be of interest for us to observe that while government for the people and in consultation with the people was a basic Confucian ideal, the further step of government by the people (that is, by election) was never considered. It was not an issue until the 20th century.
33. Bahá'u'lláh, *Gleanings*, p. 11.

34. Shoghi Effendi, *World Order*, p. 204.
35. 'Abdu'l-Bahá, *Secret*, p. 24.
36. ibid. p. 109.

15. The Winter of Chinese Religion

1. 'Abdu'l-Bahá, *Some Answered Questions*, p. 165.
2. The time of glorification, however, did not last very long. By the beginning of the first century AD, Confucianists of a more rationalistic type began to get the upper hand. Hence in later times, Confucius was no longer regarded as a divine being, although his position as that of the teacher remained.
3. Fung, *Chinese Philosophy*, p. 48.
4. Dawson, *Confucius*, p. 85.
5. In 1907 Confucius was moved up to the first class. See Thompson, *Chinese Religion*.
6. ibid. pp. 75–8.
7. Fung, *Chinese Philosophy*, p. 48.
8. ibid.
9. 'Abdu'l-Bahá, *Some Answered Questions*, p. 166.
10. See Waley, *Monkey*.
11. In fact, it may be argued that the gulf between the masses and philosophers was not really as great as between a labourer and a philosopher today, for Chinese philosophers for the most part stayed in touch with nature rather than engaged solely in abstract speculation.
12. Chan, *Religious Pluralism*, p. 142.
13. Sih, *Chinese Humanism*, p. 33.
14. Legge, *Mencius*, bk. 4, pt. 1, ch. 26, art. 1.
15. Not surprisingly, the Jesuit scholar Matteo Ricci (1552–1610) could vehemently criticize Neo-Confucianism and find substantive compatibility between classical Confucianism and Catholicism at the same time.
16. Chan, *Religious Pluralism*, p. 182.
17. For example, while Lao-tzu taught the wisdom of following nature, Taoism today teaches the doctrine of working against nature. For instance, according to Lao-tzu and Chuang-tzu, life followed by death is the course of nature, and man should follow this natural course calmly. But the main teaching of Taoist religion today appears to be the principle and technique

of how to avoid death, which is expressly working against nature.

18. 'Abdu'l-Bahá, quoted in *Compilation on China*.
19. 'Abdu'l-Bahá, *Some Answered Questions*, pp. 165–6.
20. ibid. p. 166.
21. Lao-tzu. *Tao-te ching*, ch. 38.
22. Fozdar, *God of Buddha*, p. viii.
23. Since Sung times (960–1279 AD), Confucianism (more often known as Neo-Confucianism), has broadened its theoretical scope by entertaining the Buddhist problem of mind and matter. As a system of values, Confucianism has incorporated much of the Buddhist world salvation spirit which urges people to undergo ordeals for the deliverance of mankind.
24. 'Abdu'l-Bahá, *Secret*, p. 26.
25. Lao-tzu, *Tao-te ching*, ch. 55.

16. Conclusion

1. 'Abdu'l-Bahá, *Tablets*, p. 471.
2. Chan, *Source Book*, p. 49.
3. Undeniably, humanism has been an important trend in Western thought, but it is not the same as Chinese humanism. The classical humanism promoted by Greek Sophists was one-sided. Despite his apparent emphasis on man, Socrates himself declared that philosophy was the practice of dying, and his disciple Plato quickly turned his gaze on the transcendental realm of the eternal. Scientific humanism, on the other hand, places much emphasis on matter while Marxist humanism stresses economic forces and class struggle.
4. The six arts are *li*, music, archery, chariot-driving, writing and arithmetic.
5. Chang, *Confucianism*, p. 564.
6. Quoted in ibid. p. 569.
7. Chih, *Chinese Humanism*, pp. 18–19.
8. Mao is also quoted as saying, 'I hated Confucius from the age of eight.' Payne, *Mao*, pp. 30–1.
9. *I Ching* 'Kua', 37, on *Chia Jen*/The Family.
10. Five hundred years later and in terms of present thinking, St Paul did no better in his exposition on women.
11. He did say, in fact: 'Women and children are hard to get along with. They hold a grudge on you if you keep away from them;

they act disrespectfully if you stay near them.' It is possible, however, that he had some particular women and children in mind when he made this statement. He could not have meant that all women and all children were hard to get along with. We know that he was very much attached to his widowed mother and he took very good care not only of his own daughter, but also the daughter of his older brother. It appears that others may have taken this single sentence and twisted it to bolster up some political theory.

12. See *Notes on the Li.*

13. It may be noted that this was an age of moral laxity and there was no such thing as the institution of marriage. In a way, Confucius uplifted the status of women by insisting on the strict maintenance of the marriage. Confucius really established the relationship between men and women through the institution of marriage. For example, men could not just wander off, as they had done previously. Although the wife was subservient to the husband, yet now the man was responsible for her welfare, whereas previously she had had no rights or position whatsoever and was at the mercy of 'whatever'.

14. An action which would provoke utter surprise in Mencius if he was alive today.

15. Chan, *Source Book*, pp. 69–70.

16. ibid.

17. Chen, *Confucian Way*, p. 588.

18. See the works of Arnold Toynbee.

19. 'Abdu'l-Bahá, Tablet to an individual believer, 18 July 1919.

20. 'Abdu'l-Bahá, *Some Answered Questions*, p. 214.

21. Bahá'u'lláh, *Gleanings*, p. 215.

22. ibid. p. 285.

23. Confucius, *Analects* 14:36. Jesus would have placed the emphasis differently: 'Do good to those who hate you, bless those who curse you, pray for those who abuse you.' (Luke 6:26, Matthew 5:43).

24. According to Bahá'u'lláh, 'How long will discord agitate the face of society? . . . The winds of despair are, alas, blowing from every direction . . .' (*Gleanings*, p. 216).

25. See Capra, *Turning Point*.

26. 'Abdu'l-Bahá, *Some Answered Questions*, p. 75.

Index